A Year of Poetry Tea Time Patriotism

The Essential Guide to Patriotic Poetry and Tales

Written and Edited By
Christine Owens

Illustrated by Quentin Owens

For more poetry tea time ideas

Visit www.ayearofpoetryteatime.com

A Year of Poetry Tea Time Patriotism: The Essential Guide to Patriotic Poetry and Tales

Published by Whimsy Rock Press

Any mention in this book pertaining to my experiences are purely that, my experiences, and should not be taken as legal advice when navigating your in-home educational choices. Each household must do what is best for their own family, classroom, or homeschool.

First Printing, 2022

Illustrations by Quentin Owens
Cover Art designed by Christine Owens

Owens, Christine
A Year of Poetry Tea Time Patriotism: The Essential Guide to Patriotic Poems and Tales
ISBN: 978-1-954270-17-6
ISBN: 978-1-954270-18-3 (electronic)

This book is dedicated to
My grandfather who served during WWII

Alfred Faulkner

Acknowledgments

This book was planned to be smaller and it turned out bigger than the first one. After a large loss of information and having to start over on the majority of the book, it is finally here.

Through the International Homeschooling Poetry Contest, I am able to include more current poetry along with other generous poets who were willing to share their writings with you. Congratulations to 10-year-old Jake Zesiger for being the grand prize winner. Thanks to Amelie Chindongo of Malawi, Africa and Maddox Welgan of Japan for representing international contest participants.

Thank you to the following people and their businesses for judging and promoting the
2021 International Homeschool Poetry contest

Richard Blanco
https://richard-blanco.com
2013 Presidential Inaugural poet

Kent and Amy Bowler
www.**revolutionaryheroes.com**
Freedom based classes for teens and parent mentoring

Sarah Janisse Brown
www.funschooling.com/
Owner and creator of Fun Schooling,
Thinking Tree Books and Dyslexia Games

Nephi Zufelt
www.wealthmentalityfamilies.com
Wealth education resources to help every member of your family

Nellie Johnston
www.growingthymecooking.com
Growing healthy chefs one at a time.

Sarah Watson
www.**beyondelementary.com**
Encouraging homeschooling moms

Amelia DeField
www.storyquestacademy.com
A fun reading and writing course for tweens and teens

Ellie Naomi
www.ellienaomi.com
Mystery Author

Table of Contents

Introduction

The *A Year of Poetry Tea Time* book series was designed to make poetry a fun and enjoyable experience. These poetry books should be on every home or classroom bookshelf. The series includes *A Year of Poetry Tea Time*, *A Year of Poetry Tea Time Patriotism*, *A Year of Poetry Tea Time Adventure* (coming soon), and *A Year of Poetry Tea Time Seasons* (Coming in 2023).

This book A Year of Poetry Tea Time Patriotism will provide you with over two hundred age-appropriate poems in diverse styles and themes. This second volume is designed to help introduce you and your listeners to patriotic themed poetry of many styles. The poems featured will explore the poetry of US founding fathers, soldiers, patriots from around the world and those who have a deep love for their country and culture. With all the poems tucked into one book, you won't have to search through volumes and volumes of poetry collections. Not only will it become your go-to book for patriotic themed poetry tea time, but also holidays, bedtime, mom school, classroom, homeschool, and more. You will learn how to hold a Ken Burns poetry party (popular in Scotland) as well as the basics of holding a poetry tea time. You will learn how to identify different styles of poetry, the history of poets at war, poet bios on every poet included in the book, and more. You will also find all new tea time recipes with which to adorn your table or picnic blanket.

I promise you that if you use this book for your poetry tea time you will have a plethora of patriotic poetry at your fingertips. You will be ready to explore the patriotism of Australia, Canada, England, Japan, Scotland, United States, Whales and more. You will have everything you need to make your tea time a success. Not only will it save you a lot of time, but it will make it a breeze to plan your own poetry tea time Your guests (your children, class, or friends) will have a meaningful experience, boys and girls alike. Yep! Boys love poetry tea time too. You can be ready for a quick, impromptu poetry tea time by the time the water boils.

Not only does the book provide poetry and recipes for tasty treats, it is stuffed with so much more.
Features that are included in this book:

—You can find the definition of challenging words right under the poem for quick reference
—200 poems of varying lengths
—A glossary of over 380 terms and the poems they are found in
—100+ mini poet bios stuffed full of facts
—56 quotes that will inspire ideas of freedom and cultural pride
—activity suggestions
—Poems can be looked up by poet and theme
—Poets can be looked up by country
—Chapters are organized by monthly themes for quick relevant poetry
—A section for you to write your own poetry
—A history of Poets and War
—World leaders and tea
—Learn the basic tea etiquette
—Recipes influenced by history for unique tea time fare
—Explanation of poetry styles and terms
—Field trip suggestions
—How to host a Robert Burns Night poetry party
And More

This collection will give you everything you need, neatly nestled between the covers of a single book.

After over twenty years of collecting poetry and reading it to children, in schools and at home, I have found that children of all ages enjoy poetry whether silly or thought provoking. With the right exposure, children from ages two to seventeen can learn to appreciate the poetry of Robert Louis Stevenson, as well as enjoy Moore and Yeats. Not only do children start to understand literary concepts, like imagery and rhyme, they also expand their minds with a rich vocabulary and learn the complexity of emotions.

Thousands of families around the world are already enjoying the magic that comes from sharing poetry. With a Year of Poetry Tea Time Patriotism you will sit around the table, sip tea, and ponder the lives and people who fought and loved their country. Shared glances, discussion, and smells fill the air as time is spent together. These memorable moments can be yours.

Don’t put off poetry until your children are older! Now is the time to heat up the water and pull out your tea. Establish a love for poetry now. Don’t deprive your children of this mind changing experience. This is especially good for those who are reluctant to listen to books. Build bonds, and build minds, starting today.

How to Use the Book

I created this book to take the stress out of exploring patriotic poetry and having a poetry tea time. Spending the time to find relevant and age-appropriate poetry can be very time consuming, especially if your children are young or poetry is new to you. There is nothing more frustrating than reading a poem aloud and feeling underwhelmed because you have no clue what the meaning of it was. I am confident that *A Year of Poetry Tea Time* Patriotism will prevent this problem from happening to you. So, let's learn how to use this book.

Original punctuation, spelling, and emphasis have been maintained from the original poetic works. Additionally, unique, poem formatting was kept to the original format where possible.

Poets at War
Writing was the only escape soldiers had from the unbelievable scenes and experiences they had while at war. Many soldiers wrote letters home to let family, friends and loved ones know that they were still alive. Droves of men spent their time on the front lines in the thick of battle. Sadly, many of them also lost their lives serving their countries. Some soldiers chose poetry as their form of lyrical expression. Here you will learn about the influence poetry had on war and those who wrote it.

PATRIOTIC HOLIDAYS
In this section you will find a list of holidays for each month that have a significance in a specific country. It could be related to a specific war, a day of remembrance, a day of historical significance, or national days of observance. There will also be a brief explanation of the holiday. This will help you plan a possible focus of learning for a specific month. I cannot count how many times a holiday with learning potential has snuck on me and passed leaving me disappointed that I had not noticed it. If there is anything I want to do, it is to help you be successful.

POETRY STYLES & TERMS
This section will help you learn about different poetry styles and terms. This will help you better educate yourself and children in your life. If you

run across a poetry term you are unfamiliar with just flip to this section to find a concise explanation and broaden everyone's understanding.
TIP: *Throw a sticky note in as a bookmark for lightning speed reference.*

THE POETRY CHAPTERS
This book was created with the idea that people would be using it as an educational resource with or without tea. For this reason, I have organized the chapters by month. Each month contains poetry that will line up with seasons, holidays, and related themes. Each chapter contains a minimum of 13 poems. This gives you at least three poems a week to explore. Why not a poem for every weekday like the first book in the series? Many of the patriotic themed poems are significantly longer. One alone can provide a wealth of discussion possibilities. You could choose to focus on one for an entire week, read 3-4 every week, or hold a poetry tea time once a month and select your favorites from that month's chapter to read as your listeners sip their cuppa (English slang for cup of tea) and nibble on a cookie.
TIP: *Poems could be assigned for memorization, recitation, or copy work.*

THE POETS CORNER
Here I have provided for you some blank pages for you to either write your own poetry or to give you a spot to add some of your own favorite poetry.

RECIPES
This section is to help you get started on creating tasty treats for your poetry tea time. I have included classic English tea fare to includes a few of the mainstays such as the scone. In the first book A Year of Poetry Tea Time I stuck with everything traditional to the classic English tea. This time you will find some more cakes, cookies (biscuits), cupcakes and other tantalizing treats as well as new jams, finger sandwiches and more. Recipes include unique cuisine from different time periods and popular eats from different countries that may accompany a cup of tea. You won't have any problem pleasing the tiny pallets in your home. There are many recipes that are naturally gluten free and gluten free adjustments are included for many of the recipes. All recipes are made from scratch so you can learn and apply cooking skills. Cooking from scratch is a valuable life skill and increases self-confidence.
TIP: *Use these recipes to teach cooking skills to your children.*

Herbal Teas
In the first book there was a brief section on herbal teas and some of the benefits of drinking certain herbal teas. Now we are going to take a peek

into the history of herbal teas and how they were used through time. You will also learn how to plant your very own herbal tea garden

TIP: *make a list of the plants you would want to plant in your very own tea garden.*

Poetry Tea Time

In this section you will learn the basics of hosting a poetry tea time at home for your family or for inviting friends over for a casual, intimate poetry experience. If you are interested in creating a true English Tea experience you will was to check out the book *A Year of Poetry Tea Time: The Essential Guide to Everything Poetry and Tea* (English tea etiquette, menu planning, being a gracious host, table setting and lots more). It will have everything you need to create the perfect elegant poetry tea party.

BRINGING POETRY TO LIFE

Poetry doesn't have to only be experienced at home. In this section you will learn of other creative ways to explore and share the magic of patriotic poetry.

TIP: *Pick two to four patriotic holidays or events you will feature this year. You can refer to the Patriotic Holidays Section of this book*

POETRY RABBIT TRAILS

Hop off the path and blaze your own trail as you engage in learning activities inspired by the poetry in this book. With 65+ activities to choose from you will get to explore science, art, geography, cooking, music, writing and more.

TIP: *Be prepared by reading through the activities ahead of time.*

PATRIOTIC FIELD TRIPS

This is a list of museums, childhood homes and other significant poetry and patriotic sites you can visit.

TIP: *Pick a location nearest you and plan to learn about and take a trip to learn about a poet in depth.*

PATRIOTIC QUOTES

There are a total of fifty-six patriotic quotes included in this book. Twelve of them are located at the beginning of each chapter. The rest can be found under "Patriotic Quotes." I tried to include quotes that promoted liberty, freedom, education and would inspire one to do his or her best.

TIP: *These quotes can be used to start your week off with a great message, used on a fun letter board, or even used as copy work or memorization. You can even use them to learn about additional people in history.*

MINI POET BIOS

I have included a mini bio for every single poet featured in this collection. You will find the years they were born and died along with the country they were born in or most popular in. For instance, some poets who became very popular in Australia were actually born in England. When this happens, it is mentioned in their bio where they were actually born. When able, I included what inspired the poet to write poetry and how they received their education. If any poet had a life challenge as a child, I included it so children could see others overcoming obstacles. I included the ages they were first published, especially if they were published as a child. Often you will find the names of their first publication or their most popular works. When the word "collection" is used, it is referring to a book containing a collection of poetry. Another term used often is *pseudonym* which is another term for pen name. It will also be indicated if the poet was a soldier at war and what war he or she was a part of.

TIP: *Create a poetry timeline and add a poet when you read one of their poems.*

VOCABULARY (GLOSSARY)

Poetry has stood the test of time exposing us to words that are no longer used, rarely used, or spelt differently. Some words may be familiar, but struggle to actually define them when asked by inquiring minds. To help you out, I have included vocabulary definitions for any words that are not commonly used every day. You will find this information in two places. First, they are included right below the poem for quick reference. Second, they are located in the glossary. In the glossary, not only will you find the word and definition, but also any other poems that contain that particular word. Why did I bother doing this? So, you could read another poem and experience the word in multiple contexts. I tried to include all relevant definitions so you can deduce which one it is.

TIP: *Use the vocabulary words to create a fun spelling bee, picking words that would be age appropriate for your children or class.*

Discussing Poetry with Children

You are about to enter a fun new realm of imagination and intrigue. A world that will have your children laughing, pondering, and looking forward to what they will hear next. Children are capable of having deep conversations and developing critical thinking skills that will shape their future. But remember, all children are different. To some, critical thinking will come naturally, where others need a little help to develop such skills.

Below you will find an array of questions you can ask your children about any poem. Refer to the Poetry Styles & Terms section if you are unfamiliar with any of the poetry vocabulary. The questions are in basic categories to make it easier to find questions that are relevant.

–Make sure to encourage your child to explain their answer. Giving yes or no answers does not show understanding of concepts.

–If your children are at a loss for words, after giving them some silent time to think, then share your thoughts with them and ask if they have any other ideas.

–Don't belittle your child if they don't see or understand a poem, even if it seems obvious to you.

–If you're not sure what a poem means, then give your kids a chance to figure it out.

Poetry is unique as it can mean something to one person and something completely different to another. Remind your children of this concept and embrace their different ideas.

Questions related to poetry terms and style

–Do you think the meaning of this poem is obvious or does it have hidden meanings?

–Does this poem take place in a person's mind (lyric poetry) or at a physical location?

–Does this poem use imagery?

–Does this poem use rhyming words?

–Is this poem a narrative poem, which tells a story?

–Does this poem use satire?

–Did you notice a rhyme scheme in this poem?
–Was this poem meant to be romantic?
–What symbolism was used?

Questions related to feelings
–How did this poem make you feel?
–Do you like how this poem made you feel?
–Have you ever felt this way about something?
–What do you think caused the person to write this poem?
–How do you think the poet felt when he/she wrote the poem?
–Have you ever been in the same situation as the poet?

Questions about content
–Did you hear any new words?
–Do you think the poet was writing about something real or imaginary?
–What was the coolest part of the poem?
–Did you notice a specific style of poetry?
–What was the overall theme of the poem?
–Do you like this style of poetry?
–Would you have ended the poem the same?

Questions about values/morals
–What is this poem trying to teach us?
–Do you agree with the poet's point of view?
–Does this poem align with your family's values?
–How can this poem influence your decisions?

Questions that will work for any poem
–Why do you like or dislike this poem?
–What does this poem make you think of?
–Did you hear any words that were new to you?

Poetry Styles and Terms

Alliteration—using a letter sounds repetitively to create intrigue within a written work. Tongue twisters are a good example. Check out a Dr. Seuss book and look at all of the alliteration he uses.

Abecedarius poem— an acrostic, where the first word, strophe or verse appears in the order of the alphabet.

Acrostic—a word puzzle, poem or an composition where the letter at the beginning of each line spells a word or words.

Anaphora—using the same word or phrase over and over at the beginning or end of each line.

Blank Verse—poetry that is written with a meter, but without rhyming lines. It is almost always in Iambic Pentameter. John Milton's *Paradise Lost* is an entire epic poem that was written in blank verse.

Caesura—a pause that is made purposely. Usually, you know there is this pause because of punctuation. Things like dashes, slashes, and common punctuation. These usually appear in the middle of a line. Emily Dickinson loved to use caesura.

Couplet—a short, two-line verse. A couplet on its own creates a stanza.

Enjambment—there is no punctuation at the end of lines telling the reader not to stop. Instead, they are to read continuously without pause.

Free Verse—there are no rules to bind you when writing in free verse. There is no meter or rhyming unless the poet has chosen to do so. And even if they do they do not need to stick to it. It can be as long or as short as you would like. The poet is free to use alliteration, personification, and rhyme. “Fog” by Carl Sandburg is an example of free verse.

Foot—the name given to a unit or measurement in poetry. For example, a foot can represent two or three syllables. An iamb is the most common foot where it has two syllables and has a pattern of unstressed and stressed syllables.

Georgian Poets—there was a series of poem anthologies that were published by Harold Monro during the time of King George V. The poetry included in these anthologies are referred to as Georgian poets. There were five volumes published between 1912 and 1922. The style at the time was primarily romanticism, hedonism, and sentimentality.

Haiku—a Japanese form of poetry originally written about nature. A haiku has only three lines and follows a specific syllable pattern. The first line must have five syllables, the second line must have seven syllables and the third line has another five syllables. The lines do not rhyme.

Iamb—a two syllable part of a complete meter. The first syllable being unstressed and the second being stressed. Another term for this is “a foot.” The rhythm can be compared to a heartbeat.

Iambic Pentameter—a specific meter (rhythm) found in poetry. William Shakespeare is famous for his use of Iambic Pentameter. Each line has ten syllables which switch back and forth between stressed and unstressed syllables. There are five iambs in each line of the Iambic Pentameter. For those of you who are math minded: 2 syllables per iamb X 5 iambs per line = a 10-syllable line.

Internal Rhyme—where the rhyme happens in the center of a line.

Imagery—when a poet, or writer, uses words to create an image in the reader's mind. This includes metaphorical and figurative language.

Limerick—typically limericks are comical. They always have five lines. They follow a special rhyming pattern. The first, second and fifth line must rhyme and the third and fourth line have their own rhyme.

Lyric Poetry—Poetry that focuses on the feeling and thoughts of a single speaker. For instance, a poem expressing one's feelings of love or despair.

Meter—the pattern of beats (rhythm) within a line of poetry. Sometimes people will refer to the meter as a foot, or feet. It correlates with the number of feet in a line.
–Manometer has one foot
–Dimeter has two feet
–Trimeter has three feet

Monorhyme—when the ending rhyme sound of each line is the same.

Narrative Poetry—a poem that tells a story. They contain characters and have a beginning, middle, and end like a story. An example is Edgar Allen Poe's "The Raven."

Prose Poetry – A prose is the form of written language that is not organized according to formal patterns of verse. Words and phrases that build sentences and paragraphs. This is what you would consider normal writing like fairy tales, newspaper articles, books and so on. Prose Poetry is a piece of writing in prose having obvious poetic qualities, including, but not limited to, intensity, imagery, and possible rhythms. But it does not have to follow any rules of poetry structure.

Quatrain Poetry—a four-line poem or a four-lined stanza within a poem. They can use different rhyme scheme patterns.

Satire—the use of sarcasm, humor, mockery and exaggeration to make fun of people and/or society. It is a comical way to point out flaws and provoke a person or society to act and make a change. Techniques like exaggeration and irony are used to accomplish this. A caricature is a great visual example of satire.

Renku—a poem that is collaborated on with two or more poets. So much so that they even alternate who reads each alternating line. Each stanza must be self-standing. Each stanza may seem random, but there is supposed to be an association of some sort from one stanza to the next. There needs to be contrast from stanza to stanza. This style has many additional criteria that take practice to master.

Rhyme Schemes—it identifies the set pattern of rhyming for a particular poem. Rhyme schemes are represented by a set of capital letters. These letters can be used to identify which lines have matching rhymes. Rhyme Schemes that are often used are:
AAAA: each line ends with the same rhyme like Cat, Bat, Rat, Sat
ABAB: lines one and three rhyme and line two and four rhyme like play, phone, clay, stone
AABB: the first two lines rhyme and the second two lines rhyme like book, took, hair, care
ABCB: here only the second-and fourth-lines rhyme like flower, rain, daisy, pain

Romantic Poetry—scholars looking back in time to government, poetry, and art that they considered to be a virtuous time. A time of true nobility, poets tried to bring the style and grace of the Roman Era. So the term "Romantic" has to do with the Romans not love.

Shi fu— Shi means poetry in Chinese. Fu was a popular form of poetry during the Han dynasty. Fu means "rhapsody." Fu are parts of a poem that go into extreme extensive detail about a single place, person or detail. It also goes out of its way to use rare words. These poems were chanted, not sung. This style has been around since about 3 BCE.

Sonnet—a poem with fourteen lines and uses Iambic Pentameter. William Shakespeare is well known for his sonnets. The rhyme scheme typically used was ABAB CDCD EFEF GG.

Stanza—a grouping of lines.

Strophe—divisions within a poems structure containing stanzas with lines of varying length. This occurs often in free verse poetry and odes.

Syllable—this is a part of a word that only has a single beat or sound to it.

Tercet—a three lined poem or stanza.

Trochee—a foot opposite of the Iamb. Its syllables are stressed and then unstressed. An example of this is in the first line of William Bakes "The Tyger."

Poetry and War

War poetry is not a new form of expression. Even though the First World War is known as the "poets war," war poetry has been around for thousands of years. Poetry has been a way for people to express their thoughts and feeling about war. Everything from the mundane to the gruesome has been expressed for centuries. Men and women have picked up the pen to put their thoughts and feelings to paper when emotions ran hot or nerves were wracked with fear. A love sick wife or sweetheart worried for the one she adores. A stoic mother, locked in her room, immortalizing their husband in word, pouring out her soul as tears silently run down her cheeks. A father, struggling to recall the face of his son as he mourns the news of a son's lost life on the front lines. But there is no poetry that can compare to the verses written by those who lived the life of war in person.

This brief history will be shared in chronological order so you can see how war poetry has changed over time. Not only has the content of the poetry changed drastically but the view and perspective.

War and Glory Romanticized

Before World War One there was a very idealized picture painted of battle. Those who had never experienced war first hand had been told stories of courage, victory, and dying with honor. It had been going on for longer than written history. In the Iliad, an epic poem*, it shares the story of the Trojan War, you will read phrases like "bringing glory to all men." Homer (8th century BCE) carries a theme of honor and the idealistic idea that fighting in battle with glory is more precious than life itself. It is romanticized in this passage "Let me not then die ingloriously and without a struggle, but let me first do some great thing that shall be told among men hereafter."

The Vikings (800-1050) believed that the most honorable way to die was in battle. As a reward for dying honorably, you would be rewarded by living in Valholl (Valhalla), quite literally meaning "hall of the slain." There, the warriors could fight without injury, eat great feasts and drink to their hearts content for the rest of eternity.

Shakespeare joins the ranks of battle glorification in his play King Henry V. The Saint Crispin's Day speech Is given by King Henry V (1386-1422) himself to the men who are about to follow him into battle. It shares his thoughts on how important honor is and how nothing is more important to him.

> The fewer men, the greater share of honour.
> God's will! I pray thee, wish not one man more.
> By Jove, I am not covetous for gold,
> Nor care I who doth feed upon my cost;
> It yearns me not if men my garments wear;
> Such outward things dwell not in my desires:
> But if it be a sin to covet honour,
> I am the most offending soul alive.
> No, faith, my coz, wish not a man from England:
> God's peace! I would not lose so great an honour…"

Let's not forget William Wallace (c.1270-1305), a single man who was able to lead his Scottish brothers into battle at Stirling Bridge to fight against an unwanted English rule. In the end, he values freedom over preserving his own life. He is still remembered to this day as a martyr for Scottish freedom.

In the United State Davy Crocket (1786-1836) has so many stories told about him you could wonder if he was even a real person. Thanks to a series of pamphlets published called the Crockett Almanacs, it is hard to decipher reality from fiction. There are exaggerations like being able to leap out of his crib as a new born, wrestling bears, and fighting alligators, among many other wild tales. But one thing is for sure he believed in fighting for what was right. He defended the rights of the Native American people and he even traveled to Texas to help defend the Alamo. It is known that Davy Crocket did die in battle but the big question is how?

Crocket was larger than life and people wanted to know how he died. The slave of Commander William Barret Travis, Joe, said "Davy Crockett died like a hero, surrounded by heaps of the enemy." There was another account by a servant to Santa Anna who said that they found Davy Crocked dead with "no less that 16 dead Mexicans around the corpse of Colonel Crockett and one across it with the huge knife of Davy buried in the Mexican's bosom to the hilt." The accounts go on and on. He was the last of six men protecting the Alamo and rather than surrender he leapt from the wall and charged two soldiers. He was found dead with his coon skin cap. He was executed by firing squad, he was hit with a sword in the head after wounding eight Mexican soldiers. No matter how you look at it, people look at this American icon as a man larger than life and picture that he died in battle with honor.

Young Boys and War

Throughout time, young boys have been enamored with the idea of fighting in a war. The ability to protect his family with nothing but his might and strength is an innate drive most boys are born with. They want to sleigh the dragon, protect the weak, and show the woman in their life (be it a mother or the love of their life) that they are willing to give their life in order to protect them.

During the Civil war of the United States, young boys were begging to go to war, even as a drummer boy if needs be. They wanted to be part of "the club." They wanted to prove that they were men and ready to defend their country, land, and family. These boys with drums strapped to themselves were responsible for communicating commands to the troops on the battle field. One young boy, Johnny Clem, was so eager to get on the battle field he ran away from home at age 9 and tried to join the Union troops. He was told he could not join. But he was persistent and refused to leave. So, they kept him around and he learned how to be a drummer boy. They had a tiny uniform made for him and the men even put together money from their own pay so he could make the $13 wage the other men made. He is an extreme example. At the same time, there are an unknown number of boys, throughout time, who have lied about their age to join a war.

War from the Civilians Perspective

Soldiers are out in the heat of it all, but families and civilians feel the effects of war in their own way. The loss of loved ones, being surrounded by the bombardment of artillery, and experiencing the hatred that spreads because of war are a few of the ways. It doesn't matter if you are on the side of the attacker or attacked, it creates a very different perspective. There are loved ones involved in both instances and they all delt with their altered lives in their own way.

Some people choose to honor soldiers through poetry to help lift their spirits while other used words to express their disappointment and disgust. Enheduanna was a priestess from Suma, current day Iraq, and she spoke up against war at about 2300 BCE.

> You are blood rushing down a mountain,
> Spirit of hate, greed and anger,
> dominator of heaven and earth!
>
> -Enhedianna

Henry Wadsworth Longfellow shared the aching of his heart during the Christmas season after learning his son had been injured during the Civil War. Yet even in this dark moment he hopes for peace to return to the country he loves. This is expressed in the last two stanzas of his poem *Christmas Bells*.

> *And in despair I bowed my head;*
> *"There is no peace on earth," I said;*
> *"For hate is strong,*
> *And mocks the song*
> *Of peace on earth, good-will to men!"*
>
> *Then pealed the bells more loud and deep:*
> *"God is not dead, nor doth He sleep;*
> *The Wrong shall fail,*
> *The Right prevail,*
> *With peace on earth, good-will to men."*

Then in contrast you have this poem by Madison Julius Cawein who is keeping to traditional romanticism. Boosting the moral of the hero in his poem Victory. The poem closes with the lines

Hope lit to guide you through the war:
Yet draw your sword,
And shout your word,
And plunge into the battling horde!
Give Fate the lie!
And, live or die,
Yours, yours shall be the victory!

War poetry was dominated by those experiencing war from the outside. It was not uncommon for mothers, wives, sister, uncles, and other civilians to express one's feelings on paper with pride or sadness. But messengers and newspapers shared poems and stories of glory and heroism to keep moral up on the home front, but that was about to shift.

War on the Front Lines

War poetry had a moment of change during World War One. The amazing number of soldiers who took pen to paper completely changed how people viewed war. Soldiers describing things that few people had ever experienced. The carnage, fear and danger of war was piercing people to their core as they read the accounts of soldier life and the front lines. Poetry and verse describing lost friends, sights and sounds in a way that had never been written before. The glorified idea of battle was forever changed.

The First World War involved 16 nations resulting in a horrific 8 million deaths and over 21 million wounded. In the first day alone, 60 thousand British troops were lost. Warfare had changed dramatically and this created an unexpected stage of horror for all who were involved. Machine guns, poisoned gas, tanks and bomber planes were all new and unexpected foes to face. Wilfred Owen experienced all of this first hand. After being blown into the air by a bombardment of shells he was taken to Scotland to recover after lying in a hole of rubble for days with the remains of another comrade. There he met Siegfried Sassoon, an English poet.

To help Owen, he suggested that he write about his experiences through poetry to help work through the trauma of his experience. He wrote the poems *Arms and the Boys*, *Anthem For Doomed Youth*, and *Dulce Et Decorum Est* among others. For Owen, war numbed the soul and killed one's moral feelings. He believed that "the true poet must be truthful…" and felt that the original idea of fighting for glory was a waste. This sentiment was shared by many of his generation. At the same time, he wanted to continue to share what war was like and returned to battle after he had recovered.

Siegfried Sassoon has a very interesting story of his own. You can actually see his progression from idealistic naivety to harsh reality. He was born into a wealthy family and new nothing of hardship. He played tennis and golf and would go hunting with his brother. He enjoyed writing poetry but his mundane, sheltered, Edwardian life lent to very little inspiration. He decided to go to London for adventure and to study poetry. In 1914 when he arrived, he found a city in a tizzy over the coming war. People were excited to sign up for the adventure. Sassoon got caught up in the frenzy and enlisted into the British army. With anticipation he wrote the poem France:

FRANCE
By Siegfried Sassoon
She triumphs, in the vivid green
Where sun and quivering foliage meet;
And in each soldier's heart serene;
When death stood near them they have seen
The radiant forests where her feet
Move on a breeze of silver sheen.

And they are fortunate, who fight
For gleaming landscapes swept and shafted
And crowned by cloud pavilions white;
Hearing such harmonies as might

Only from Heaven be downward wafted—
Voices of victory and delight.

This is a prime example of the glorification of war. Sassoon, and all the other men who had enlisted, had no idea what they had signed up for. Dreams of grand adventure and being a war hero were still the common ideas people had of going to battle. Sadly, his idealistic view did not last long with the delivery of a telegram revealing the death of his brother Hamo. This changed Sassoon and made the reality of war impossible to ignore. In 1915 he was put in charge of a platoon and he was stationed at a supply station not far from the front lines. Day after day droves of injured men would walk past the depot. He kept a journal of his day-to-day experiences and tasks. During this time, he found another poet by the name Robert Graves. They enjoyed sneaking off from others to talk poetry. And they both made friends with David Thomas. When David lost his life both Sassoon and Graves were deeply hurt and it changed Sassoon forever. He recorded in his journal "today I knew what it means to find the soul washed pure with tears and the load of death was lifted from my heart."

Now moved to the front lines, Sassoon got to see what Graves had been writing about in his poetry (Graves had already fought on the front lines). Death was everywhere that he looked and it inspired the poem The Redeemer. It stated:

Darkness: the rain sluiced down; the mire was deep;
It was past twelve on a mid-winter night,
When peaceful folk in beds lay snug asleep;
There, with much work to do before the light,
We lugged our clay-sucked boots as best we might
Along the trench; sometimes a bullet sang,
And droning shells burst with a hollow bang;
We were soaked, chilled and wretched, every one;
Darkness; the distant wink of a huge gun.

Sassoon, once naive to the reality of his surroundings once said "I used to say I couldn't kill anyone in this war..." but after the loss of both his brother Hamo and friend David he no longer doubted his ability to take another man's life. With little care of whether he lived or died he started to take enormous risks and this once mild tempered man earned the name "Mad Jack." He would rush into dangerous situations, such as running strait into a trench full of Germans and it catching them so off guard so that they retreated.

In England, people were becoming aware of the dangers and they were no longer voluntarily signing up to fight. Poets like Sassoon and Graves had poetry published specifically to awaken the people back home to the realities of war. They wanted people to see the truth. Sassoon wrote the poem *In the Pink* and it was the first poem to truly create controversy.

In the Pink
By Siegfried Sassoon
So Davies wrote: ' This leaves me in the pink. '
Then scrawled his name: ' Your loving sweetheart Willie '
With crosses for a hug. He'd had a drink
Of rum and tea; and, though the barn was chilly,
For once his blood ram warm; he had pay to spend,
Winter was passing; soon the year would mend.

He couldn't sleep that night. Stiff in the dark
He groaned and thought of Sundays at the farm,
When he'd go out as cheerful as a lark
In his best suit to wander arm-in-arm
With brown-eyed Gwen, and whisper in her ear
The simple, silly things she liked to hear.

And then he thought: to-morrow night we trudge
Up to the trenches, and my boots are rotten.
Five miles of stodgy clay and freezing sludge,
And everything but wretchedness forgotten.
To-night he's in the pink; but soon he'll die.
And still the war goes on; he don't know why.

People didn't like to think of what was really happening. The idea of a young men dressed neatly in their uniforms and performing acts of valor was a much more pleasant sentiment than a young man mourning the inevitable loss of his life. For this reason, many papers didn't publish all of the poems he sent in, for fear it would make recruitment even harder.

Sassoon and Owen are only two of many soldiers who suffered and shared their experience through poetry. But through their example, we can see the transformation that can happen when young men experience life on the battlefield.

Nobody wants to go to war, but it is necessary to protect those who cannot protect themselves. It makes no difference if the war is current or long in the past. It doesn't matter if the war is near your home or in a distant land. War affects many, and with that comes a host of emotions. Poets throughout time have shared their thoughts from pomp and pride to melancholy and malice. They immortalize those who have bravely fought for freedom and to protect the liberty of others. Soldiers throughout time have been a part of this great woven tapestry of honor that none of us should take for granted. They are those who have fought for the dream of freedom. Thanks to poets throughout time, they will be remembered and we too can have a glimpse into the sacrifices they have made.

---

*Epic Poem—a long poem, written in a narrative form to tell of a journey, physical or mental.

The Boston Tea Party

Boston Gazette BOSTON, *December* 20. [1773] (see original clip below)

On Tuesday last the body of the people of this and all the adjacent towns, and others from the distance of twenty miles, assembled at the old south meeting-house, to inquire the reason of the delay in sending the ship Dartmouth, with the East-India Tea back to London, and having found that the owner had not taken the necessary steps for that purpose, they enjoin'd him at his peril to demand of the collector of the customs a clearance for the ship, and appointed a comm [it]tee of ten to see it performed ; after which they adjourn'd to the Thursday following ten o'clock. They then met and being inform'd by Mr. Rotch, that a clearance was refus'd him, they enjoyn'd him immediately to enter a protest and apply to the governor for a pass port by the castle, and adjourn'd again till three o'clock for the same day. At which time they again met and after waiting till near sunset Mr. Rotch came in and inform'd them that he had accordingly enter'd his protest and waited on the governor for a pass, but his excellency told him he could not consistent with his duty grant it until his vessel was qualified. The people finding all their efforts to preserve the property of the East India company and return it safely to London, frustrated by the tea consignees, the collector of the customs and the governor of the province, DISSOLVED their meeting. -- But, BEHOLD what followed ! A number of brave & resolute men, determined to do all in their power to save their country from the ruin which their enemies had plotted, in less than four hours, emptied every chest of tea on board the three ships commanded by the captains Hall, Bruce, and Coffin, amounting to 342 chests, into the sea ! ! without the least damaged done to the ships or any other property. The masters and owners are well pleas'd that their ships are thus clear'd ; and the people are almost universally congratulating each other on this happy event.

January

"We make war that we may live in peace."
-Aristotle

The Year
By Ella Wheeler Wilcox

What can be said in New Year rhymes,
That's not been said a thousand times?
The new years come, the old years go,
We know we dream, we dream we know.
We rise up laughing with the light,
We lie down weeping with the night.
We hug the world until it stings,
We curse it then and sigh for wings.
We live, we love, we woo, we wed,
We wreathe our brides, we sheet our dead.
We laugh, we weep, we hope, we fear,
And that's the burden of the year.

The Present Crisis
By James Russell Lowell

When a deed is done for Freedom, through the broad earth's aching breast
Runs a thrill of joy prophetic, trembling on from east to west,
And the slave, where'er he cowers, feels the soul within him climb
To the awful verge of manhood, as the energy sublime
Of a century bursts full-blossomed on the thorny stem of Time.
Through the walls of hut and palace shoots the instantaneous throe,
When the travail of the Ages wrings earth's systems to and fro;
At the birth of each new Era, with a recognizing start,
Nation wildly looks at nation, standing with mute lips apart,
And glad Truth's yet mightier man-child leaps beneath the Future's heart.
So the Evil's triumph sendeth, with a terror and a chill,
Under continent to continent, the sense of coming ill,
And the slave, where'er he cowers, feels his sympathies with God

In hot tear-drops ebbing earthward, to be drunk up by the sod,
Till a corpse crawls round unburied, delving in the nobler clod.
For mankind are one in spirit, and an instinct bears along,
Round the earth's electric circle, the swift flash of right or wrong;
Whether conscious or unconscious, yet Humanity's vast frame
Through its ocean-sundered fibres feels the gush of joy or shame;—
In the gain or loss of one race all the rest have equal claim.
Once to every man and nation comes the moment to decide,
In the strife of Truth with Falsehood, for the good or evil side;
Some great cause, God's new Messiah, offering each the bloom or blight,
Parts the goats upon the left hand, and the sheep upon the right,
And the choice goes by forever 'twixt that darkness and that light.
Hast thou chosen, O my people, on whose party thou shalt stand,
Ere the Doom from its worn sandals shakes the dust against our land?
Though the cause of Evil prosper, yet 'tis Truth alone is strong,
And, albeit she wander outcast now, I see around her throng
Troops of beautiful, tall angels, to enshield her from all wrong.
Backward look across the ages and the beacon-moments see,
That, like peaks of some sunk continent, jut through Oblivion's sea;
Not an ear in court or market for the low, foreboding cry
Of those Crises, God's stern winnowers, from whose feet earth's chaff must fly;
Never shows the choice momentous till the judgment hath passed by.
Careless seems the great Avenger; history's pages but record
One death-grapple in the darkness 'twixt old systems and the Word;
Truth forever on the scaffold, Wrong forever on the throne,—
Yet that scaffold sways the future, and, behind the dim unknown,
Standeth God within the shadow, keeping watch above his own.
We see dimly in the Present what is small and what is great,
Slow of faith how weak an arm may turn the iron helm of fate,
But the soul is still oracular; amid the market's din,
List the ominous stern whisper from the Delphic cave within,—
"They enslave their children's children who make compromise with sin."

Slavery, the earth-born Cyclops, fellest of the giant brood,
Sons of brutish Force and Darkness, who have drenched the earth with blood,
Famished in his self-made desert, blinded by our purer day,
Gropes in yet unblasted regions for his miserable prey;—
Shall we guide his gory fingers where our helpless children play?
Then to side with Truth is noble when we share her wretched crust,
Ere her cause bring fame and profit, and 'tis prosperous to be just;

Then it is the brave man chooses, while the coward stands aside,
Doubting in his abject spirit, till his Lord is crucified,
And the multitude make virtue of the faith they had denied.
Count me o'er earth's chosen heroes,—they were souls that stood alone,
While the men they agonized for hurled the contumelious stone,
Stood serene, and down the future saw the golden beam incline
To the side of perfect justice, mastered by their faith divine,
By one man's plain truth to manhood and to God's supreme design.
By the light of burning heretics Christ's bleeding feet I track,
Toiling up new Calvaries ever with the cross that turns not back,
And these mounts of anguish number how each generation learned
One new word of that grand *Credo* which in prophet-hearts hath burned
Since the first man stood God-conquered with his face to heaven upturned.
For Humanity sweeps onward: where to-day the martyr stands,
On the morrow crouches Judas with the silver in his hands;
Far in front the cross stands ready and the crackling fagots burn,
While the hooting mob of yesterday in silent awe return
To glean up the scattered ashes into History's golden urn.
'Tis as easy to be heroes as to sit the idle slaves
Of a legendary virtue carved upon our fathers' graves,
Worshippers of light ancestral make the present light a crime;—
Was the Mayflower launched by cowards, steered by men behind their time?
Turn those tracks toward Past or Future, that made Plymouth Rock sublime?
They were men of present valor, stalwart old iconoclasts,
Unconvinced by axe or gibbet that all virtue was the Past's;
But we make their truth our falsehood, thinking that hath made us free,
Hoarding it in mouldy parchments, while our tender spirits flee
The rude grasp of that great Impulse which drove them across the sea.
They have rights who dare maintain them; we are traitors to our sires,
Smothering in their holy ashes Freedom's new-lit altar-fires;
Shall we make their creed our jailer? Shall we, in our haste to slay,
From the tombs of the old prophets steal the funeral lamps away
To light up the martyr-fagots round the prophets of to-day?
New occasions teach new duties; Time makes ancient good uncouth;
They must upward still, and onward, who would keep abreast of Truth;
Lo, before us gleam her camp-fires! we ourselves must Pilgrims be,
Launch our Mayflower, and steer boldly through the desperate winter sea,
Nor attempt the Future's portal with the Past's blood-rusted key.

abreast—facing the same direction side by side with others

prophetic—something that is described or predicted to happen in the future.
cowers—to act or shrink away in fear.
throe—a struggle that is painful or a violent struggle
ebbing—something that is becoming less or moving away or receding
sunder—to be taken or smashed apart
blight—a plant disease caused by a fungus
albeit—same meaning as although
foreboding—having a feeling that something bad will happen
winnower—a person who fishes for minnows.
oracular—related to an oracle, something representing or holding the powers of an oracle.
Delphic—related to the antient Greek oracle Delphi
contumelious —acting insulting, scornful and/or insulting
heretic —beliefs different than those commonly accepted or believing and doing things contrary to religious beliefs.
calvaries —referring to a representation of the crucifixion of Christ.
Credo —This is a Latin word referring to a statement of beliefs, a creed
martyr —a person who is killed for what they believe.
iconoclast —a person who attacks popular beliefs or destroys religious images.
mouldy —another spelling of moldy
faggots —a bundle of sticks to use as fuel.
uncouth —bad behavior or poor manners

Character of the Happy Warrior
By William Wordsworth

Who is the happy Warrior? Who is he
That every man in arms should wish to be?
—It is the generous Spirit, who, when brought
Among the tasks of real life, hath wrought
Upon the plan that pleased his boyish thought:
Whose high endeavours are an inward light
That makes the path before him always bright;
Who, with a natural instinct to discern
What knowledge can perform, is diligent to learn;
Abides by this resolve, and stops not there,
But makes his moral being his prime care;
Who, doomed to go in company with Pain,

And Fear, and Bloodshed, miserable train!
Turns his necessity to glorious gain;
In face of these doth exercise a power
Which is our human nature's highest dower:
Controls them and subdues, transmutes, bereaves
Of their bad influence, and their good receives:
By objects, which might force the soul to abate
Her feeling, rendered more compassionate;
Is placable—because occasions rise
So often that demand such sacrifice;
More skillful in self-knowledge, even more pure,
As tempted more; more able to endure,
As more exposed to suffering and distress;
Thence, also, more alive to tenderness.
—'Tis he whose law is reason; who depends
Upon that law as on the best of friends;
Whence, in a state where men are tempted still
To evil for a guard against worse ill,
And what in quality or act is best
Doth seldom on a right foundation rest,
He labours good on good to fix, and owes
To virtue every triumph that he knows:
—Who, if he rise to station of command,
Rises by open means; and there will stand
On honourable terms, or else retire,
And in himself possess his own desire;
Who comprehends his trust, and to the same
Keeps faithful with a singleness of aim;
And therefore does not stoop, nor lie in wait
For wealth, or honours, or for worldly state;
Whom they must follow; on whose head must fall,
Like showers of manna, if they come at all:
Whose powers shed round him in the common strife,
Or mild concerns of ordinary life,
A constant influence, a peculiar grace;
But who, if he be called upon to face
Some awful moment to which Heaven has joined
Great issues, good or bad for human kind,
Is happy as a Lover; and attired
With sudden brightness, like a Man inspired;
And, through the heat of conflict, keeps the law
In calmness made, and sees what he foresaw;

Or if an unexpected call succeed,
Come when it will, is equal to the need:
—He who, though thus endued as with a sense
And faculty for storm and turbulence,
Is yet a Soul whose master-bias leans
To homefelt pleasures and to gentle scenes;
Sweet images! which, wheresoe'er he be,
Are at his heart; and such fidelity
It is his darling passion to approve;
More brave for this, that he hath much to love:—
'Tis, finally, the Man, who, lifted high,
Conspicuous object in a Nation's eye,
Or left unthought-of in obscurity,—
Who, with a toward or untoward lot,
Prosperous or adverse, to his wish or not—
Plays, in the many games of life, that one
Where what he most doth value must be won:
Whom neither shape or danger can dismay,
Nor thought of tender happiness betray;
Who, not content that former worth stand fast,
Looks forward, persevering to the last,
From well to better, daily self-surpast:
Who, whether praise of him must walk the earth
For ever, and to noble deeds give birth,
Or he must fall, to sleep without his fame,
And leave a dead unprofitable name—
Finds comfort in himself and in his cause;
And, while the mortal mist is gathering, draws
His breath in confidence of Heaven's applause:
This is the happy Warrior; this is he
That every man in arms should wish to be.

---

wrought—to be formed and shaped
dower—a widows share in her husband's estate. Noun for the word dowery.
transmute— changes in form
bereave—actively suffering from the loss of a loved one.
placable—forgiving, calmed, easily pacified

Sailing to Byzantium
By William Butler Yeats
I

That is no country for old men. The young
In one another's arms, birds in the trees,
—Those dying generations—at their song,
The salmon-falls, the mackerel-crowded seas,
Fish, flesh, or fowl, commend all summer long
Whatever is begotten, born, and dies.
Caught in that sensual music all neglect
Monuments of unageing intellect.

II

An aged man is but a paltry thing,
A tattered coat upon a stick, unless
Soul clap its hands and sing, and louder sing
For every tatter in its mortal dress,
Nor is there singing school but studying
Monuments of its own magnificence;
And therefore I have sailed the seas and come
To the holy city of Byzantium.

III

O sages standing in God's holy fire
As in the gold mosaic of a wall,
Come from the holy fire, perne in a gyre,
And be the singing-masters of my soul.
Consume my heart away; sick with desire
And fastened to a dying animal
It knows not what it is; and gather me
Into the artifice of eternity.

IV

Once out of nature I shall never take
My bodily form from any natural thing,
But such a form as Grecian goldsmiths make
Of hammered gold and gold enamelling
To keep a drowsy Emperor awake;

Or set upon a golden bough to sing
To lords and ladies of Byzantium
Of what is past, or passing, or to come.

---

sensual—Having great satisfaction of the senses
tatter—when cloth is torn irregularly
Byzantium—later known as Constantinople, Byzantium was an ancient Greek city that existed during the classical antiquity.
perne—power, glory, rank
gyre—to whirl or gyrate
Grecian—referring to ancient Greece and often refers to the architecture of the time.
bough—the larger branches of a tree

Address to Edinburgh
By Robert Burns
Written in Augustian English

I.

Edina! Scotia's darling seat!
   All hail thy palaces and tow'rs,
Where once beneath a monarch's feet
   Sat Legislation's sov'reign pow'rs!
From marking wildly-scatter'd flow'rs,
   As on the banks of Ayr I stray'd,
And singing, lone, the ling'ring hours,
   I shelter in thy honour'd shade.

II.

Here wealth still swells the golden tide,
   As busy Trade his labour plies;
There Architecture's noble pride
   Bids elegance and splendour rise;
Here Justice, from her native skies,
   High wields her balance and her rod;
There Learning, with his eagle eyes,
   Seeks Science in her coy abode.

III.

Thy sons, Edina! social, kind,
   With open arms the stranger hail;
Their views enlarg'd, their liberal mind,
   Above the narrow, rural vale;
Attentive still to sorrow's wail,
   Or modest merit's silent claim;
And never may their sources fail!
   And never envy blot their name!

IV.

Thy daughters bright thy walks adorn,
   Gay as the gilded summer sky,
Sweet as the dewy milk-white thorn,

Dear as the raptur'd thrill of joy!
Fair Burnet strikes th' adoring eye,
Heav'n's beauties on my fancy shine;
I see the Sire of Love on high,
And own his work indeed divine!

V.

There, watching high the least alarms,
Thy rough, rude fortress gleams afar,
Like some bold vet'ran, gray in arms,
And mark'd with many a seamy scar:
The pond'rous wall and massy bar,
Grim-rising o'er the rugged rock,
Have oft withstood assailing war,
And oft repell'd th' invader's shock.

VI.

With awe-struck thought, and pitying tears,
I view that noble, stately dome,
Where Scotia's kings of other years,
Fam'd heroes! had their royal home:
Alas, how chang'd the times to come!
Their royal name low in the dust!
Their hapless race wild-wand'ring roam,
Tho' rigid law cries out, 'twas just!

VII.

Wild beats my heart to trace your steps,
Whose ancestors, in days of yore,
Thro' hostile ranks and ruin'd gaps
Old Scotia's bloody lion bore:
Ev'n I who sing in rustic lore,
Haply, my sires have left their shed,
And fac'd grim danger's loudest roar,
Bold-following where your fathers led!

VIII.

Edina! Scotia's darling seat!
   All hail thy palaces and tow'rs,
Where once beneath a monarch's feet
   Sat Legislation's sov'reign pow'rs!
From marking wildly-scatter'd flow'rs,
   As on the hanks of Ayr I stray'd,
And singing, lone, the ling'ring hours,
   I shelter in thy honour'd shade.

---

sov'reign—(sovereign) A ruler such as a monarch like a king, queen or emporer.
coy—To act shy or modest in the effort to draw attention.
gay—happy
gilded—covered in gold, traditionaly thought of as gold leaf (real gold). gold paint
rapture—an intense feeling of joy
Fair Burnet—this is referring to Eliza Burnett (1766-1790) who was the daughter of a Scottish philosopher (Lord Monboddo) and she was one of the most popular young ladies of Edinburgh.
pond'rous—very heavy in weight
hapless—unfortunate

Address to a Haggis
By Robert Burns

Fair fa' your honest, sonsie face,
Great chieftain o' the pudding-race!
Aboon them a' ye tak your place,
   Painch, tripe, or thairm:
Weel are ye wordy o' a grace
   As lang's my arm.

The groaning trencher there ye fill,
Your hurdies like a distant hill,
Your pin wad help to mend a mill
   In time o' need,
While thro' your pores the dews distil
   Like amber bead.

His knife see rustic-labour dight,
An' cut you up wi' ready slight,
Trenching your gushing entrails bright
   Like onie ditch;
And then, O what a glorious sight,
   Warm-reekin, rich!

Then horn for horn they stretch an' strive,
Deil tak the hindmost, on they drive,
'Till a' their weel-swall'd kytes belyve
   Are bent like drums;
Then auld Guidman, maist like to rive,
   Bethankit hums.

Is there that o'er his French ragout,
Or olio that wad staw a sow,
Or fricassee wad mak her spew
   Wi' perfect sconner,
Looks down wi' sneering, scornfu' view
   On sic a dinner?

Poor devil! see him owre his trash,
As feckless as a wither'd rash,
His spindle shank a guid whip-lash,
   His nieve a nit;

Thro' bloody flood or field to dash,
   O how unfit!

But mark the rustic, haggis-fed,
The trembling earth resounds his tread,
Clap in his walie nieve a blade,
   He'll mak it whissle;
An' legs, an' arms, an' heads will sned,
   Like taps o' thrissle.

Ye pow'rs wha mak mankind your care,
And dish them out their bill o' fare,
Auld Scotland wants nae stinking ware
   That jaups in luggies;
But, if ye wish her gratefu' pray'r,
   Gie her a Haggis!

---

sonsie—Having a healthy and attractive look
painch—the first stomach section (rumen) of the sheep's digestive system.
thairm—intestines, in this instance it is referring to a sheep's intestines.
hurdies—the buttocks
onie—any
reekin—not smelling good or stinking

BALTO
By Dorothy Parker

I think that you could only pity me
Who'd want to weep and stroke your head and coo
And murmur little names, mellifluously,
And know no other thing to do.

What should I do, but drop my eyes, and strain
To cloak the meanness of my offerings,
Who an aggrieved at cold, and hide from pain,
And live with little, little things.

My days slip by in thin and wavering line;
Softened my life to such as sick men lead.
And sharp there cuts across dimmed hours like mine
The cold white radiance of your deed.

Outraging cornered Death, you held the course
Against the whining night, the whirling day.
When man gave over to the inhuman force,
Then it was you who led the way.

Though never trumpet urged you to the fight,
And roystering rush of war was not your part,
Your spirit was a rocket in the night,
You bore a banner in your heart.

Not hope of cited glory led you then,
Simply, so went your days since they began.
You did the thing, not thought of it again,
A very gallant gentleman.

---

mellifluous(ly)—a smooth rich sound like a voice, soothing
aggrieved—when someone feels as if they have been treated unfairly or feel resentment towards a person or specific outcome.
roystering— to be a part of a noisy revelry, merrymaking
gallant—to be brave or heroic

Receipt To Make A Sally Lun
By Major Drewe of Exeter

NO more I heed the muffin zest
The Yorkshire cake or bun
Sweet Muse of Pastry teach me how
To make a Sally Lun.

Take thou of luscious wholesome cream
What the full pint contains
Warm as the native Mood which glows
In youthful virgin's veins

Hast thou not seen in olive rind
The wall-tree's rounded nut
Of juicy butter just its size
In thy clean pastry put

Hast thou not seen the golden yolk
In Chrystal shrine immur'd
Whence brooded o'er by sostring wing
Forth springs the warrior bird?

Oh save three birds from savage man
And combat's sanguine hour
Cush in three yolk, the seeds of life
And on the butter pour

Take then a cup that hold the juice
Fam'd China's fairest pride
Let foaming yeast its concave fill
And froth adown its side

But seek thou first for neatness sake
The Naiad's crystal stream
Swift let it round the concave play
And o'er the surface gleam

Of salt more keen than that of Greece
Which cooks not poets use
Sprinkle thou then with sparing hand
And thro the mass diffuse

Then let it rest disturb'd no more
Safe in its steady feat
Till thrice Time's warning bell hath struck
Nor yet the hour compleat

And now let Fancy revel free
By no stern rule confin'd
On glittr'ing tin in varied form
Each Sally-Lun be twin'd

But heed thou west to lift thy thought
To me thy power divine
Then to the oven's glowing mouth
The woud'rous work consign

Sally Lun—this is a sweet bun mad popular in Bath, England made by Solange Luyon, a French immigrant who moved to Bath in 1680. Learn more about the sweet bun in the bread recipe section of this book.
Sanguine—having a positive attitude, even in a bad situation

The Four Ages of Man
By William Butler Yeats

He with body waged a fight,
But body won; it walks upright.
Then he struggled with the heart;
Innocence and peace depart.
Then he struggled with the mind;
His proud heart he left behind.
Now his wars on God begin;
At stroke of midnight God shall win.

The Rule of Life
By Johann Wolfgang von Goethe

If thou wouldst live unruffled by care,
Let not the past torment thee e'er;
As little as possible be thou annoy'd,
And let the present be ever enjoy'd;
Ne'er let thy breast with hate be supplied,
And to God the future confide.

Bolt That Door!
William Arthur Dunkerley
Also known as John Oxenham

Each sin has its door of entrance.
Keep--that--door--closed!
Bolt it tight!
Just outside, the wild beast crouches
In the night.
Pin the bolt with a prayer,
God will fix it there.

Mark Twain and Joan of Arc
By Vachel Lindsay

When Yankee soldiers reach the barricade
Then Joan of Arc gives each the accolade.

For she is there in armor clad, today,
All the young poets of the wide world say.

Which of our freemen did she greet the first,
Seeing him come against the fires accurst?

Mark Twain, our Chief, with neither smile nor jest,
Leading to war our youngest and our best.

The Yankee to King Arthur's court returns.
The sacred flag of Joan above him burns.

For she has called his soul from out the tomb.
And where she stands, there he will stand till doom.

But I, I can but mourn, and mourn again
At bloodshed caused by angels, saints, and men.

---

accolade—an award given to acknowledge great merit as a special honor. This can be an award or a ceremony like being knighted.
clad—clothed
jest—joke
mourn—deep sorrow over the loss of someone

The Song of Australia

By Caroline Carleton

There is a land where summer skies
Are gleaming with a thousand eyes,
Blending in witching harmonies ;
And grassy knoll and forest height,
Are flushing in the rosy light,
And all above is azure bright — Australia!
There is a land where honey flows,
Where laughing corn luxuriant grows,
Land of the myrtle and the rose;
On hill and plain the clust'ring vine
Is gushing out with purple wine,
And cups are quaffed to thee and thine — Australia!
There is a land where treasures shine
Deep in the dark unfathom'd mine
For worshippers at Mammon's shrine;
Where gold lies hid, and rubies gleam,
And fabled wealth no more doth seem
The idle fancy of a dream — Australia!
There is a land where homesteads peep
From sunny plain and woodland steep,
And love and joy bright vigils keep;
Where the glad voice of childish glee
Is mingling with the melody
Of nature's hidden minstrelsy — Australia!
There is a land where, floating free,
From mountain-top to girdling sea,
A proud flag waves exultingly;
And FREEDOM'S sons the banner bear,
No shackled slave can breathe the air,
Fairest of Britain's daughters fair — Australia!

---

knoll—a small mound or hill
harmonies—a combination of notes sounded at the same time to create cords having a pleasant sound to the ear.
azure—a blue hugh like a sky on a clear day
luxuriant—lavish or lush growth
myrtle—an evergreen shrub
quaffed—to drink in large quantities
Mammon—A biblical term for riches
vigil—waiting in prayer or peace
minstrelsy—a wandering musician of medieval time
girdling—to encircle like a belt

George Washington
Inspiration unknown

Oh Ye Gods why should my Poor Resistless Heart
Stand to oppose thy might and Power
At Last surrender to cupids feather'd Dart
And now lays Bleeding every Hour
For her that's Pityless of my grief and Woes
And will not on me Pity take
Ill sleep amongst my most Inviterate Foes
And with gladness never with to Wake
In deluding sleepings let my Eyelids close
That in an enraptured Dream I may
In a soft lulling sleep and gentle repose
Possess those joys denied by Day

---

pityless (pitiless)—cruel; showing no compassion
inviterate (inveterate)—a habit that someone has had for a long time and unlikely to change.
deluding—to be deceived by a misleading belief; foolish
enraptured—extremely pleasant; full of joy or pleasure

We Are America
By Joshua Pung

The green grass lush as the treetops.
The mountains calling,
Pointing to the heavens.
The clouds as blue as the ocean,
Winds whirling.
My land.
Your land.
From which we, as the foundation of our great country
Rebuild.
Reviving,
From the imminent doom that surrounds us
We emerge.
The victors.
Making the dark seem even dimmer in our light.
A fire,
Unquenchable,

Shining brighter than the sun.
The Son of God
Lending us strength
We. Are. America.
A place where everybody is welcome.
And we are welcome to them.
Together, In union,
We. Are. America.

---

imminent—something that is anticipated or about to happen
unquenchable—unable to be satisfied or extinguished

Winter
By H. P. Nichols

With my breath so keen and chilling,
  I have stripped the branches bare;
And my snow-flakes white are filling,
  Feather-like, the frosty air.

Coming o'er the lofty mountains,
  There I left a robe of white;
I have locked the sparkling fountains,
  I have chained the river bright.

O'er the quiet valley winging,
  There I left my traces, too;
Hark! the merry sleigh-bells ringing,
  With their music call on you.

I have come! The school-boy shouting,
  Joyfully brings out his sled;
He has seen me, nothing doubting,
  As across the fields he sped.

I have come; but shall I find you
  Better than the former year?
If you've cast your faults behind you,
  I shall gladly greet you here.

February

"The life of the nation is secure only while the nation is honest, truthful, and virtuous."
–Frederick Douglas

America
By Claude McKay

Although she feeds me bread of bitterness,
And sinks into my throat her tiger's tooth,
Stealing my breath of life, I will confess
I love this cultured hell that tests my youth!
Her vigour flows like tides into my blood,
Giving me strength erect against her hate.
Her bigness sweeps my being like a flood.
Yet as a rebel fronts a king in state,
I stand within her walls with not a shred
Of terror, malice, not a word of jeer.
Darkly I gaze into the days ahead,
And see her might and granite wonders there,
Beneath the touch of Time's unerring hand,
Like priceless treasures sinking in the sand.

---

malice—wanting to do evil; ill will
jeer—to make mocking or rude remarks towards someone
unerring—to always be right; not in error

On Being Brought from Africa to America
By Phillis Wheatley

Twas mercy brought me from my *Pagan* land,
Taught my benighted soul to understand
That there's a God, that there's a *Saviour* too:
Once I redemption neither sought nor knew.
Some view our sable race with scornful eye,
"Their colour is a diabolic die."
Remember, *Christians, Negros,* black as *Cain,*
May be refin'd, and join th' angelic train.

---

benighted—a state of moral ignorance; a state of pitifulness
sable—a color that is dark brown or black
diabolical—unpleasant, extremely bad; like the devil
Cain—biblical name of a person who killed his own brother.

Cotton King
By Horatio Alger Jr.

King Cotton looks from his window
Towards the westering sun,
And he marks, with an anguished horror,
That his race is almost run.

His form is thin and shrunken;
His cheek is pale and wan;
And the lines of care on his furrowed brow
Are dread to look upon.

But yesterday a monarch,
In the flush of his pomp and pride,
And, not content with his own broad lands,
He would rule the world beside.

He built him a stately palace,
With gold from beyond the sea;
And he laid with care the corner-stone,
And he called it Slavery:

He summoned an army with banners,
To keep his foes at bay;
And, gazing with pride on his palace walls,

He said, "They will stand for aye!"

But the palace walls are shrunken,
And partly overthrown,
And the storms of war, in their violence,
Have loosened the corner-stone.

Now Famine stalks through the palace halls,
With her gaunt and pallid train;
You can hear the cries of famished men,
As they cry for bread in vain.

The king can see, from his palace walls.
A land by his pride betrayed;
Thousands of mothers and wives bereft.
Thousands of graves new-made.

And he seems to see, in the lowering sky,
The shape of a flaming sword;
Whereon he reads, with a sinking heart,
The anger of the Lord.

God speed the time when the guilty king
Shall be hurled from his blood-stained throne;
And the palace of Wrong shall crumble to dust,
With its boasted corner-stone.

A temple of Freedom shall rise instead,
On the desecrated site:
And within its shelter alike shall stand
The black man and the white.

---

wan—pale skin like someone who is sick
monarch—a ruler of a land such as a king, queen, or emperor
gaunt—a person who is thin and suffering from age, hunger, or neglect.
bereft—deprived or lacking in something

Occasioned by George Washington's Arrival in Philadelphia, on his way to Residence in Virginia
By Philip Freneau

The great, unequal conflict past,
The Briton banish'd from our shore,
Peace, heav'n-descended, comes at last,
And hostile nations rage no more;
From fields of death the weary swain
Returning, seeks his native plain.

In every vale she smiles serene,
Freedom's bright stars more radiant rise,
New charms she adds to every scene,
Her brighter sun illumes our skies;
Remotest realms admiring stand,
And hail the *Hero* of our land:

He comes!—the Genius of these lands—
Fame's thousand tongues his worth confess,
Who conquered with his suffering bands,
And grew immortal by distress:
Thus calms succeed the stormy blast,
And valour is repaid at last.

O Washington!—thrice glorious name,
What due rewards can man decree—
Empires are far below thy aim,
And sceptres have no charms for thee;
Virtue alone has thy regard,
And she must be thy great reward.

Encircled by extorted power,
Monarchs must envy thy Retreat,
Who cast, in some ill fated hour,
Their country's freedom at their feet;
'Twas thine to act a nobler part
For injur'd Freedom had thy heart.

For ravag'd realms and conquer'd seas
Borne gave the great imperial prize,
And, swelTd with pride, for feats like these,

Transferr'd her heroes to the skies:—
A brighter scene your deeds display,
You gain those heights a different way.

When *Faction* rear'd her bristly head,
And join'd with tyrants to destroy,
Where'er you march' d the monster fled,
Tim'rous her arrows to employ;
Hosts catch'd from you a bolder flame,
And despots trembled at your name.

Ere war's dread horrors ceas'd to reign,
What leader could your place supply?—
Chiefs crowded to the embattled plain,
Prepaid to conquer or to die—
Heroes arose— but none like yon
Could save our lives and freedom too.

In swelling verse let kings be read,
And princes shine in polish'd prose;
Without such aid your triumphs spread
Where'er the convex ocean flows,
To Indian worlds by seas embrac'd,
And Tartar, tyrant of the waste.

Throughout the east you gain applause,
And soon the *Old World*, taught by you,
Shall blush to own her barbarous laws,
Shall learn instruction from the *New*:
Monarchs shall hear the humble plea,
Nor urge too far the proud decree.

Despising pomp and vain parade,
At home you stay, while France and Spain
The secret, ardent wish convey'd,
And hail'd you to their shores in vain:
In *Vernon's* groves you shun the throne,
Admir'd by kings, but seen by none.

Your fame, thus spread to distant lands,
May envy's fiercest blasts endure,
Like Egypt's pyramids it stands,

Built on a basis more secure;
Time's latest age shall own in you
The patriot and the statesman too.

Now hurrying from the busy scene,
Where thy *Potowmack's* waters flow,
Mayt thou enjoy thy rural reign,
And every earthly blessing know;
Thus He whom Rome's proud legions sway'd,
Beturn'd, and sought his sylvan shade.

Not less in wisdom than in war
Freedom shall still employ your mind,
Slavery shall vanish, wide and far,
'Till not a trace is left behind;
Your counsels not bestow'd in vain
Shall still protect this infant reign,

So when the bright, all-cheering sun
From our contracted view retires,
Though fools may think his race is run,
On other worlds he lights his fires:
Cold climes beneath his influence glow,
And frozen rivers learn to flow.

O say, thou great, exalted name!
What Muse can boast of equal lays,
Thy worth disdains all vulgar fame,
Transcends the noblest poet's praise,
Art soars, unequal to the flight,
And genius sickens at the height.

For States redeem'd— our western reign
Restored by thee to milder sway,
Thy conscious glory shall remain
When this great globe is swept away,
And *all* is lost that pride admires,
And all the pageant scene expires.

---

sceptres—a decorative and ornamental staff carried by rulers for ceremonies.
monarch—a ruler such as a king, queen or emperor

extorted—to obtain something in an unfair way like threatening or by force.
convex—when something is curved outwards like the exterior of a circle or like the lens of a telescope or glasses.
barbarous—primitive, uncivilized, and very brutal; savage
patriot(s)—a person(s) devoted to supporting his country and willing to defend it.
pomp—elaborate ceremony meant for show that are ostentatious and boastful.
Vernon—the home of George Washington was named Mount Vernon
sylvan—a rural wooded area
lays—in this instance the word lays refers to a sound of a musical quality

A Nation's Strength
By William Ralph Emerson

What makes a nation's pillars high
And its foundations strong?
What makes it mighty to defy
The foes that round it throng?

It is not gold. Its kingdoms grand
Go down in battle shock;
Its shafts are laid on sinking sand,
Not on abiding rock.

Is it the sword? Ask the red dust
Of empires passed away;
The blood has turned their stones to rust,
Their glory to decay.

And is it pride? Ah, that bright crown
Has seemed to nations sweet;
But God has struck its luster down
In ashes at his feet.

Not gold but only men can make
A people great and strong;
Men who for truth and honor's sake
Stand fast and suffer long.

Brave men who work while others sleep,
Who dare while others fly...
They build a nation's pillars deep
And lift them to the sky.

---

abiding—an object or feeling that lasts a long time like a rock or a memory.
luster—a gentle sheen or glow or luster often from light reflecting off an object.

Washington's Monument, February, 1885
By Walt Whitman

Ah, not this marble, dead and cold:
Far from its base and shaft expanding—the round zones circling, comprehending,
Thou, Washington, art all the world's, the continents' entire—not yours alone, America,
Europe's as well, in every part, castle of lord or laborer's cot,
Or frozen North, or sultry South—the African's—the Arab's in his tent,
Old Asia's there with venerable smile, seated amid her ruins;
(Greets the antique the hero new? 'tis but the same—the heir legitimate, continued ever,
The indomitable heart and arm—proofs of the never-broken line,
Courage, alertness, patience, faith, the same—e'en in defeat defeated not, the same:)
Wherever sails a ship, or house is built on land, or day or night,
Through teeming cities' streets, indoors or out, factories or farms,
Now, or to come, or past—where patriot wills existed or exist,

Wherever Freedom, pois'd by Toleration, sway'd by Law,
Stands or is rising thy true monument.

---

sultry—humid and hot
venerable—respect because of age, character, or wisdom
indomitable—Impossible to defeat or subdue
patriot(s)—a person(s) devoted to supporting his country and willing to defend it.

A Soldier's Valentine
By Horatio Alger Jr.

Just from the sentry's tramp
(I must take it again at ten),
I have laid my musket down,
And seized instead my pen;
For, pacing my lonely round
In the chilly twilight gray,
The thought, dear Mary, came,
That this is St. Valentine's Day.

And with the thought there came
A glimpse of the happy time
When a school-boy's first attempt
I sent you, in borrowed rhyme,
On a gilt-edged sheet, embossed
With many a quaint design,
And signed, in school-boy hand,
"Your loving Valentine."

The years have come and gone,--
Have flown, I know not where, --
And the school-boy's merry face
Is grave with manhood's care;
But the heart of the man still
beats
At the well-remembered name,
And on this St. Valentine's Day
His choice is still the same.

There was a time-- ah, well!
Think not that I repine
When I dreamed this happy day
Would smile on you as mine;
But I heard my country's call;
I knew her need was sore.
Thank God, no selfish thought
Withheld me from the war.

But when the dear old flag
Shall float in its ancient pride,
When the twain shall be made
one,
And feuds no more divide,--
I will lay my musket down,
My martial garb resign,
And turn my joyous feet
Toward home and Valentine.

---

sentry—a soldier standing guard
gilt— covered in gold, traditionally thought of as gold leaf (real gold). gold paint.

Lincoln
By Vachel Lindsay

Would I might rouse the Lincoln in you all,
That which is gendered in the wilderness
From lonely prairies and God's tenderness.
Imperial soul, star of a weedy stream,
Born where the ghosts of buffaloes still dream,
Whose spirit hoof-beats storm above his grave,
Above that breast of earth and prairie-fire—
Fire that freed the slave.

**Abraham Lincoln is the 16th president of the United Sates and he was Born on February 12th 1809*

Greater Love
By Wilfred Edward Salter Owen

Red lips are not so red
As the stained stones kissed by the English dead.
Kindness of wooed and wooer
Seems shame to their love pure.
O Love, your eyes lose lure
When I behold eyes blinded in my stead!

Your slender attitude
Trembles not exquisite like limbs knife-skewed,
Rolling and rolling there
Where God seems not to care;
Till the fierce Love they bear
Cramps them in death's extreme decrepitude.

Your voice sings not so soft,--
Though even as wind murmuring through raftered loft,--
Your dear voice is not dear,
Gentle, and evening clear,
As theirs whom none now hear
Now earth has stopped their piteous mouths that coughed.

Heart, you were never hot,
Nor large, nor full like hearts made great with shot;
And though your hand be pale,
Paler are all which trail
Your cross through flame and hail:
Weep, you may weep, for you may touch them not.

---

decrepitude—A state of being decrepit, frail and worn out because of age or neglect.
Murmuring—a person or group of people talking quietly about their dislike of something; complaining
piteous—causing or deserving pity

On Liberty and Slavery
By George Moses Horton

Alas! and am I born for this,
  To wear this slavish chain?
Deprived of all created bliss,
  Through hardship, toil and pain!

How long have I in bondage lain,
  And languished to be free!
Alas! and must I still complain—
  Deprived of liberty.

Oh, Heaven! and is there no relief
  This side the silent grave—
To soothe the pain—to quell the grief
  And anguish of a slave?

Come Liberty, thou cheerful sound,
  Roll through my ravished ears!
Come, let my grief in joys be drowned,
  And drive away my fears.

Say unto foul oppression, Cease:
  Ye tyrants rage no more,
And let the joyful trump of peace,
  Now bid the vassal soar.

Soar on the pinions of that dove
  Which long has cooed for thee,
And breathed her notes from Afric's grove,
  The sound of Liberty.

Oh, Liberty! thou golden prize,
  So often sought by blood—
We crave thy sacred sun to rise,
  The gift of nature's God!

Bid Slavery hide her haggard face,
  And barbarism fly:
I scorn to see the sad disgrace
  In which enslaved I lie.

Dear Liberty! upon thy breast,
  I languish to respire;
And like the Swan unto her nest,
  I'd like to thy smiles retire.

Oh, blest asylum—heavenly balm!
  Unto thy boughs I flee—
And in thy shades the storm shall calm,
  With songs of Liberty!

---

languished—lacking vitality; something or someone loosing strength or feeble
oppression—when anyone is treated unjustly or has cruel control forced upon them.
tyrant—a ruler that is cruel to his subjects
trump—a sound like a trumpet calling to all to hear.
pinions—the outer parts of a birds wings; a wings pinions are cut to prevent a bird from flying.
cooed—A soft sound a dove or pigeon makes; talking with a soft gentle voice
liberty—the ability to do be free to make choices without the fear of oppression.
respire—breath
balm—an ointment to place on the skin or wound to aid in healing.
bough—the larger branches of a tree

The King's Breakfast
By A. A. Milne

The King asked
The Queen, and
The Queen asked
The Dairymaid:
"Could we have some butter for
The Royal slice of bread?"
The Queen asked the Dairymaid,
The Dairymaid
Said, "Certainly,
I'll go and tell the cow
Now
Before she goes to bed."

The Dairymaid
She curtsied,
And went and told
The Alderney:
"Don't forget the butter for
The Royal slice of bread."
The Alderney
Said sleepily:
"You'd better tell
His Majesty
That many people nowadays
Like marmalade
Instead."

The Dairymaid
Said, "Fancy!"
And went to
Her Majesty.
She curtsied to the Queen, and
She turned a little red:
"Excuse me,
Your Majesty,
For taking of
The liberty,
But marmalade is tasty, if
It's very
Thickly
Spread."

The Queen said
"Oh!:
And went to
His Majesty:
"Talking of the butter for
The royal slice of bread,
Many people
Think that
Marmalade
Is nicer.
Would you like to try a little
Marmalade
Instead?"

The King said,
"Bother!"
And then he said,
"Oh, deary me!"
The King sobbed, "Oh, deary
me!"
And went back to bed.
"Nobody,"
He whimpered,
"Could call me
A fussy man;
I only want
A little bit
Of butter for
My bread!"

The Queen said,
"There, there!"
And went to
The Dairymaid.
The Dairymaid
Said, "There, there!"
And went to the shed.
The cow said,
"There, there!

I didn't really
Mean it;
Here's milk for his porringer,
And butter for his bread."

The Queen took
The butter
And brought it to
His Majesty;
The King said,
"Butter, eh?"
And bounced out of bed.
"Nobody," he said,
As he kissed her
Tenderly,
"Nobody," he said,
As he slid down the banisters,
"Nobody,
My darling,
Could call me
A fussy man -

BUT
I do like a little bit of butter to
my bread!"

Alderney—a breed of dairy cow that is extinct
marmalade—A jelly preserve made with orange or other citrus rind and juice.
porringer—a shallow bowl no more than 6 inches in diameter and between 1.5 inches and 3 inches deep. Used in Europe during the Middle Ages.

Songs for the People
By Frances Ellen Watkins Harper

Let me make the songs for the people,
  Songs for the old and young;
Songs to stir like a battle-cry
  Wherever they are sung.

Not for the clashing of sabres,
  For carnage nor for strife;
But songs to thrill the hearts of men
  With more abundant life.

Let me make the songs for the weary,
  Amid life's fever and fret,
Till hearts shall relax their tension,
  And careworn brows forget.

Let me sing for little children,
  Before their footsteps stray,

Sweet anthems of love and duty,
  To float o'er life's highway.

I would sing for the poor and aged,
  When shadows dim their sight;
Of the bright and restful mansions,
  Where there shall be no night.

Our world, so worn and weary,
  Needs music, pure and strong,
To hush the jangle and discords
  Of sorrow, pain, and wrong.

Music to soothe all its sorrow,
  Till war and crime shall cease;
And the hearts of men grown tender
  Girdle the world with peace.

---

girdle—a garment that wraps around one's mid-section from the torso down to the hips.

A Poem Written In a Journal (untitled)
By George Washington

About Frances Alexander, a women he had a crush on while he was on a surveying trip in Northern Virginia.

From your bright sparkling Eyes, I was undone;
Rays, you have, more transparent than the sun,
Amidst its glory in the rising Day,
None can you equal in your bright array;
Constant in your calm and unspotted Mind;
Equal to all, but will to none Prove kind,
So knowing, seldom one so Young, you'l Find
Ah! woe's me that I should Love and conceal,
Long have I wish'd, but never dare reveal,
Even though severely Loves Pains I feel;
Xerxes that great, was't free from Cupids Dart,
And all the greatest Heroes, felt the smart.

Xerxes—known as Xerxes the Great and son of Darius the Great. The fourth king of kings from the Achaemenid Empire from 486-465 BC.

Aunt Chloe's Politics
By Frances Ellen Watkins Harper

Of course, I don't know very much
  About these politics,
But I think that some who run 'em
  Do mighty ugly tricks.
I've seen 'em honey-fugle round,
  And talk so awful sweet,
That you'd think them full of kindness,
  As an egg is full of meat.
Now I don't believe in looking
  Honest people in the face,
And saying when you're doing wrong,
  That "I haven't sold my race."
When we want to school our children,
  If the money isn't there,
Whether black or white have took it,
  The loss we all must share.
And this buying up each other
  Is something worse than mean,
Though I thinks a heap of voting,
  I go for voting clean.

---

honey-fugle—to cheat or deceive

The Hunter's Wooing
By Ruth Muskrat Bronson

Come roam the wild hills, my Cherokee Rose,
Come roam the wild hills with me.
We'll follow the path where the Spavinaw flows,
Dashing wild on its way to the sea,
On its wearisome way to the sea.
We'll chase the fleet deer from its lair in the woods;
We'll follow the wolf to his den.
When the sun hides his face, we'll rest in the woods;
Hid away from the worry of men.
Hid away from the bother of men.
And then we'll go home, my Cherokee Rose,
Where the Senecas live in the heart of the hills
By the rippling Cowskin, where the Saulchana grows,

We'll go home to the Coyauga hills,
To the sheltering Coyauga hills.

Cherokee—the largest Native American Indian Tribe in the United States
Spavinaw—a creek in Eastern Oklahoma, USA
lair—where a wild animal lives
Senecas—a group of Native American Indians also known as the Mingo.
Cowskin—a creek in Eastern Oklahoma
Saulchana—a plant native to Eastern Oklahoma

Swiss Air-"Ranz Des Vaches
By Thomas Moore

But wake, the trumpet's blast again,
And rouse the ranks of warrior-men!
Oh War, when Truth thy arm employs,
And Freedom's spirit guides the laboring storm,
'Tis then thy vengeance takes a hallowed form,
And like Heaven's lightning sacredly destroys.
Nor, Music, thro' thy breathing sphere,
Lives there a sound more grateful to the ear
Of Him who made all harmony,
Than the blest sound of fetters breaking,
And the first hymn that man awaking
From Slavery's slumber breathes to Liberty.

---

vengeance—punishing someone out of revenge for doing something to you.
hallowed—a holy place
harmony (ies)—a combination of notes sounded at the same time to create cords having a pleasant sound to the ear.
fetters—chains and shackles used to bind the hands and feet of a prisoner

The Maple Leaf Forever
By Alexander Muir

In Days of yore, from Britain's shore
Wolfe the dauntless hero came
And planted firm Britannia's flag
On Canada's fair domain.
Here may it wave, our boast, our pride
And joined in love together,
The thistle, shamrock, rose entwined,
The Maple Leaf Forever.
[CHORUS]
The Maple Leaf
Our Emblem Dear,
The Maple Leaf Forever.
God save our Queen and heaven bless,
The Maple Leaf Forever.
At Queenston Heights and Lundy's Lane
Our brave fathers side by side
For freedom's home and loved ones dear,
Firmly stood and nobly died.
And so their rights which they maintained,
We swear to yield them never.
Our watchword ever more shall be
The Maple Leaf Forever
[CHORUS]
Our fair Dominion now extends
From Cape Race to Nootka Sound
May peace forever be our lot
And plenty a store abound
And may those ties of love be ours
Which discord cannot sever
And flourish green for freedom's home
The Maple Leaf Forever
[CHORUS]

---

yore—a long time past
dauntless—to have no fear, nothing holds you back, unstoppable.
Britannia—derived from the Latin word "Britannicae" and was the term the Romans used when speaking of the British Isles.

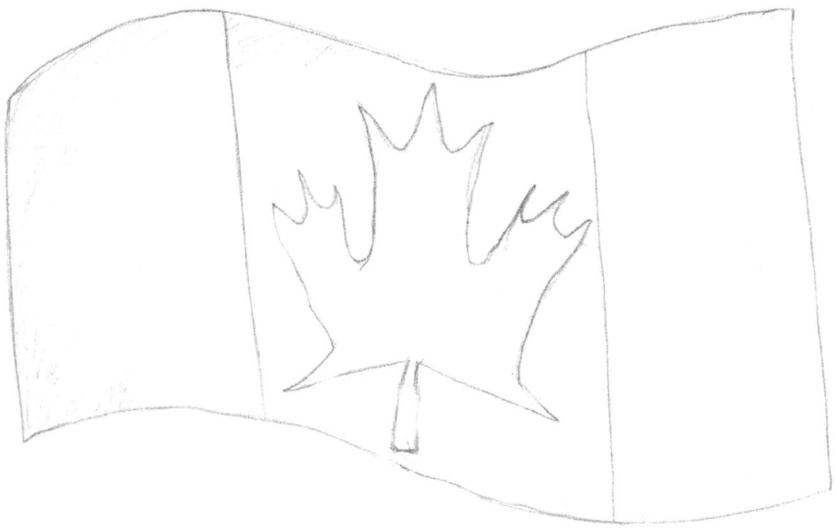

March

"The only thing necessary for the triumph of evil is for good men to do nothing.
-Edmund Burke

Sonnet to Liberty
Oscar Wilde

Not that I love thy children, whose dull eyes
See nothing save their own unlovely woe,
Whose minds know nothing, nothing care to know,—
But that the roar of thy Democracies,
Thy reigns of Terror, thy great Anarchies,
Mirror my wildest passions like the sea,—
And give my rage a brother——! Liberty!
For this sake only do thy dissonant cries
Delight my discreet soul, else might all kings
By bloody knout or treacherous cannonades
Rob nations of their rights inviolate
And I remain unmoved—and yet, and yet,
These Christs that die upon the barricades,
God knows it I am with them, in some things.

---

democracies—government run by the people
anarchies—when there is no law or government in power
knout—a punishment inflicted by a whip
cannonades—continuous gun fire

The American Flag
Joseph Rodman Drake

I.

When Freedom from her mountain height
Unfurled her standard to the air,
She tore the azure robe of night,
And set the stars of glory there.
She mingled with its gorgeous dyes
The milky baldric of the skies,
And striped its pure celestial white,
With streakings of the morning light;
Then from his mansion in the sun
She called her eagle bearer down,
And gave into his mighty hand,
The symbol of her chosen land.

II.

Majestic monarch of the cloud,
Who rear'st aloft thy regal form,
To hear the tempest trumpings loud
And see the lightning lances driven,
When strive the warriors of the storm,
And rolls the thunder-drum of heaven,
Child of the sun! to thee 'tis given
To guard the banner of the free,
To hover in the sulphur smoke,
To ward away the battle stroke,
And bid its blendings shine afar,
Like rainbows on the cloud of war,
The harbingers of victory!

III.

Flag of the brave! thy folds shall fly,
The sign of hope and triumph high,
When speaks the signal trumpet tone,
And the long line comes gleaming on.
Ere yet the life-blood, warm and wet,
Has dimm'd the glistening bayonet,
Each soldier eye shall brightly turn
To where thy sky-born glories burn;
And as his springing steps advance,
Catch war and vengeance from the glance.

And when the cannon-mouthings loud
Heave in wild wreaths the battle shroud,
And gory sabres rise and fall
Like shoots of flame on midnight's pall;
Then shall thy meteor glances glow,
And cowering foes shall shrink beneath
Each gallant arm that strikes below
That lovely messenger of death.

IV.

Flag of the seas! on ocean wave
Thy stars shall glitter o'er the brave;
When death, careering on the gale,
Sweeps darkly round the bellied sail,
And frighted waves rush wildly back
Before the broadside's reeling rack,
Each dying wanderer of the sea
Shall look at once to heaven and thee,
And smile to see thy splendours fly
In triumph o'er his closing eye.

V.

Flag of the free heart's hope and home!
By angel hands to valour given;
The stars have lit the welkin dome,
And all thy hues were born in heaven.
For ever float that standard sheet!
Where breathes the foe but falls before us,
With Freedom's soil beneath our feet,
And Freedom's banner streaming o'er us?

---

azure—a blue hugh like a sky on a clear day
baldric—a strap or belt worn over the shoulder to hold a weapon like a sword, drum or bugle.
celestial—related to heaven; heavenly
bearer—a person who holds something
monarch—a ruler of a land such as a king, queen, or emperor
trump(ings)—a sound like a trumpet calling to all to hear.
lance—a long pointed weapon for jousting
harbinger—a person or thing that announces when a person arrives or approaches.
bayonet—a pointed weapon that can be attached to the end of a rifle.
vengeance—punishing someone out of revenge for doing something to you.

gallant—brave and heroic
shroud—shelter, covering
gale—a very strong wind
splendours—wonderful, grandeur
welkin—heaven or the sky
hue—shades of color
foe—enemy

Expectans Expectavi
By Charles Hamilton Sorley

From morn to midnight, all day through,
I laugh and play as others do,
I sin and chatter, just the same
As others with a different name.

And all year long upon the stage
I dance and tumble and do rage
So vehemently, I scarcely see
The inner and eternal me.

I have a temple I do not
Visit, a heart I have forgot,
A self that I have never met,
A secret shrine—and yet, and yet

This sanctuary of my soul
Unwitting I keep white and whole,
Unlatched and lit, if Thou should'st care
To enter or to tarry there.

With parted lips and outstretched hands
And listening ears Thy servant stands,
Call Thou early, call Thou late,
To Thy great service dedicate.

---

vehemently—intense and passionate; strong feelings
shrine—a holy place to worship that contains a relic or representation of a deity or person
sanctuary—a safe place to go
unwittingly—unaware of the full facts
tarry—to stay or abide in a place

Cannon Fodder
Katharine Lee Bates

Bodies glad, erect,
Beautiful with youth,
Life's elect,
Nature's truth,
Marching host on host,
Those bright, unblemished ones,
Manhood's boast,
Feed them to the guns.

Hearts and brains that teem
With blessing for the race,
Thought and dream,
Vision, grace,
Oh, love's best and most,
Bridegrooms, brothers, sons,
Host on host
Feed them to the guns.

---

fodder—food
erect—very upright and strait
boast—to brag pridefully out ones self
grace—showing goodwill
bridegrooms—the title given to a man on his wedding day

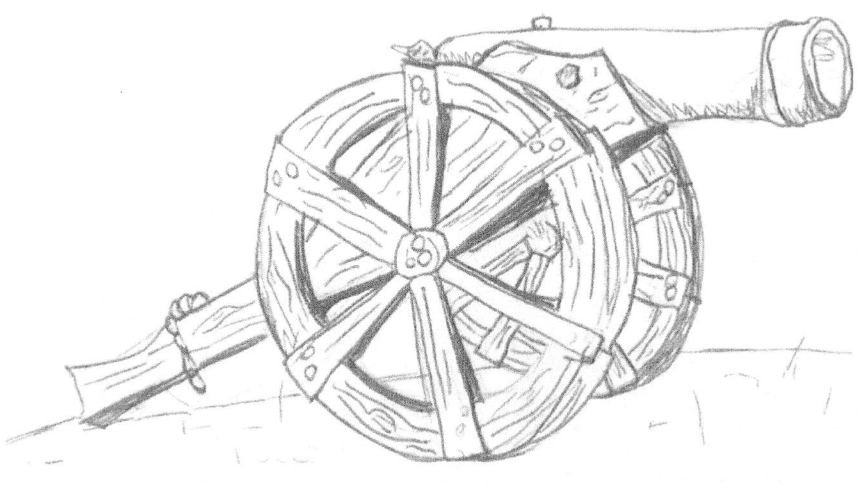

The Dead Kings
By Francis Ledwidge

All the dead kings came to me
At Rosnaree, where I was dreaming,
A few stars glimmered through the morn,
And down the thorn the dews were streaming.

And every dead king had a story
Of ancient glory, sweetly told.
It was too early for the lark,
But the starry dark had tints of gold.

I listened to the sorrows three
Of that Eire passed into song.
A cock crowed near a hazel croft,
And up aloft dim larks winged strong.

And I, too, told the kings a story
Of later glory, her fourth sorrow:
There was a sound like moving shields
In high green fields and the lowland furrow.

And one said: 'We who yet are kings
Have heard these things lamenting inly.'
Sweet music flowed from many a bill
And on the hill the morn stood queenly.

And one said: 'Over is the singing,
And bell bough ringing, whence we come;
With heavy hearts we'll tread the shadows,
In honey meadows birds are dumb.'

And one said: 'Since the poets perished
And all they cherished in the way,
Their thoughts unsung, like petal showers
Inflame the hours of blue and grey.'

And one said: 'A loud tramp of men
We'll hear again at Rosnaree.'
A bomb burst near me where I lay.
I woke, 'twas day in Picardy.

Rosnaree—a small village in Ireland
lark—a small song bird
Eire—the Gaelic word for Ireland
cock—a rooster
furrow—a long trench plowed into the ground for planting
inly—inwardly
perished—something that died suddenly
tramp—noisy, heavy walking
Picardy—a region of France

Liberty – A Fragment
By Robert Burns

Thee, Caledonia, thy wild heaths among,
Thee, fam'd for martial deed and sacred song,
To thee I turn with swimming eyes;
Where is that soul of freedom fled?
Immingled with the mighty dead!
Beneath the hallow'd turf where Wallace lies!
Hear it not, Wallace, in thy bed of death!
Ye babbling winds, in silence sweep;
Disturb not ye the hero's sleep,
Nor give the coward secret breath.
Is this the power in freedom's war,
That wont to bid the battle rage?
Behold that eye which shot immortal hate,
Crushing the despot's proudest bearing!

Caledonia—a Latin name used by the Roman Empire to refer to the area in Great Britain North of the River Forth including the majority of Scotland.
heaths—uncultivated land characteristic of Britain that would grow heather and grasses.
immingled—mixed or blended together
Wallace—A famous historical hero of Scotland
babbling—the bubbling sound of running water.

The Power of Armies is a Visible Thing
By William Wordsworth

The power of Armies is a visible thing,
Formal and circumscribed in time and space;
But who the limits of that power shall trace
Which a brave People into light can bring
Or hide, at will,—for freedom combating
By just revenge inflamed? No foot may chase,
No eye can follow, to a fatal place
That power, that spirit, whether on the wing
Like the strong wind, or sleeping like the wind
Within its awful caves.—From year to year
Springs this indigenous produce far and near;
No craft this subtle element can bind,
Rising like water from the soil, to find
In every nook a lip that it may cheer.

---

circumscribed—restricted within limits
indigenous—something that is native to a certain area

The Road to Old Man’s Town
By Andrew Barton Andrew

The fields of youth are filled with flowers,
The wine of youth is strong:
What need have we to count the hours?
The summer days are long.

But soon we find to our dismay
That we are drifting down
The barren slopes that fall away
Towards the foothills grim and grey
That lead to Old Man's Town.

And marching with us on the track
Full many friends we find:
We see them looking sadly back
For those who've dropped behind

But God forfend a fate so dread,
Alone to travel down
The dreary toad we all must tread,
With faltering steps and whitening head,
The road to Old Man's Town!

Ireland
By Francis William Lauderdale Adams

O we have loved you through cold and rain
  And pitiless frost,
Consuming our offering of blood and of brain
Gladly again and again and again,
  Though it all seemed lost,
    Ireland, Ireland!

O we will fight, fight on for you till
  Your anguish is past,
The wronged ones righted, the tyrants still. -
Though God has not saved you, yet we will,
  At the last, at the last,
    Ireland, Ireland!

O we will love you in warmth and light
  And the happy day,
When you have forgotten the terrible night,
Standing proud and beautiful bright
  For ever and aye,
    Ireland, Ireland!

---

pitiless—cruel; showing no compassion
tyrants—a ruler that is cruel to his subjects

A Nation Once Again
By Thomas Osborne Davis

I.

When boyhood's fire was in my blood
I read of ancient freemen
For Greece and Rome who bravely stood,
THREE HUNDRED MEN AND THREE MEN.[1]
And then I prayed I yet might see
Our fetters rent in twain,
And Ireland, long a province, be
A NATION ONCE AGAIN.

II.

And, from that time, through wildest woe,
That hope has shone, a far light;
Nor could love's brightest summer glow
Outshine that solemn starlight:
It seemed to watch above my head
In forum, field and fane;
Its angel voice sang round my bed,
"A NATION ONCE AGAIN."

III.

It whispered, too, that "freedom's ark
And service high and holy,
Would be profaned by feelings dark
And passions vain or lowly:
For freedom comes from God's right hand,
And needs a godly train;
And righteous men must make our land
A NATION ONCE AGAIN."

IV.

So, as I grew from boy to man,
I bent me to that bidding--
My spirit of each selfish plan
And cruel passion ridding;
For, thus I hoped some day to aid--
Oh! can *such* hope be vain?--
When my dear country shall be made
A NATION ONCE AGAIN.

fane—a temple or church
profaned—disrespected and irreverence
ridding—getting rid of; setting free

The Kangaroo
By Barron Fields

Kanagaroo, Kangaroo!
Thou Spirit of Australia,
That redeems from utter failure,
From perfect desolation,
And warrants the creation
Of this fifth part of the Earth,
Which would seem an after-birth,
Not conceiv'd in the Beginning
(For GOD bless'd His work at first,
And saw that it was good),
But emerg'd at the first sinning,
When the ground was therefore curst; —
And hence this barren wood!

Kangaroo, Kangaroo!
Tho' at first sight we should say,
In thy nature that there may
Contradiction be involv'd,
Yet, like discord well resolv'd,
It is quickly harmonized.
Sphynx or mermaid realiz'd,
Or centaur unfabulous,
Would scarce be more prodigious,
Or Pegasus poetical,
Or hippogriff — chimeras all!
But, what Nature would compile,
Nature knows to reconcile;
And Wisdom, ever at her side,
Of all her children's justified.

She had made the squirrel fragile;
She had made the bounding hart;
But a third so strong and agile

Was beyond ev'n Nature's art;
So she join'd the former two
In thee, Kangaroo!
To describe thee, it is hard:
Converse of the camélopard,
Which beginneth camel-wise,
But endeth of the panther size,
Thy fore half, it would appear,
Had belong'd to some "small deer,"
Such as liveth in a tree;
By thy hinder, thou should'st be
A large animal of chace,
Bounding o'er the forest's space; —
Join'd by some divine mistake,
None but Nature's hand can make —
Nature, in her wisdom's play,
On Creation's holiday.

For howsoe'er anomalous,
Thou yet art not incongruous,
Repugnant or preposterous.
Better-proportion'd animal,
More graceful or ethereal,
Was never follow'd by the hound,
With fifty steps to thy one bound.
Thou can'st not be amended: no;
Be as thou art; thou best art so.

When sooty swans are once more rare,
And duck-moles the Museum's care,
Be still the glory of this land,
Happiest Work of finest Hand!

---

desolation—destruction and complete emptiness
discord—a disagreement
contradiction—two opposing ideas
centaur—mythological Greek creature that is half man on top and half horse on bottom.
prodigious—impressive by size
Pegasus—winged flying horse
hippogriff—a feathered creature with an eagles head and a horse like body with talons on its front legs.

chimeras—mythological Greek monster part lion, goat, and dragon that breaths fire.
camelopard—a giraffe
converse—the reverse of something
anomalous—deviating from what is expected or normal
incongruous—not keeping in harmony with its surroundings
preposterous—opposite of common sense; ridiculous and absurd

At the Tug-O-War
By Henry Lawson

'Twas in a tug-of-war where I, the guvnor's hope and pride,
Stepped proudly on the platform as the ringer on my side;
Old dad was in his glory there, it gave the old man joy
To fight a passage through the crowd and barrack for his boy.

A friend came up and said to me, Put out your muscles, John,
And pull them to eternity, your guvnor's looking on.
I paused before I grasped the rope, and glanced around the place,
And, foremost in the waiting crowd, I saw the old man's face.

My mates were strong and plucky chaps, but very soon I knew
That our opponents had the weight and strength to pull them through;
The boys were losing surely and defeat was very near,
When, high above the mighty roar, I heard the old man cheer!

I felt my muscles swelling when the old man cheer'd for me,
I felt as though I'd burst my heart, or gain the victory!
I shouted, Now! Together! and a steady strain replied,
And, with a mighty heave, I helped to beat the other side!

Oh! how the old man shouted in his wild, excited joy!
I thought he'd burst his boiler then, a-cheering for his boy;
The chaps, oh! how they cheered me, while the girls all smiled so kind,
They praised me, little dreaming, how the old man pulled behind.

He barracks for his boy no more, his grave is old and green,
And sons have grown up round me since he vanished from the scene;
But, when the cause is worthy where I fight for victory,
In fancy still I often hear the old man cheer for me.

plucky—being determined and showing courage in difficulty
barrack—typically housing for soldiers but in this case, it is when someone is shouting and making fun of someone who is performing, speaking or doing a play.

A Poem Against the Tories
By James Madison

Of late our muse keen satire drew
And humourous thoughts in vollies flew
Because we took our foes for men
Who might deserve a decent pen
A gross mistake with brutes we fight
And [goblins?] from the realms of night
Where Spring & Craig lay down their heads
Sometimes a goat steps on the pump
Which animates old Warford's trunk
Sometimes a poisonous toad appears
Which Eckley's yellows carcuss bears
And then to grace us with a bull
Forsooth they show McOrkles skull
And that the Ass may not escape
He take the poet Laureat's shape
The screech owl too comes in the train
Which leap'd from Alexander's brain
Just as he scratch'd his grisly head
Which people say is made of lead.
Come noble whigs, disdain these sons
Of screech owls, monkeys, & baboons
Keep up you[r] minds to humourous themes
And verdant meads & flowing streams
Untill this tribe of dunces find
The baseness of their grovelling mind
And skulk within their dens together
Where each ones stench will kill his brother;

---

muse—
satire—humor that uses exaggeration, irony and bring attention to a persons stupidity. Often used in political humor and shakespeare
vollies—
carcuss—a dead animals body or remains

laureat(e)—a person who receives an honor or receives recognition for a great achievement
disdain—feeling that a person does not deserve respect; to hold someone in contempt.
Verdant—to be covered in green grass or other lush green vegetation
dunce–a person who is slow to learn
skulk—to hide out of sight; often for a sinister reason.

Choice
By Lucy Becker

Ignorance is bliss,
Because there's only you
What do you know to seek?
There's no burn to be better
It's survival of the fittest, might makes right
Responsibility isn't acknowledged, isn't owned
Because there isn't knowledge
Because there isn't knowledge.
Responsibility isn't acknowledged, isn't owned
It's survival of the fittest, might makes right
There's no burn to be better
What do you know to seek?
Because there's only you
Ignorance is bliss
CHOICE
Knowledge is power
Because you have learned
What is the good and the beautiful
It ignites a quest, a desire
To start another's fire, because
With great power comes great responsibility
Because there is knowledge.
Because there is knowledge
With great power comes great responsibility
To start another's fire, because
Ignited is a quest, a desire:
What is the good and the beautiful?
Because you have learned
Knowledge is power

---

ignorance—lacking or not having knowledge
bliss—being perfectly happy

The Parting Before the Battle
By Thomas Moore

HE.
On to the field, our doom is sealed,
   To conquer or be slaves:
This sun shall see our nation free,
   Or set upon our graves.

SHE.
Farewell, oh farewell, my love,
   May heaven thy guardian be,
And send bright angels from above
   To bring thee back to me.

HE.
On to the field, the battle-field,
   Where freedom's standard waves,
This sun shall see our tyrant yield,
   Or shine upon our graves.

---

tyrant— a ruler that is cruel to his subjects

The Western Window
By Edward Powys Mathers
From the Chinese of Wang Ch'ang Ling (eighth century)

At the head of a thousand roaring warriors,
With the sound of gongs,
My husband has departed
Following glory.

At first I was overjoyed
To have a young girl's liberty.

Now I look at the yellowing willow-leaves;
They were green the day he left.

I wonder if he also was glad?

God Save the Flag
By Oliver Wendell Holmes

Washed in the blood of the brave and the blooming,
Snatched from the altars of insolent foes,
Burning with star-fires, but never consuming,
Flash its broad ribbons of lily and rose.

Vainly the prophets of Baal would rend it,
Vainly his worshippers pray for its fall;
Thousands have died for it, millions defend it,
Emblem of justice and mercy to all;

Justice that reddens the sky with her terrors,
Mercy that comes with her white-handed train,
Soothing all passions, redeeming all errors,
Sheathing the sabre and breaking the chain.

Borne on the deluge of all usurpations,
Drifted our Ark o'er the desolate seas,
Bearing the rainbow of hope to the nations,
Torn from the storm-cloud and flung to the breeze!

God bless the Flag and its loyal defenders,
While its broad folds o'er the battle-field wave,
Till the dim star-wreath rekindle its splendors,
Washed from its stains in the blood of the brave.

Baal—an ancient Middle Eastern God
insolent—being arrogant and rude; showing disrespect
foe—enemy
vainly—when something does not produce a result one hopes for no matter what you do.
sheath(ing)—a covering for a blade or sword; a protective covering
deluge—a flood; to be inundated with a large quantity of something
desolate—void of people; empty
usurpations—taking a throne illegally; usurping is wrongful seizure of a throne.

April

"Once we have a war there is only one thing to do. It must be won. For defeat brings worse things that any that can ever happen in war."
-Earnest Hemmingway

Paul Revere's Ride
By Henry Wadsworth Longfellow

Listen, my children, and you shall hear
Of the midnight ride of Paul Revere,
On the eighteenth of April, in Seventy-Five:
Hardly a man is now alive
Who remembers that famous day and year.
He said to his friend, "If the British march
By land or sea from the town to-night,
Hang a lantern aloft in the belfry-arch
Of the North-Church-tower, as a signal-light,—
One if by land, and two if by sea;
And I on the opposite shore will be,
Ready to ride and spread the alarm
Through every Middlesex village and farm,
For the country-folk to be up and to arm."
Then he said "Good night!" and with muffled oar
Silently rowed to the Charlestown shore,
Just as the moon rose over the bay,
Where swinging wide at her moorings lay
The Somerset, British man-of-war:
A phantom ship, with each mast and spar
Across the moon, like a prison-bar,
And a huge black hulk, that was magnified
By its own reflection in the tide.
Meanwhile, his friend, through alley and street
Wanders and watches with eager ears,
Till in the silence around him he hears

The muster of men at the barrack door,
The sound of arms, and the tramp of feet,
And the measured tread of the grenadiers
Marching down to their boats on the shore.
Then he climbed to the tower of the church,
Up the wooden stairs, with stealthy tread,
To the belfry-chamber overhead,
And startled the pigeons from their perch
On the sombre rafters, that round him made
Masses and moving shapes of shade,—
By the trembling ladder, steep and tall,
To the highest window in the wall,
Where he paused to listen and look down
A moment on the roofs of the town,
And the moonlight flowing over all.
Beneath, in the churchyard, lay the dead,
In their night-encampment on the hill,
Wrapped in silence so deep and still
That he could hear, like a sentinel's tread,
The watchful night-wind, as it went
Creeping along from tent to tent,
And seeming to whisper, "All is well!"
A moment only he feels the spell
Of the place and the hour, and the secret dread
Of the lonely belfry and the dead;
For suddenly all his thoughts are bent
On a shadowy something far away,
Where the river widens to meet the bay,—
A line of black, that bends and floats
On the rising tide, like a bridge of boats.
Meanwhile, impatient to mount and ride,
Booted and spurred, with a heavy stride,
On the opposite shore walked Paul Revere.
Now he patted his horse's side,
Now gazed on the landscape far and near,
Then impetuous stamped the earth,
And turned and tightened his saddle-girth;
But mostly he watched with eager search
The belfry-tower of the old North Church,
As it rose above the graves on the hill,
Lonely and spectral and sombre and still.
And lo! as he looks, on the belfry's height,

A glimmer, and then a gleam of light!
He springs to the saddle, the bridle he turns,
But lingers and gazes, till full on his sight
A second lamp in the belfry burns!
A hurry of hoofs in a village-street,
A shape in the moonlight, a bulk in the dark,
And beneath from the pebbles, in passing, a spark
Struck out by a steed that flies fearless and fleet:
That was all! And yet, through the gloom and the light,
The fate of a nation was riding that night;
And the spark struck out by that steed, in his flight,
Kindled the land into flame with its heat.
He has left the village and mounted the steep,
And beneath him, tranquil and broad and deep,
Is the Mystic, meeting the ocean tides;
And under the alders, that skirt its edge,
Now soft on the sand, now loud on the ledge,
Is heard the tramp of his steed as he rides.
It was twelve by the village clock
When he crossed the bridge into Medford town.
He heard the crowing of the cock,
And the barking of the farmer's dog,
And felt the damp of the river-fog,
That rises when the sun goes down.
It was one by the village clock,
When he galloped into Lexington.
He saw the gilded weathercock
Swim in the moonlight as he passed,
And the meeting-house windows, blank and bare,
Gaze at him with a spectral glare,
As if they already stood aghast
At the bloody work they would look upon.
It was two by the village clock,
When be came to the bridge in Concord town.
He heard the bleating of the flock,
And the twitter of birds among the trees,
And felt the breath of the morning breeze
Blowing over the meadows brown.
And one was safe and asleep in his bed
Who at the bridge would be first to fall,
Who that day would be lying dead,
Pierced by a British musket-ball.

You know the rest. In the books you have read,
How the British Regulars fired and fled,—
How the farmers gave them ball for ball,
From behind each fence and farmyard-wall,
Chasing the red-coats down the lane,
Then crossing the fields to emerge again
Under the trees at the turn of the road,
And only pausing to fire and load.
So through the night rode Paul Revere;
And so through the night went his cry of alarm
To every Middlesex village and farm,—
A cry of defiance, and not of fear,
A voice in the darkness, a knock at the door,
And a word that shall echo forevermore!
For, borne on the night-wind of the Past,
Through all our history, to the last,
In the hour of darkness and peril and need,
The people will waken and listen to hear
The hurrying hoof-beats of that steed,
And the midnight message of Paul Revere.

---

eager—when someone really wants something or wants to do something
barrack— typically housing for soldiers
muster—collect; gather before battle
moorings—the place a boat is docked or the items used to dock a boat.
grenadiers—soldiers that are armed with a grenade launcher
stealthy—to move in a manner or behave in a way as to not be seen.
sombre—gloomy, dull color
sentinel—a soldier who stands guard
impetuous—acting without contemplating the consequences; forcful and rapid movement
bridle—the headgear used to control a horse that includes
cock—rooster
gilded— covered in gold, traditionally thought of as gold leaf (real gold). gold paint.
defiance—choosing to be disobedient

The Death of Lincoln
By William Cullen Bryant

Oh, slow to smite and swift to spare,
Gentle and merciful and just!
Who, in the fear of God, didst bear
The sword of power, a nation's trust!
In sorrow by thy bier we stand,
Amid the awe that hushes all,
And speak the anguish of a land
That shook with horror at thy fall.

Thy task is done; the bond are free:
We bear thee to an honored grave,
Whose proudest monument shall be
The broken fetters of the slave.

Pure was thy life; its bloody close
Hath placed thee with the sons of light,
Among the noble host of those
Who perished in the cause of Right.

**Abraham Lincoln was the 16th president of the United State and he saw assassinated on April 15th 1865*
smite—to hit hard
bier—o place where a coffin is placed before burial or to be moved to the grave.
fetters— chains and shackles used to bind the hands and feet of a prisoner.

O Captain! My Captain!
By Walt Whitman

O Captain! my Captain! our fearful trip is done,
The ship has weather'd every rack, the prize we sought is won,
The port is near, the bells I hear, the people all exulting,
While follow eyes the steady keel, the vessel grim and daring;
But O heart! heart! heart!
O the bleeding drops of red,
Where on the deck my Captain lies,
Fallen cold and dead.

O Captain! my Captain! rise up and hear the bells;
Rise up—for you the flag is flung—for you the bugle trills,
For you bouquets and ribbon'd wreaths—for you the shores a-crowding,
For you they call, the swaying mass, their eager faces turning;
Here Captain! dear father!
This arm beneath your head!
It is some dream that on the deck,
You've fallen cold and dead.

My Captain does not answer, his lips are pale and still,
My father does not feel my arm, he has no pulse nor will,
The ship is anchor'd safe and sound, its voyage closed and done,
From fearful trip the victor ship comes in with object won;
Exult O shores, and ring O bells!
But I with mournful tread,
Walk the deck my Captain lies,
Fallen cold and dead.

---

exulting—feeling elation
keel—a ridge or blade that runs along the bottom of a boat for stability
trills—a rhythmic vibrating sound
eager— when someone really wants something or wants to do something

Spring in War-Time

By Sara Teasdale

I feel the spring far off, far off,
   The faint, far scent of bud and leaf—
Oh, how can spring take heart to come
   To a world in grief,
   Deep grief?
The sun turns north, the days grow long,
   Later the evening star grows bright—
How can the daylight linger on
   For men to fight,
   Still fight?
The grass is waking in the ground,
   Soon it will rise and blow in waves—
How can it have the heart to sway
   Over the graves,
   New graves?
Under the boughs where lovers walked
   The apple-blooms will shed their breath—
But what of all the lovers now
   Parted by Death,
   Grey Death?

bough—the larger branches of a tree

To My Country
By Katharine Lee Bates

O dear my Country, beautiful and dear,
Love cloth not darken sight.
God looketh through Love's eyes, whose vision clear
Beholds more flaws than keenest Hate hath known.
Nor is Love's judgment gentle, but austere;
The heart of Love must break ere it condone
One stain upon the white.

There comes an hour when on the parent turns
The challenge of the child;
The bridal passion for perfection burns;

Life gives her last allegiance to the best;
Each sweet idolatry the spirit spurns,
Once more enfranchised for its starry quest
Of beauty undefiled.

Love must be one with honor; yet to-day
Love liveth by a sign;
Allows no lasting compromise with clay,
But tends the mounting miracle of gold,
Content with service till the bud make way
To the rejoicing sunbeams that unfold
Its culminant divine.

There is a rumoring among the stars,
A trouble in the sun.
Freedom, most holy word, hath fallen at jars
With her own deeds; 'tis Mammon's jubilee;
Again the cross contends with scimitars;
The seraphim look down with dread to see
Earth's noblest hope undone.

O dear my Country, beautiful and dear,
Ultimate dream of Time,
By all thy millions longing to revere
A pure, august, authentic commonweal,
Climb to the light. Imperiled Pioneer
Of Brotherhood among the nations, seal
Our faith with thy sublime.

---

austere—very strict attitude or deminer
condone—permit or approve
allegiance—showing loyalty
idolatry—love or admiration for something or someone or the worship of anything other than God.
spurn—to reject someone or something with great contempt
enfranchised—given the right to vote
undefiled—pure
culminant—the highest point; reaching full development
seraphim a deity creature with two to three pairs of wings in by the Jewish, Christian, and Islamic literature.
commonweal—public welfare

To Germany
By Charles Hamilton Sorley

You are blind like us. Your hurt no man designed,
And no man claimed the conquest of your land.
But gropers both through fields of thought confined
We stumble and we do not understand.
You only saw your future bigly planned,
And we, the tapering paths of our own mind,
And in each other's dearest ways we stand,
And hiss and hate. And the blind fight the blind.

When it is peace, then we may view again
With new-won eyes each other's truer form
And wonder. Grown more loving-kind and warm
We'll grasp firm hands and laugh at the old pain,
When it is peace. But until peace, the storm
The darkness and the thunder and the rain.

---

conquest—seeking after control of an geographical area or people using the military.
gropers—A large warm sea fish in the bass family
tapering—shrinking from wide to narrow

The Wild Honeysuckle
By Philip Freneau

Fair flower, that dost so comely grow,
Hid in this silent, dull retreat,
Untouch'd thy honey'd blossoms blow,
Unseen thy little branches greet:
  No roving foot shall crush thee here,
  No busy hand provoke a tear.

By Nature's self in white array'd,
She bade thee shun the vulgar eye,
And planted here the guardian shade,
And sent soft waters murmuring by;
  Thus quietly thy summer goes,
  Thy days declining to repose.

Smit with those charms, that must decay,
I grieve to see thy future doom;
They died—nor were those flowers more gay,
(The flowers that did in Eden bloom)
  Unpitying frosts and Autumn's power
  Shall leave no vestige of this flower.

From morning suns and evening dews
At first thy little being came:
If nothing once, you nothing lose,
For when you die you are the same;
  The space between is but an hour,
  The mere idea of a flower.

---

roving—always wandering from one place to another
provoke—purposefully bother or annoy someone
murmuring— a person or group of people talking quietly about their dislike of something; complaining
gay—happy
vestige—a trace left behind, showing that something used to exist. Like a dead dried up flower stem after the flower has died off. It can also mean a very small amount.
dews—droplets of water left on a surface from moisture in the air.

On the Death of Dr. Benjamin Franklin
By Philip Freneau

Thus, some tall tree that long hath stood
The glory of its native wood,
By storms destroyed, or length of years,
Demands the tribute of our tears.

The pile, that took long time to raise,
To dust returns by slow decays:
But, when its destined years are o'er,
We must regret the loss the more.

So long accustomed to your aid,
The world laments your exit made;
So long befriended by your art,
Philosopher, 'tis hard to part!—

When monarchs tumble to the ground,
Successors easily are found:
But, matchless Franklin! what a few
Can hope to rival such as you,
Who seized from kings their sceptred pride,
And turned the lightning's darts aside!

---

destined—something unfolding as if it was planned; fate
laments—deep grief; mourning
philosopher—a person who learns about philosophy; a deep thinker
monarch(s)— a ruler of a land such as a king, queen, or emperor
sceptred—bestowed with legal power and often symbolized with the holding of a sceptor

To God and the Soldier
By Anonymous

God and the soldier
All men adore
In time of trouble,
And no more;
For when war is over
And all things righted,
God is neglected -
The old soldier slighted.

---

slighted—to feel disrespected by how someone speaks to or treats you

The Union
By Alfred Noyes

You that have gathered together the sons of all races,
  And welded them into one,
Lifting the torch of your Freedom on hungering faces
  That sailed to the setting sun;

You that have made of mankind in your own proud regions
  The music of man to be,
How should the old earth sing of you, now, as your legions
  Rise to set all men free?

How should the singer that knew the proud vision and loved it,
  In the days when not all men knew,
Gaze through his tears, on the light, now the world has approved it;
  Or dream, when the dream comes true?

How should he sing when the Spirit of Freedom in thunder
  Speaks, and the wine-press is red;
And the sea-winds are loud with the chains that are broken asunder
  And nations that rise from the dead?

Flag of the sky, proud flag of that wide communion,
  Too mighty for thought to scan;
Flag of the many in one, and that last world-union
  That kingdom of God in man;

Ours was a dream, in the night, of that last federation,
  But yours is the glory unfurled--
The marshalled nations and stars that shall make one nation
  One singing star of the world.

---

asunder—to be put into pieces; divided apart
communion—thoughts and feelings on an intimate level, often related to spirituality. A Christian worship service in many religions
federation—A group of geographical areas with a central government while still retaining autonomy to a certain degree

Mrs. Earth
By Walter De La Mare

Mrs. Earth makes silver black,
  Mrs. Earth makes iron red
But Mrs. Earth can not stain gold,
  Nor ruby red.
Mrs. earth the slenderest bone
  Whitens in her bosom cold,
But Mrs. Earth can change my dreams
  No more than ruby or gold.
Mrs. Earth and Mr. Sun
  Can tan my skin, and tire my toes,
But all that I'm thinking of, ever shall think,
  Why, either knows.

---

bosom—a woman's chest

The Fairies Dancing
By Walter De La Mare

I heard along the early hills,
  Ere yet the lark was risen up,
Ere yet the dawn with firelight fills
  The night-dew of the bramble-cup, -
I heard the fairies in a ring
  Sing as they tripped a lilting round
Soft as the moon on wavering wing.
  The starlight shook as if with sound,
As if with echoing, and the stars
  Prankt their bright eyes with trembling gleams
While red with war the gusty Mars
  Rained upon earth his ruddy beams.
He shone alone, low down the West,
  While I, behind a hawthorn-bush,
Watched on the fairies flaxen-tressed
  The fires of the morning flush.
Till, as a mist, their beauty died,
  Their singing shrill and fainter grew;
And daylight tremulous and wide
  Flooded the moorland through and through;

Till Urdon's copper weathercock
  Was reared in golden flame afar,
And dim from moonlit dreams awoke
  The towers and groves of Arroar.

lark—a small song bird
bramble—a prickly bush like a berry or wild thorned bush
dew— droplets of water left on a surface from moisture in the air.
lilting—when someone is speaking or singing and their voice rises and falls pleasantly
prankt—when someone has had a trick or prank done upon them
flaxen—a pale yellow color
tressed—refers to hair long hair being arranged in some organized way.
tremulous—when a voice is trembling or nervous

Concord Hymn
By Ralph Waldo Emerson
SUNG AT THE COMPLETION OF THE BATTLE MONUMENT, JULY 4, 1837

By the rude bridge that arched the flood,
Their flag to April's breeze unfurled,
Here once the embattled farmers stood
And fired the shot heard round the world.

The foe long since in silence slept;
Alike the conqueror silent sleeps;
And Time the ruined bridge has swept
Down the dark stream which seaward creeps.

On this green bank, by this soft stream,
We set to-day a votive stone;
That memory may their deed redeem,
When, like our sires, our sons are gone.

Spirit, that made those heroes dare
To die, and leave their children free,
Bid Time and Nature gently spare
The shaft we raise to them and thee.

embattled—either preparing for or involved in war; surrounded by enemies
foe—enemies
votive—something received in fulfillment of a vow like a candle.

The Land of the Free
By Juliette Hiller

The dark was too dark around the old ship
As she sailed 'cross the churning sea
But a light shone in the heart of the ship
Of a hope in the land of the free

The people were abused and downtrodden
So they had a party with Tea
A young man sat with a parchment and pen
And wrote of the land of the free

The mourning sky was streaked with gray and blue
A mother's heart was torn in grief
A tall man lead with wisdom and in truth
A nation where humans were free

Truth and lies are distorted with deceit
The people stand, but cannot see
Some have trust in God for our souls to keep
And to save the land of the free

And bring us home to the land of the free

---

churning—agitate; to move about vigorously
downtrodden—treated poorly
mourning— deep sorrow over the loss of someone

Foreign Lands
By Robert Lewis Stevenson

Up into the cherry tree
Who should climb but little me?
I held the trunk with both my hands
And looked abroad in foreign lands.

I saw the next door garden lie,
Adorned with flowers, before my eye,
And many pleasant places more
That I had never seen before.

I saw the dimpling river pass
And be the sky's blue looking-glass;
The dusty roads go up and down
With people tramping in to town.

If I could find a higher tree
Farther and farther I should see,
To where the grown-up river slips
Into the sea among the ships,

To where the roads on either hand
Lead onward into fairy land,
Where all the children dine at five,
And all the playthings come alive.

---

adorned—to make more appealing or attractive with decoration or objects.
tramping—noisy, heavy walking

Newton
By Alfred Noyes

A single excerpt: Section I

If I saw farther, 'twas because I stood
On giant shoulders," wrote the king of thought,
Too proud of his great line to slight the toils
Of his forebears. He turned to their dim past,
Their fading victories and their fond defeats,
And knelt as at an altar, drawing all
Their strengths into his own; and so went forth
With all their glory shining in his face,
To win new victories for the age to come.
So, where Copernicus had destroyed the dream
We called our world; where Galileo watched
Those ancient firmaments melt, a thin blue smoke
Into a vaster night; where Kepler heard
Only stray fragments, isolated chords
Of that tremendous music which should bind
All things anew in one, Newton arose
And carried on their fire.
Around him reeled
Through lingering fumes of hate and clouds of doubt,
Lit by the afterglow of the Civil War,
The dissolute throngs of that Walpurgis night
Where all the cynical spirits that deny
Danced with the vicious lusts that drown the soul
In flesh too gross for Circe or her swine.
But, in his heart, he heard one instant voice.
"On with the torch once more, make all things new,
Build the new heaven and earth, and save the world."

Ah, but the infinite patience, the long months
Lavished on tasks that, to the common eye,
Were insignificant, never to be crowned
With great results, or even with earth's rewards.
Could Rembrandt but have painted him, in those hours
Making his first analysis of light
Alone, there, in his darkened Cambridge room
At Trinity! Could he have painted, too,
The secret glow, the mystery, and the power,

The sense of all the thoughts and unseen spires
That soared to heaven around him!
                He stood there,
Obscure, unknown, the shadow of a man
In darkness, like a grey dishevelled ghost,
--Bare-throated, down at heel, his last night's supper
Littering his desk, untouched; his glimmering face,
Under his tangled hair, intent and still,--
Preparing our new universe.
        He caught
The sunbeam striking through that bullet-hole
In his closed shutter--a round white spot of light
Upon a small dark screen.
                    He interposed
A prism of glass. He saw the sunbeam break
And spread upon the screen its rainbow band
Of disentangled colours, all in scale
Like notes in music; first, the violet ray,
Then indigo, trembling softly into blue;
Then green and yellow, quivering side by side;
Then orange, mellowing richly into red.
Then, in the screen, he made a small, round hole
Like to the first; and through it passed once more
Each separate coloured ray. He let it strike
Another prism of glass, and saw each hue
Bent at a different angle from its path,
The red the least, the violet ray the most;
But all in scale and order, all precise
As notes in music. Last, he took a lens,
And, passing through it all those coloured rays,
Drew them together again, remerging all
On that dark screen, in one white spot of light.

So, watching, testing, proving, he resolved
The seeming random glories of our day
Into a constant harmony, and found
How in the whiteness of the sunlight sleep
Compounded, all the colours of the world.
He saw how raindrops in the clouds of heaven
Breaking the light, revealed that sevenfold arch
Of colours, ranged as on his own dark screen,
Though now they spanned the mountains and wild seas.

Then, where that old-world order had gone down
Beneath a darker deluge, he beheld
Gleams of the great new order and recalled
--Fraught with new meaning and a deeper hope--
That covenant which God made with all mankind
Throughout all generations: *I will set*
My bow in the cloud, that henceforth ye may know
How deeper than the wreckage of your dreams
Abides My law, in beauty and in power.

---

forebears—an ancestor
firmament—the sky or the heavens
Copernicus—a Polish mathematician of the Renaissance who created a model of the solar system with the sun at the center.
Galileo—an Italian astronomer and scientist and refered to as the father of astronomy.
Kepler—a German astronomer best known for his study of planetary movement.
dissolute—not having restraint, over indulgent and with little morals
Circe— a minor Greek mythology goddess
Rembrandt—Dutch painter from the Baroque era
dishevelled—unkept; disorderly and messy
disentangled—untangled; free of knots
sevenfold—seven times more (X7)
indigo—a dark blue color created from the indigo plant

Canada's Glory
By Dr. L. Allen Homan

Crowned with arctic's icy glory,
Holding great oceans in her hands,
Stands above the Americas,
Canada's wide and pleasant lands.

Clothed with splendour by the forests
Of green their colour is displayed,
While the grain fields of the midwest
In golden glory are arrayed.

With joy her cities are displayed
As jewels upon her regal gown.
Placed within the precious setting
Of her small villages and town.

The heart of a hundred nations
Is heard to beat within her breast
Proclaiming freedom and justice
From rocky east to mountains west.

Her tender heart of compassion
To ward the people beyond her shores
Is seen as she gives her children
In time of peace and tragic wars.

Yet calling to her from above
Is the God who makes her free
Pleading for her to turn to Christ's
Who died upon that cruel tree.

May

War is an ugly thing, but not the ugliest of things. The decayed and degraded state of moral and patriotic feeling which thinks that nothing is worth war is much worse. The person who has nothing for which he is willing to fight, nothing which is more important than his own personal safety, is a miserable creature and has no chance of being free unless made and kept so by the exertions of better men than himself.

-John Stewart Mill

A Prophecy to George Keats in America
By John Keats

'Tis the witching time of night,
Orbed is the moon and bright,
And the Stars they glisten, glisten,
Seeming with bright eyes to listen.
For what listen they?
For a song and for a charm,
See they glisten in alarm,
And the Moon is waxing warm
To hear what I shall say.
Moon! keep wide thy golden ears—
Hearken, Stars! and hearken, Spheres!—
Hearken, thou eternal Sky!
I sing an infant's Lullaby,
O pretty lullaby!
Listen, listen, listen, listen,
Glisten, glisten, glisten, glisten,
And hear my Lullaby!
Though the Rushes, that will make
Its cradle, still are in the lake—
Though the linen that will be
Its swathe, is on the cotton tree—
Though the woollen that will keep
It warm, is on the silly sheep—
Listen, Starlight, listen, listen,
Glisten, glisten, glisten, glisten,
And hear my lullaby!
Child, I see thee! Child, I've found thee
Midst of the quiet all around thee!
Child, I see thee! Child, I spy thee
And thy mother sweet is nigh thee!
Child, I know thee! Child no more,
But a Poet evermore!
See, see the Lyre, the Lyre,
In a flame of fire,
Upon the little cradle's top
Flaring, flaring, flaring,
Past the eyesight's bearing.
Awake it from its sleep,

And see if it can keep
Its eyes upon the blaze—
Amaze, amaze!
It stares, it stares, it stares,
It dares what no one dares!
It lifts its little hand into the flame
Unharm'd, and on the strings
Paddles a little tune, and sings,
With dumb endeavor sweetly—
Bard art thou completely!
Little child
O' th' western wild,
Bard art thou completely!
Sweetly with dumb endeavor.
A poet now or never,
Little child
O' th' western wild,
A Poet now or never!

---

swathe (swath)—a long strip of land
lyre—an ancient Greek harp

In Flanders Field
By John McCrae

In Flanders fields the poppies blow
Between the crosses, row on row,
That mark our place; and in the sky
The larks, still bravely singing, fly
Scarce heard amid the guns below.

We are the Dead. Short days ago
We lived, felt dawn, saw sunset glow,
Loved and were loved, and now we lie,
In Flanders fields.

Take up our quarrel with the foe:
To you from failing hands we throw
The torch; be yours to hold it high.
If ye break faith with us who die
We shall not sleep, though poppies grow
In Flanders fields.

Flanders Field—one of the eight World War I American cemeteries that are oversees. Located in Belgium.
quarrel—a heated argument between two people

On Cissarat Kalifa
By Nimbo (an unknown soldier)
36th French Colonial Infantry

We're just the same - there's nothing queer
Except a bit more black!
We found that you weren't in the rear
The night of our attack!

You've been the same just all alone
Amidst the bullet showers
Your grin the night when all went wrong
Was just the same of ours!

Though doubly white the snow-flakes glance
Against your swarthy head
The blood you lost down there in France
Was just the same old red!

---

queer—strange
swarthy—dark colored skin

The Soldier
By Rupert Brooke

If I should die, think only this of me:
    That there's some corner of a foreign field
That is for ever England. There shall be
    In that rich earth a richer dust concealed;
A dust whom England bore, shaped, made aware,
    Gave, once, her flowers to love, her ways to roam;
A body of England's, breathing English air,
    Washed by the rivers, blest by suns of home.

And think, this heart, all evil shed away,
    A pulse in the eternal mind, no less
        Gives somewhere back the thoughts by England given;
Her sights and sounds; dreams happy as her day;
    And laughter, learnt of friends; and gentleness,
        In hearts at peace, under an English heaven.

The French Revolution as It Appeared to Enthusiasts at Its Commencement
By William Wordsworth

Oh! pleasant exercise of hope and joy!
For mighty were the auxiliars which then stood
Upon our side, we who were strong in love!
Bliss was it in that dawn to be alive,
But to be young was very heaven!—Oh! times,
In which the meagre, stale, forbidding ways
Of custom, law, and statute, took at once
The attraction of a country in romance!
When Reason seemed the most to assert her rights,
When most intent on making of herself
A prime Enchantress—to assist the work
Which then was going forward in her name!
Not favoured spots alone, but the whole earth,
The beauty wore of promise, that which sets
(As at some moment might not be unfelt
Among the bowers of paradise itself)
The budding rose above the rose full blown.
What temper at the prospect did not wake
To happiness unthought of? The inert
Were roused, and lively natures rapt away!
They who had fed their childhood upon dreams,
The playfellows of fancy, who had made
All powers of swiftness, subtilty, and strength
Their ministers,—who in lordly wise had stirred
Among the grandest objects of the sense,
And dealt with whatsoever they found there
As if they had within some lurking right
To wield it;—they, too, who, of gentle mood,
Had watched all gentle motions, and to these
Had fitted their own thoughts, schemers more wild,
And in the region of their peaceful selves;—
Now was it that both found, the meek and lofty
Did both find, helpers to their heart's desire,
And stuff at hand, plastic as they could wish;
Were called upon to exercise their skill,
Not in Utopia, subterranean fields,
Or some secreted island, Heaven knows where!
But in the very world, which is the world

Of all of us,—the place where in the end
We find our happiness, or not at all!

---

auxiliars—a soldier who is serving along-side a nation other than his own
bowers—a shady place under a tree
Utopia—the idea of a society that lives in perfect harmony
subterranean—things occurring under the surface of the Earth

Opportunity
By John James Ingalls

Master of human destinies am I;
Fame, love and fortune on my footsteps wait.
Cities and fields I walk. I penetrate
Deserts and seas remote, and, passing by
Hovel and mart and palace, soon or late,
I knock unbidden once at every gate.

If sleeping, wake; if feasting, rise, before
I turn away. It is the hour of fate,
And they who follow me reach every state
Mortals desire, and conquer every foe
Save death; but those who hesitate
Condemned to failure, penury and woe,
Seek me in vain, and uselessly implore.
I answer not, and I return no more.

---

penury—very poor, destitute

The Old Soldier
By Walter De La Mare

There came an Old Soldier to my door,
Asked a crust, and asked no more;
The wars had thinned him very bare,
Fighting and marching everywhere,
With a Fol rol dol rol di do.

With nose stuck out, and cheek sunk in,
A bristling beard upon his chin -
Powder and bullets and wounds and drums
Had come to that Soldier as suchlike comes -
With a Fol rol dol rol di do.

'Twas sweet and fresh with buds of May,
Flowers springing from every spray;
And when he had supped the Old Soldier trolled
The song of youth that never grows old,
Called Fol rol dol rol di do.

Most of him rags, and all of him lean,
And the belt round his belly drawn tightsome in
He lifted his peaked old grizzled head,
And these were the very same words he said-
A Fol-rol-dol-rol-di-do.

---

bristling—hairs that are stiff and spiky

War
By Hedd Wyn (Ellis Evans)
Translated by A.Z. Foreman

Woe that I live in bitter days,
As God is setting like a sun
And in his place, as lord and slave,
Man raises forth his heinous throne.

When he thought God was gone at last
He put his brother to the sword.
Now death is roaring in our ears,
Shadowing the shanties of the poor.

The old and silenced harps are hung
On yonder willow trees again.
The bawl of boys is on the wind.
Their blood is blended in the rain.

---

heinous—an absolutely horrible act
shanties—a poorly built shack

The Original in Welsh

Rhyfel

Gwae fi fy myw mewn oes mor ddreng
A Duw ar drai ar orwel pell;
O'i ôl mae dyn, yn deyrn a gwreng,
Yn codi ei awdurdod hell.

Pan deimlodd fyned ymaith Dduw
Cyfododd gledd i ladd ei frawd;
Mae swn yr ymladd ar ein clyw,
A'i gysgod ar fythynnod tlawd.

Mae'r hen delynau genid gynt
Ynghrog ar gangau'r helyg draw,
A gwaedd y bechgyn lond y gwynt,
A'u gwaed yn gymysg efo'r glaw.

Away to Canada
By Joshua McCarter Simpson

'm on my way to Canada,
That cold and dreary land;
The dire effects of slavery,
I can no longer stand.
My soul is vexed within me so,
To think that I'm a slave;
I've now resolved to strike the blow
For freedom or the grave.

0 righteous Father,
Wilt thou not pity me?
And aid me on to Canada,
Where colored men are free.

I heard Victoria plainly say,
If we would all forsake
Our native land of slavery,
And come across the Lake.
That she was standing on the shore,
With arms extended wide,
To give us all a peaceful home,
Beyond the rolling tide.

Farewell, old master!
That's enough for me—
I'm going straight to Canada,
Where colored men are free.

I heard old master pray last night—
I heard him pray for me;
That God would come, and in his might
From Satan set me free;
So I from Satan would escape,
And flee the wrath to come—
If there's a fiend in human shape,
Old master must be one.

O! old master,?
While you pray for me,
I'm doing all I can to reach
The land of Liberty.

Ohio's not the place for me;
For I was much surprised,
So many of her sons to see
In garments of disguise.
Her name has gone out through the world,
Free Labor, Soil, and Men;
But slaves had better far be hurled
Into the Lion's Den.

Farewell, Ohio!
I am not safe in thee;
I'll travel on to Canada,
Where colored men are free.

I've now embarked for yonder shore,
Where man's a man by law,
The vessel soon will bear me o'er,
To shake the Lion's paw.
I no more dread the Auctioneer,
Nor fear the master's frowns,
I no more tremble when I hear
The beying negro-hounds.

O! old Master,
Don't think hard of me —
I'm just in sight of Canada,
Where colored men are free.

I've landed safe upon the shore,
Both soul and body free;
My blood and brain, and tears no more

Will drench old Tennessee.
But I behold the scalding tear,
Now stealing from my eye,
To think my wife — my only dear,
A slave must live and die.

0, Susannah!
Don't grieve after me—
For ever at a throne of grace,
I will remember thee.

vexed—troubled about something that is annoying or problematic; to be worried
beying—a howling sound made by a dog

At Home
By A. A. Milne

I want a soldier
(A soldier in a busby).
I want a soldier to come and play with me.
I'd give him cream-cakes
(Big ones, sugar ones),
I'd give him cream-cakes and cream for his tea.

I want a soldier
(A tall one, a red one),
I want a soldier who plays on the drum.
Daddy's going to get onc
(He's written to the shopman)
Daddy's going to get one as soon as he can come.

busby—a black fur military hat

A Song of Sydney
By Ethel Castille

High headlands all jealously hide thee,
  O fairest of sea-girdled towns!
Thine Ocean-spouse smileth beside thee,
  While each headland threatens and frowns.
Like Venice, upheld on sea-pinion,
  And fated to reign o'er the free,
Thou wearest, in sign of dominion,
  The zone of the sea.

No winter thy fertile slope hardens,
  O new Florence, set in the South!
All lands give their flowers to thy gardens,
  That glow to thy bright harbour's mouth;
The waratah and England's red roses
  With stately magnolias entwine,
Gay sunflowers fill sea-scented closes,
  All sweet with woodbine.

Thy harbour's fair flower-crowned islands
  See flags of all countries unfurled,
Thou smilest from green, sunlit highlands
  To open thine arms to the world!
Dark East's and fair West's emulations
  Resound from each hill-shadowed quay,
And over the songs of all nations,
  The voice of the sea.

---

girdled— a garment that wraps around one's mid-section from the torso down to the hips; to be gird about, wrapped
emulation(s)—when someone or something is imitated
gay—happy
woodbine—a common plant name
quay—a platform used for loading cargo on and off a ship

Heavy is the Crown
By Elijah Strong

Heavy are the heads, that wear the crown,
That turned the whole world upside down.
Heavy are the hearts, of those who grieve,
Who's friends fell, like autumn leaves.

Heavy is the toll, the crown exacts,
Our lives and our freedom, are its tax.
Heavy is the burden, that we must bear,
As family is thrust into the hospital's care.

Heavy are the minds, that are filled with fear,
Who cower at home, saying "Don't let it near."
Heavy are the thoughts, that reek of despair,
That say, "No escape from this global nightmare."

Heavy is the weight, of this deadly crown,
That rests on this world, pushing everything down.
But pressure and heat make the Refiner's fire,
That makes strength, out of the dark and the dire.

Heavy is the weight of this deadly crown,
But nothing on this earth can keep us down.
Though heavy is the burden, that bear we must,
Strength will rise from perseverance and trust.

And so we will rise from the ash of before,
And rebuild our world into something more.
As we steadily advance, out of this long night,
We leave the crown behind and move into the light.

Perhaps as we leave the long shadow of our past,
We'll build a new world, something that will last.
With lessons learned through fear and strife,
Let us work together, to build a brand new life.

---

perseverance—never giving up to achieve a goal

Freedom
By Brock Zesiger

Flags flying proudly high
Represent power in the sky
Every time I see this sight
Eternally grateful to those who fight
Doing unselfishly what is right
Over clouds jets fly, defend in the sky
Making sure our freedoms never die!

Dual
By Louise Dyson

Dual, it's what I am
But what does it mean?
It's not something
Outwardly seen.

Living in my country of birth
Yet always feeling somewhat out of place.
Although I blend in here
"American" isn't stamped on my face.

Cut me through to the core though,
And then you will see,
It's not the bull dog
But stars and stripes at the heart of me.

Torn between the physical and emotional homes
Separated by vast depths.
Home is where the heart is,
But my heart is 3000 miles out of my chest.

Here it's not all downpours,
Or afternoon tea.
I'll be the first to admit that I do have

The best of friends and a loving family.

Yet I hear a calling deep in my soul
From across the deep blue sea.
Indiana is the place
Where I'll finally be me.

I don't know what the future holds.
Either which way the following is true;
Flying the Union flag alongside Old Glory,
Cut my veins and they bleed red, white and blue.

Indiana—a state in the Unites States of America
Old Glory—another name for the United States flag

A Mixed Battle Song
By Henry Lawson

Lo! the Boar's tail is salted, and the Kangaroo's exalted,
And his right eye is extinguished by a man-o'-warsman's cap;
He is flying round the fences where the Southern Sea commences,
And he's very much excited for a quiet sort of chap.
For his ships have had a scrap and they've marked it on the map
Where the H.M.A.S. Sydney dropped across a German trap.
So the Kangaroo's a-chasing of his Blessed Self, and racing
From Cape York right round to Leeuwin, from the coast to Nevertire;
And of him need be no more said, save that to the tail aforesaid
Is the Blue Australian Ensign firmly fixed with copper wire.
(When he's filled the map with white men there'll be little to desire.)
I was sulky, I was moody (I'm inclined to being broody)
When the news appeared in Sydney, bringing joy and bringing tears,
(There's an undertone of sorrow that you'll understand to-morrow)
And I felt a something in me that had not been there for years.
Though I lean in the direction of most absolute Protection
(And of wheat on the selection)
And, considering Congestion and the hopeless unemployed,
I'd a notion (but I hid it) that, the way the Emden did it,
'Twould be better for Australia if her "commerce" was destroyed.

You may say that war's a curse, but the peace curse may be worse,
When it's lasted till it's rotten—rotten from the inmost core,

To the mouldy skin which we are, in the land we call the freer—
And I almost feel inclined to call for "Three Cheers for the War!"
For I think, when all is over, from Magellan's Straits to Dover,
Things will be a great deal better than they ever were before.
But, since "Peace" and "Right" are squalling, I'll content myself with calling
For three rousers—like the ringing cheers we used to give of yore—
For the Emden!
For the Sydney!
And their gallant crews and captains—both of whom we've met before!
And, for Kaiser William's nevvy, we shall venture three cheers more!
Cheers that go to end a war.

aforesaid—something mentioned beforehand
mouldy—another spelling of moldy
squalling—constant noisy crying
rousers—a person who rouses or stirs people up
gallant— to be brave or heroic

Morning on the Shinnecock
By Olivia Ward Bush-Banks

The rising sun had crowned the hills,
        And added beauty to the plain;
O grand and wondrous spectacle!
        That only nature could explain.
I stood within a leafy grove,
        And gazed around in blissful awe;
The sky appeared one mass of blue,
        That seemed to spread from sea to shore.
Far as the human eye could see,
        Were stretched the fields of waving corn.
Soft on my ear the warbling birds
        Were heralding the birth of morn.
While here and there a cottage quaint
        Seemed to repose in quiet ease
Amid the trees, whose leaflets waved
        And fluttered in the passing breeze.
O morning hour! so dear thy joy,
        And how I longed for thee to last;
But e'en thy fading into day
        Brought me an echo of the past.
'Twas this,—how fair my life began;
        How pleasant was its hour of dawn;
But, merging into sorrow's day,
        Then beauty faded with the morn.

---

spectacle—something drawing attention; visually striking
blissful—being perfectly happy
warbling—a sting of softly sung notes
quaint—old-fashioned
fluttered—flapping wings quickly

Both the Victor and the Vanquished
By Ouchi Yoshitaka
Both the victor and the vanquished are
but drops of dew, but bolts of lightning –
thus should we view the world.

---

vanquished—defeated
dew— droplets of water left on a surface from moisture in the air.

June

"Liberty without learning is always in peril;
learning without liberty is always in vain."
-John F. Kennedy

Men of England
By Percy Bysshe Shelley

Men of England, wherefore plough
For the lords who lay ye low?
Wherefore weave with toil and care
The rich robes your tyrants wear?

Wherefore feed and clothe and save
From the cradle to the grave
Those ungrateful drones who would
Drain your sweat—nay, drink your blood?

Wherefore, Bees of England, forge
Many a weapon, chain, and scourge,
That these stingless drones may spoil
The forced produce of your toil?

Have ye leisure, comfort, calm,
Shelter, food, love's gentle balm?
Or what is it ye buy so dear
With your pain and with your fear?

The seed ye sow, another reaps;
The wealth ye find, another keeps;
The robes ye weave, another wears;
The arms ye forge, another bears.

Sow seed—but let no tyrant reap:
Find wealth—let no imposter heap:
Weave robes—let not the idle wear:
Forge arms—in your defence to bear.

Shrink to your cellars, holes, and cells—
In hall ye deck another dwells.
Why shake the chains ye wrought? Ye see
The steel ye tempered glance on ye.

With plough and spade and hoe and loom
Trace your grave and build your tomb
And weave your winding-sheet—till fair
England be your Sepulchre.

---

balm–an ointment to sooth or heal skin
tyrant— a ruler that is cruel to his subjects
forge—a space to heat metal
scourge—a whip that is used to inflict pain as a punishment; something that causes trouble or suffering
reaps—to cut or harvest a crop
tempered—to be made stronger by heating and cooling, like with the metal of a sword.
sepulchre—a small space built as a monument to bury a person

D-Day
By Mason Shackleford

The soldiers advanced with courage true
In defense of what is right.
Some wore the colors red, white and blue,
Never looked back or took flight.

Facing enemies in front of them,
Comrades falling at their side.
Though the future ahead looked so dim,
They kept our freedom alive.

---

comrade—another person who belongs to or participates in the same group or organization like the military, a club or a society.

Des Croix de Bois Blanc
By Julien Vocance

White wooden crosses
Bursting from the soil,
Each day, here and there

In French
Des croix de bois blanc
Surgissent du sol,
Chaque jour, ça et là.

Everyone Sang
By Siegfried Sassoon

Everyone suddenly burst out singing;
And I was filled with such delight
As prisoned birds must find in freedom,
Winging wildly across the white
Orchards and dark-green fields; on - on - and out of sight.

Everyone's voice was suddenly lifted;
And beauty came like the setting sun:
My heart was shaken with tears; and horror
Drifted away ... O, but Everyone
Was a bird; and the song was wordless; the singing will never be done.

I Hear America Singing

By Walt Whitman

I hear America singing, the varied carols I hear,
Those of mechanics, each one singing his as it should be blithe
and strong,
The carpenter singing his as he measures his plank or beam,
The mason singing his as he makes ready for work, or leaves off
work,
The boatman singing what belongs to him in his boat,
the deckhand singing on the steamboat deck,
The shoemaker singing as he sits on his bench, the hatter singing
as he stands,
The wood-cutter's song, the ploughboy's on his way in the
morning, or at noon intermission or at sundown,
The delicious singing of the mother, or of the young wife at work,
or of the girl sewing or washing,
Each singing what belongs to him or her and to none else,
The day what belongs to the day—at night the party of young fellows,
robust, friendly,
Singing with open mouths their strong melodious songs.

---

blithe—cheerful and casual indifference; joyous

Cavalry Crossing the Ford

By Walt Whitman

A line in long array where they wind betwixt green islands,
They take a serpentine course, their arms flash in the sun—hark to the
musical clank,
Behold the silvery river, in it the splashing horses loitering stop to
drink,
Behold the brown-faced men, each group, each person a picture, the
negligent rest on the saddles,
Some emerge on the opposite bank, others are just entering the ford—
while,
Scarlet and blue and snowy white,
The guidon flags flutter gayly in the wind.

---

betwixt—between two things or two people
serpentine—snake shaped
gay(ly)—happily
guidon—a flag that narrows to a point, often used by a cavalry regiment

Gone to the War
By Horatio Alger Jr.

My Charlie has gone to the war,
My Charlie so brave and tall;
He left his plough in the furrow,
And flew at his country's call.
May God in safety keep him,--
My precious boy--my all!

My heart is pining to see him;
I miss him every day;
My heart is weary with waiting,
And sick of the long delay,--
But I know his country needs him,
And I could not bid him stay.

I remember how his face flushed,
And how his color came,
When the flash from the guns of Sumter
Lit the whole land with flame,
And darkened our country's banner
With the crimson hue of shame.

"Mother," he said, then faltered,--
I felt his mute appeal;
I paused-- if you are a mother,
You know what mothers feel,
When called to yield their dear ones
To the cruel bullet and steel.

My heart stood still for a moment,
Struck with a mighty woe;
A faint as of death came o'er me,
I am a mother, you know,
But I sternly checked my weakness,
And firmly bade him "Go."

Wherever the fight is fiercest
I know that my boy will be;
Wherever the need is sorest
Of the stout arms of the free.

May he prove as true to his country
As he has been true to me.

My home is lonely without him,
My hearth bereft of joy,
The thought of him who has left me
My constant sad employ;
But God has been good to the mother,--
She shall not blush for her boy.

---

pining—suffering a mental or physical decline often caused by a broken heart.
Sumter—a city in South Carolina
Falter(ed)—loosing strength
bereft—loosing or lacking something; sad or lonely

Anthem for Doomed Youth
By Wilfred for Doomed Youth

What passing-bells for these who die as cattle?
Only the monstrous anger of the guns.
Only the stuttering rifles' rapid rattle
Can patter out their hasty orisons.
No mockeries for them; no prayers nor bells,
Nor any voice of mourning save the choirs,--
The shrill, demented choirs of wailing shells;
And bugles calling for them from sad shires.

What candles may be held to speed them all?
Not in the hands of boys, but in their eyes
Shall shine the holy glimmers of goodbyes.
The pallor of girls' brows shall be their pall;
Their flowers the tenderness of patient minds,
And each slow dusk a drawing-down of blinds.

---

orisons—prayer
mourning— deep sorrow over the loss of someone
wailing—crying out loud in great pain
shire—English countryside
pallor—pale appearance

The King of England
By Sir Henry John Newbolt

In that eclipse of noon when joy was hushed
Like the bird's song beneath unnatural night,
And Terror's footfall in the darkness crushed
The rose imperial of our delight,
Then, even then, though no man cried "He comes,"
And no man turned to greet him passing there,
With phantom heralds challenging renown
And silent-throbbing drums
I saw the King of England, hale and fair,
Ride out with a great train through London town.

Unarmed he rode, but in his ruddy shield
The lions bore the dint of many a lance,
And up and down his mantle's azure field
Were strewn the lilies plucked in famous France.
Before him went with banner floating wide
The yeoman breed that served his honour best,
And mixed with these his knights of noble blood;
But in the place of pride
His admirals in billowy lines abreast
Convoyed him close like galleons on the flood.

Full of a strength unbroken showed his face
And his brow calm with youth's unclouded dawn,
But round his lips were lines of tenderer grace
Such as no hand but Time's hath ever drawn.
Surely he knew his glory had no part
In dull decay, nor unto Death must bend,
Yet surely too of lengthening shadows dreamed
With sunset in his heart,
So brief his beauty now, so near the end,
And now so old and so immortal seemed.

O King among the living, these shall hail
Sons of thy dust that shall inherit thee:
O King of men that die, though we must fail
Thy life is breathed from thy triumphant sea.
O man that servest men by right of birth,
Our hearts' content thy heart shall also keep,

Thou too with us shalt one day lay thee down
In our dear native earth,
Full sure the King of England, while we sleep,
For ever rides abroad, through London town.

---

renown—fame; when lots of people know who you are
ruddy— a person having a healthy red color
abreast—facing the same direction side by side with others
azure— a blue hugh like a sky on a clear day
plucked—to be pulled out
servest—serve

Tipperary
By Thomas Osborne Davis

I.

Let Britain boast her British hosts,
About them all right little care we;
Not British seas nor British coasts
Can match the Man of Tipperary!

II.

Tall is his form, his heart is warm,
His spirit light as any fairy--
His wrath is fearful as the storm
That sweeps the Hills of Tipperary!

III.

Lead him to fight for native land,
His is no courage cold and wary;
The troops live not on earth would stand
The headlong charge of Tipperary!

IV.

Yet meet him in his cabin rude,
Or dancing with his dark-haired Mary,
You'd swear they knew no other mood
But Mirth and Love in Tipperary!

V.

You're free to share his scanty meal,
His plighted word he'll never vary--
In vain they tried with gold and steel
To shake the Faith of Tipperary!

VI.

Soft is his *cailin's* sunny eye,
Her mien is mild, her step is airy,

Her heart is fond, her soul is high--
Oh! she's the Pride of Tipperary!

VII.

Let Britain brag her motley rag;
We'll lift the Green more proud and airy--
Be mine the lot to bear that flag,
And head the Men of Tipperary!

VIII.

Though Britain boasts her British hosts,
About them all right little care we--
Give us, to guard our native coasts,
The matchless Men of Tipperary!

Tipperary—A county in Ireland
native—naturally from a specific geographical area
mirth—amusement often expressed in laughter
scanty—a very small amount
plight—a situation that is challenging or difficult

The Invaders
By A. A. Milne

In careless patches through the wood
The clumps of yellow primrose stood
And sheets of white anemones,
Like driven snow against the trees,
Had covered up the violet,
But left the blue bell bluer yet.

Along the narrow carpet ride,
With primroses on either side,
Between their shadows and the sun
The cows came slowly, one by one,
Breathing the early morning air
And leaving it still sweeter there
And, one by one, intent upon
Their purposes, they followed on
In ordered silence... and were gone.

But all the little wood was still
As if it waited so, until
Some blackbirds on an outpost yew
Watching the slow procession through
Lifted his yellow beak at last
To whistle that the line had passed...
Then all the wood began to sing
Its morning anthem to the spring.

anemones—a flower

yew—a conifer tree that can have little red berries with a very poisonous seed.

Reign of Our Voice
By Mary Flanagan

Our silent hearts, are now bursting.
Though we know, our vengeful cries only fill your heart with a sickening sense of content, for you firmly believe you have won.
But, our pleads will end your reign.
Your throne will be forgotten, as we join our voices that ring throughout the land proclaiming our victory, as you grieve in bloody defeat.

Glimpses
By Nellie Boyer

In a church pew, my Mother
Stands up first when the Anthem
Is played. Tears in her eyes.

Before the state finals, my nerves
Electric, the stadium pauses as
One voice sings. Honoring home.

Flags line the streets on that September day,
Doors and arms open, hearts
Break and we Remember.

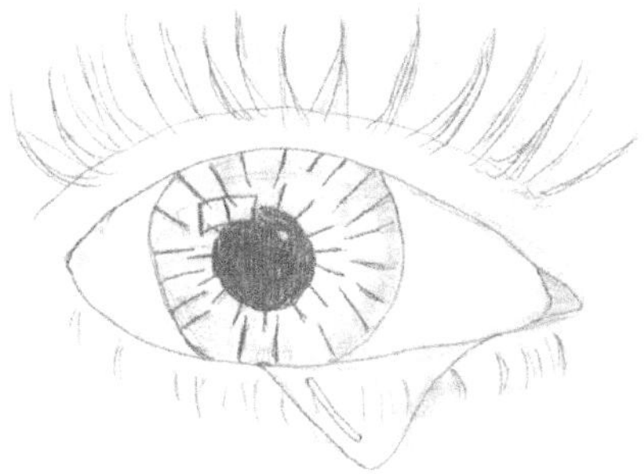

On a base far from home
A camo-clad father salutes
As a young boy looks on.

Sending my own Love off to war
Six months away, praying everyday,
Fearing the gift of a
Folded flag.

Home again. Familiar streets.
Open arms. Open hearts.
Flag flying on my front stoop.

Now in my church pew, I stand up
First when the anthem begins.
Tears on my cheeks and little hands
In mine.

A Song of the Republic
By Henry Lawson

Poem about the Australian South

Sons of the South, awake! arise!
Sons of the South, and do.
Banish from under your bonny skies
Those old-world errors and wrongs and lies.
Making a hell in a Paradise
That belongs to your sons and you.

Sons of the South, make choice between
(Sons of the South, choose true),
The Land of Morn and the Land of E'en,
The Old Dead Tree and the Young Tree Green,
The Land that belongs to the lord and the Queen,
And the Land that belongs to you.

Sons of the South, your time will come,
Sons of the South, 'tis near,
The "Signs of the Times", in their language dumb,
Fortell it, and ominous whispers hum
Like sullen sounds of a distant drum,
In the ominous atmosphere.

Sons of the South, aroused at last!
Sons of the South are few!
But your ranks grow longer and deeper fast,
And ye shall swell to an army vast,
And free from the wrongs of the North and Past
The land that belongs to you.

---

ominous—The feeling or impression that something unpleasant is going to happen.

Sunlight and Sea
By Alfred Noyes

Give me the sunlight and the sea
And who shall take my heaven from me?

Light of the Sun, Life of the Sun,
O happy, bold companion,
Whose golden laughters round me run,
Making wine of the blue air
With wild-rose kisses everywhere,
Browning the limb, flushing the cheek,
Apple-fragrant, leopard-sleek,
Dancing from thy red-curtained East
Like a Nautch-girl to my feast,
Proud because her lord, the Spring,
Praised the way those anklets ring;
Or wandering like a white Greek maid
Leaf-dappled through the dancing shade,
Where many a green-veined leaf imprints
Breast and limb with emerald tints,
That softly net her silken shape
But let the splendour still escape,
While rosy ghosts of roses flow
Over the supple rose and snow.

But sweetest, fairest is thy face,
When we meet, when we embrace,
Where the white sand sleeps at noon
Round that lonely blue lagoon,
Fringed with one white reef of coral
Where the sea-birds faintly quarrel
And the breakers on the reef
Fade into a dream of grief,
And the palm-trees overhead
Whisper that all grief is dead.

Sister Sunlight, lead me then
Into thy healing seas again....
For when we swim out, side by side,
Like a lover with his bride,
When thy lips are salt with brine,

And thy wild eyes flash in mine,
The music of a mightier sea
Beats with my blood in harmony.
I breast the primal flood of being,
Too clear for speech, too near for seeing;
And to his heart, new reconciled,
The Eternal takes his earth-bound child.

Who the essential secret spells
In those gigantic syllables,--
Flowing, ebbing, ebbing, flowing,--
Gathers wisdom past all knowing.
Song of the Sea, I hear, I hear,
That deeper music of the sphere,
Catch the rhythm of sun and star,
And know what light and darkness are;
Ay, faint beginnings of a rhyme
That swells beyond the tides of time;
Beat with thy rhythm in blood and breath,
And make one song of life and death.
I hear, I hear, and rest content,
Merged in the primal element,
The old element whence life arose,
The fount of youth, to which it goes.

Give me the sunlight and the sea
And who shall take my heaven from me?

Nautch-girl—girls who dance for entertaining others in India. The dancing would be for royalty or cultural and religious ceremonies.
dappled—marked with spots or splotches of color

To the King's Most Excellent Majesty 1768
By Phillis Wheatley

Your subjects hope, dread Sire--
The crown upon your brows may flourish long,
And that your arm may in your God be strong!
O may your sceptre num'rous nations sway,
And all with love and readiness obey!
But how shall we the British king reward!
Rule thou in peace, our father, and our lord!
Midst the remembrance of thy favours past,
The meanest peasants most admire the last
May George, beloved by all the nations round,
Live with heav'ns choicest constant blessings crown'd!
Great God, direct, and guard him from on high,
And from his head let ev'ry evil fly!
And may each clime with equal gladness see
A monarch's smile can set his subjects free

---

sceptre— a decorative and ornamental staff carried by rulers for ceremonies.
monarch— a ruler of a land such as a king, queen, or emperor

The Summer Grass
By Matsuo Basho

The summer grasses.
All that remains
Of warriors' dreams.

In Japanese

夏草や 兵どもが 夢の跡

Natsu kusa ya/ Tsuwamono domo ga/ Yume no ato

July

"A land without memories is a people without liberty"
-General Robert E. Lee

Boston Hymn
By Ralph Waldo Emerson

The word of the Lord by night
To the watching Pilgrims came,
As they sat by the seaside,
And filled their hearts with flame.

God said, I am tired of kings,
I suffer them no more;
Up to my ear the morning brings
The outrage of the poor.

Think ye I made this ball
A field of havoc and war,
Where tyrants great and tyrants small
Might harry the weak and poor?

My angel,—his name is Freedom,—
Choose him to be your king;
He shall cut pathways east and west,
And fend you with his wing.

Lo! I uncover the land
Which I hid of old time in the West,
As the sculptor uncovers the statue
When he has wrought his best;

I show Columbia, of the rocks
Which dip their foot in the seas,
And soar to the air-borne flocks
Of clouds, and the boreal fleece.

I will divide my goods;
Call in the wretch and slave:
None shall rule but the humble,
And none but Toil shall have.

I will have never a noble,
No lineage counted great;
Fishers and choppers and ploughmen
Shall constitute a state.

Go, cut down trees in the forest,
And trim the straightest boughs;
Cut down trees in the forest,
And build me a wooden house.

Call the people together,
The young men and the sires,
The digger in the harvest field,
Hireling, and him that hires;

And here in a pine state-house
They shall choose men to rule
In every needful faculty,
In church, and state, and school.

Lo, now! if these poor men
Can govern the land and sea,
And make just laws below the sun,
As planets faithful be.

And ye shall succor men;
'T is nobleness to serve;
Help them who cannot help again:
Beware from right to swerve.

I break your bonds and masterships,
And I unchain the slave:
Free be his heart and hand henceforth
As wind and wandering wave.
I cause from every creature
His proper good to flow:

As much as he is and doeth,
So much he shall bestow.

But, laying hands on another
To coin his labor and sweat,
He goes in pawn to his victim
For eternal years in debt.

To-day unbind the captive,
So only are ye unbound;
Lift up a people from the dust,
Trump of their rescue, sound!

Pay ransom to the owner,
And fill the bag to the brim.
Who is the owner? The slave is owner,
And ever was. Pay him.

North! give him beauty for rags,
And honor, South! for his shame;
Nevada! coin thy golden crags
With Freedom's image and name.

Up! and the dusky race
That sat in darkness long,—
Be swift their feet as antelopes,
And as behemoth strong.

Come, East and West and North,
By races, as snow-flakes,
And carry my purpose forth,
Which neither halts nor shakes.

My will fulfilled shall be,
For, in daylight or in dark,
My thunderbolt has eyes to see
His way home to the mark.

---

bough— the larger branches of a tree
hireling—a person who does low level/menial work
succor—helping a person in a time of difficulty and distress
behemoth—a very large creature

Freedom Fighters
By Maddox Welgan

The people who fought for our freedom,
Well, I would certainly like to meet 'em.
Freedom was their main concern,
But it was something they had to earn.
They were fighting so we could be free,
So that we could have Liberty. Many people gave their lives, But it was worth it for the Fourth of July.

A Daughter Of The States
By Madison Julius Cawein

She has the eyes of some barbarian Queen
Leading her wild tribes into battle; eyes,
Wherein th' unconquerable soul defies,
And Love sits throned, imperious and serene.

And I have thought that Liberty, alone
Among the mountain stars, might look like her,
Kneeling to GOD, her only emperor,
Kindling her torch on FREEDOM'S altar-stone.

For in herself, regal with riches of
Beauty and youth, again those Queens seem born -
BOADICEA, meeting scorn with scorn,
And ERMENGARDE, returning love for love.

---

imperious—arrogant and domineering authoritarian power
serene—calm and peaceful
Boadicea—Queen of the British Iceni and led and uprising against the Roman Empire about 60AD.

Canada, 1882
By John Campbell

"Are hearts here strong enough to found
A glorious people's sway?"
Ask of our rivers as they bound
From hill to plain, or ocean-sound,
If they are strong to-day?
If weakness in their floods be found,
Then may ye answer "Nay!"

"Is union yours? may foeman's might
Your love ne'er break or chain?"
Go see if o'er our land the flight
Of Spring be stayed by blast or blight;
If Fall bring never grain;
If Summer suns deny their light,
Then may our hope be vain!

"Yet far too cramped the narrow space
Your country's rule can own?"
Ah! travel all its bounds and trace
Each Alp unto its fertile base,
Our realm of forests lone,
Our world of prairie, like the face
Of ocean, hardly known!

"Yet for the arts to find a shrine,
Too rough, I ween, and rude?"
Yea, if you find no flower divine
With prairie grass or hardy pine.
No lilies with the wood,
Or on the water-meadows' line
No purple Iris' flood!

"You deem a nation here shall stand,
United, great, and free?"
Yes, see how Liberty's own hand
With ours the continent hath spanned,
Strong-arched, from sea to sea:
Our Canada's her chosen land,
Her roof and crown to be!

Marching
By Isaac Rosenberg

My eyes catch ruddy necks
Sturdily pressed back.
All a red-brick moving glint.
Like flaming pendulums, hands
Swing across the khaki—
Mustard coloured khaki—
To the automatic feet.

We husband the ancient glory
In these bared necks and hands.
Not broke is the forge of Mars;
But a subtler brain beats iron
To shoe the hoofs of death.
Who pays dynamic air now?—
Blind fingers loose an iron cloud
To rain immortal darkness
On strong eyes.

---

ruddy— a person having a healthy red color
pendulums—an item swinging from a fixed point under the effects of gravity.

America the Beautiful
By Katharine Lee Bates

O beautiful for spacious skies,
For amber waves of grain,
For purple mountain majesties
Above the fruited plain!
America! America!
God shed His grace on thee
And crown thy good with brotherhood
From sea to shining sea!

O beautiful for pilgrim feet,
Whose stern, impassioned stress
A thoroughfare for freedom beat
Across the wilderness!
America! America!
God mend thine every flaw,
Confirm thy soul in self-control,
Thy liberty in law!

O beautiful for heroes proved
In liberating strife,
Who more than self their country loved,
And mercy more than life!
America! America!
May God thy gold refine,
Till all success be nobleness,
And every gain divine!

O beautiful for patriot dream
That sees beyond the years
Thine alabaster cities gleam
Undimmed by human tears!
America! America!
God shed His grace on thee
And crown thy good with brotherhood
From sea to shining sea!

---

patriot(s)—a person(s) devoted to supporting his country and willing to defend it.

Pioneer! O Pioneer!
By Walt Whitman

COME my tan-faced children,
Follow well in order, get your weapons ready,
Have you your pistols? have you your sharp-edged axes?
Pioneers! O pioneers!

For we cannot tarry here,
We must march my darlings, we must bear the brunt of danger,
We the youthful sinewy races, all the rest on us depend,
Pioneers! O pioneers!

O you youths, Western youths,
So impatient, full of action, full of manly pride and friendship,
Plain I see you Western youths, see you tramping with the fore-
most,
Pioneers! O pioneers!

Have the elder races halted?
Do they droop and end their lesson, wearied over there beyond
the seas?
We take up the task eternal, and the burden and the lesson,
Pioneers! O pioneers!

All the past we leave behind,
We debouch upon a newer mightier world, varied world,
Fresh and strong the world we seize, world of labor and the march,
Pioneers! O pioneers!

We detachments steady throwing,
Down the edges, through the passes, up the mountains steep,
Conquering, holding, daring, venturing as we go the unknown ways,
Pioneers! O pioneers!

We primeval forests felling,
We the rivers stemming, vexing we and piercing deep the mines
within,
We the surface broad surveying, we the virgin soil upheaving,
Pioneers! O pioneers!

A

Song For The Irish Militia
By Thomas Osborne Davis

I.

The tribune's tongue and poet's pen
May sow the seed in prostrate men;
But 'tis the soldier's sword alone
Can reap the crop so bravely sown!
No more I'll sing nor idly pine,
But train my soul to lead a line--
A soldier's life's the life for me--
A soldier's death, so Ireland's free!

II.

No foe would fear your thunder words,
If 'twere not for your lightning swords--
If tyrants yield when millions pray,
'Tis less they link in war array;
Nor peace itself is safe, but when
The sword is sheathed by fighting men--
A soldier's life's the life for me--
A soldier's death, so Ireland's free!

III.

The rifle brown and sabre bright
Can freely speak and nobly write--
What prophets preached the truth so well
As HOFER, BRIAN, BRUCE, and TELL?
God guard the creed these heroes taught--
That blood-bought Freedom's cheaply bought
A soldier's life's the life for me--
A soldier's death, so Ireland's free!

IV.

Then, welcome be the bivouac,
The hardy stand, and fierce attack,
Where pikes will tame their carbineers,
And rifles thin their bay'neteers,
And every field the island through
Will show "what Irishmen can do!"
A soldier's life's the life for me--
A soldier's death so Ireland's free!

V.

Yet, 'tis not strength and 'tis not steel
Alone can make the English reel;
But wisdom, working day by day,
Till comes the time for passion's sway--
The patient dint and powder shock,
Can blast an empire like a rock.
A soldier's life's the life for me--
A soldier's death, so Ireland's free!

VI.

The tribune's tongue and poet's pen
May sow the seed in slavish men;
But 'tis the soldier's sword alone
Can reap the harvest when 'tis grown.
No more I'll sing, no more I'll pine,
But train my soul to lead a line--
A soldier's life's the life for me--
A soldier's death, so Ireland's free.

---

pine— suffering a mental or physical decline often caused by a broken heart.
sheath— a covering for a blade or sword; a protective covering
carbineers—a soldier armed with a carbine

Sea-Magic
By Walter De La Mare

My heart faints in me for the distant sea.
   The roar of London is the roar of ire
   The lion utters in his old desire
For Libya out of dim captivity.
The long bright silver of Cheapside I see,
   Her gilded weathercocks on roof and spire
   Exulting eastward in the western fire;
All things recall one heart-sick memory: -

Ever the rustle of the advancing foam,
   The surges' desolate thunder, and the cry
   As of some lone babe in the whispering sky;
Ever I peer into the restless gloom
   To where a ship clad dim and loftily
Looms steadfast in the wonder of her home.

---

gilded— covered in gold, traditionally thought of as gold leaf (real gold). gold paint.

If I Were King
By A. A. Milne

I often wish I were a King,
And then I could do anything.

If only I were King of Spain,
I'd take my hat off in the rain.

If only I were King of France,
I wouldn't brush my hair for
aunts.

I think, if I were King of Greece,
I'd push things off the
mantelpiece.

If I were King of Norroway,
I'd ask an elephant to stay.

If I were King of Babylon,
I'd leave my button gloves
undone.

If I were King of Timbuctoo,
I'd think of lovely things to do.

If I were King of anything,
I'd tell the soldiers, "I'm the
King!"

The Cowboy
By Richard Hunter

There was a bold cowboy
  Came out of the west;
Of all the bold riders,
  This cowboy's the best.

The horse he brought with him
  Will not run away;
But stands by the side of
  His master all day.

The Picnic Battle
By Anicka Melville

The people gather on this eventful day,
Gray against blue,
Father against son.
The citizens and reporters and watchers.
They come with sandwiches and nice suits and dresses.
They hold up their glasses
To watch the skirmish,
To see the side that they are sure will win.
"Oh I'll wipe up all the blood that is to be spilled today
With my pocket handkerchief."

And they did not find what they expected.
They did not anticipate
The grief or sadness,
The regret that comes with any fight.
The battle much bloodier than expected,
The dawning realization:
War, this war, all war, is no picnic.

They started to move, to get up, to run.
To get away from the war that was no picnic.
The panic to see the other side winning,
The horror to see the lives that were lost.
Gray against blue.
Brother against brother.

Father against son.
Never again see any dispute as a reason to party.
Never again see any conflict as a joke.
War is no picnic.

---

skirmish—an unplanned fight between small armies or fleets

The first land battle of the United States Civil War was fought on July 21, 1861 near the town on Centreville, Virginia where people gathered to watch the battle while having a picnic.

The Captain
By John Alexander McCrea

Here all the day she swings from tide to tide,
Here all night long she tugs a rusted chain,
A masterless hulk that was a ship of pride,
Yet unashamed: her memories remain.

It was Nelson in the 'Captain', Cape St. Vincent far alee,
With the 'Vanguard' leading s'uth'ard in the haze --
Little Jervis and the Spaniards and the fight that was to be,
Twenty-seven Spanish battleships, great bullies of the sea,
And the 'Captain' there to find her day of days.

Right into them the 'Vanguard' leads, but with a sudden tack
The Spaniards double swiftly on their trail;
Now Jervis overshoots his mark, like some too eager pack,
He will not overtake them, haste he e'er so greatly back,
But Nelson and the 'Captain' will not fail.

Like a tigress on her quarry leaps the 'Captain' from her place,
To lie across the fleeing squadron's way:
Heavy odds and heavy onslaught, gun to gun and face to face,
Win the ship a name of glory, win the men a death of grace,
For a little hold the Spanish fleet in play.

Ended now the "Captain"'s battle, stricken sore she falls aside
Holding still her foemen, beaten to the knee:
As the 'Vanguard' drifted past her, "Well done, 'Captain'," Jervis cried,
Rang the cheers of men that conquered, ran the blood of men that died,
And the ship had won her immortality.

Lo! here her progeny of steel and steam,
A funnelled monster at her mooring swings:
Still, in our hearts, we see her pennant stream,
And "Well done, 'Captain'," like a trumpet rings.

progeny—a descendant

In a Hole In the Ground, At Night
By Julien Vocance

In a hole in the ground, at night,
Facing an immense army
Two men

In the original French
Les cadavres entre les tranchées,
Depuis trois mois noircissant,
Ont attrapé la pelade

Love for My Country
By Lily Hall

Patriotism means
Love for your home, your country
Your legacy, your history
And everything in between
For me, it's the fact that I'm free
The red, white, and blue
Faithful and true,
My country, I love you

---

patriotism—devotion to one country

Drummer's Lament
By Niccole Perrine

The price is too dear,
Daughters and Sons.

The danger too near,
Daughters and Sons.

The sacrifice too grave,
Daughters and Sons.

The march-time's been clave,
Daughters and Sons.

Will you stand, be brave?
Daughters and Sons.

Apathy lingers.
Daughters and Sons

Remove your blinkers.
Daughters and Sons.

Will you heed the call?
Daughters and Sons.

Seek freedom for all?
Daughters and Sons.

The price is too dear
Daughters and Sons.

To dear, to fear.
Daughters and Sons.

clave—cleaver

August

"Live as if you were to die tomorrow. Learn as if you were to live forever."
-Mahatma Gandhi

Long Island Sound
Emma Lazarus

I see it as it looked one afternoon
In August,— by a fresh soft breeze o'erblown.
The swiftness of the tide, the light thereon,
A far-off sail, white as a crescent moon.
The shining waters with pale currents strewn,
The quiet fishing-smacks, the Eastern cove,
The semi-circle of its dark, green grove.
The luminous grasses, and the merry sun
In the grave sky; the sparkle far and wide,
Laughter of unseen children, cheerful chirp
Of crickets, and low lisp of rippling tide,
Light summer clouds fantastical as sleep
Changing unnoted while I gazed thereon.
All these fair sounds and sights I made my own.

August 1914
By Isaac Rosenberg

What in our lives is burnt
In the fire of this?
The heart's dear granary?
The much we shall miss?

Three lives hath one life—
Iron, honey, gold.
The gold, the honey gone—
Left is the hard and cold.

Iron are our lives
Molten right through our youth.
A burnt space through ripe fields,
A fair mouth's broken tooth.

1942
By Emma Lazarus

Thou two-faced year, Mother of Change and Fate,
Didst weep when Spain cast forth with flaming sword,
The children of the prophets of the Lord,
Prince, priest, and people, spurned by zealot hate.
Hounded from sea to sea, from state to state,
The West refused them, and the East abhorred.
No anchorage the known world could afford,
Close-locked was every port, barred every gate.
Then smiling, thou unveil'dst, O two-faced year,
A virgin world where doors of sunset part,
Saying, "Ho, all who weary, enter here!
There falls each ancient barrier that the art
Of race or creed or rank devised, to rear
Grim bulwarked hatred between heart and heart!"

spurn—to reject with extreme dislike and disdain
zealot—a person who is a fanatic about something like religion, politics or anything else he/she has stonge feeling about
Abhorred—feeling of hatred and discuss towards something or someone
bulwarked—a defense created by an embankment or wall

Arms and the Boy
By Wilfred Edward Salter Owen

Let the boy try along this bayonet-blade
How cold steel is, and keen with hunger of blood;
Blue with all malice, like a madman's flash;
And thinly drawn with famishing for flesh.

Lend him to stroke these blind, blunt bullet-heads
Which long to muzzle in the hearts of lads.
Or give him cartridges of fine zinc teeth,
Sharp with the sharpness of grief and death.

For his teeth seem for laughing round an apple.
There lurk no claws behind his fingers supple;
And God will grow no talons at his heels,
Nor antlers through the thickness of his curls.

---

bayonet—a pointed weapon that can be attached to the end of a rifle.
malice—wanting to do evil; ill will
supple—flexible or bending easily

Vitai Lampada
By Sir Henry Newbolt

THERE'S a breathless hush in the Close to-night -
Ten to make and the match to win -
A bumping pitch and a blinding light,
An hour to play and the last man in.
And it's not for the sake of a ribboned coat,
Or the selfish hope of a season's fame,
But his Captain's hand on his shoulder smote
"Play up! play up! and play the game!"

The sand of the desert is sodden red, -
Red with the wreck of a square that broke; -
The Gatling's jammed and the colonel dead,
And the regiment blind with dust and smoke.
The river of death has brimmed his banks,
And England's far, and Honour a name,
But the voice of schoolboy rallies the ranks,
"Play up! play up! and play the game!"

This is the word that year by year
While in her place the School is set
Every one of her sons must hear,
And none that hears it dare forget.
This they all with a joyful mind
Bear through life like a torch in flame,
And falling fling to the host behind -
"Play up! play up! and play the game!"

---

sodden—soaked or saturated with liquid

The British Tar
By William Schwenck Gilbert

A British tar is a soaring soul,
As free as a mountain bird,
His energetic fist should be ready to resist
A dictatorial word
His nose should pant and his lips should curl,
His cheeks should flame and his brow should furl,
His bosom should heave and his heart should glow,
And his fist be ever ready for a knock-down blow.

His eyes should flash with an inborn fire,
His brow with scorn be rung;
He never should bow down to a domineering frown,
Or the tang of a tyrant tongue.
His foot should stamp and his throat should growl,
His hair should twirl and his face should scowl:
His eyes should flash and his breast protrude,
And this should be his customary attitude!

William Wallace
By Francis William Lauderdale Adams
This is Scotch William Wallace. It was he
Who in dark hours first raised his face to see:
Who watched the English tyrant nobles spurn,
Steel-clad, with iron hoofs the Scottish free:

Who armed and drilled the simple footman Kern,
Yea, bade in blood and rout the proud Knight learn
His Feudalism was dead, and Scotland stand
Dauntless to wait the day of Bannockburn!

O Wallace, peerless lover of thy land,
We need thee still, thy moulding brain and hand!
For us, thy poor, again proud tyrants spurn,
The robber rich, a yet more hateful band!

---

spurn—to reject someone or something with great contempt
mould(ing)—another spelling of moldy
Feudalism—a class system in medieval Europe where nobility held land and serfs were indebted.

The Dreamer
By Walter De La Mare
O thou who giving helm and sword,
  Gav'st, too, the rusting rain,
And starry dark's all tender dews
  To blunt and stain:

Out of the battle I am sped,
  Unharmed, yet stricken sore;
A living shape amid whispering shades
  On Lethe's shore.

No trophy in my hands I bring,
  To this sad, sighing stream,
The neighings and the trumps and cries
  Were but a dream.

Traitor to life, of life betrayed:
  O, of thy mercy deep,
A dream my all, the all I ask
  Is sleep.

The Marsh Of Rhuddlan
By Evan Evans (Ievan Glan Geirionydd)

OVER Eryri the setting sun flashes,
Night's curtain closes o'er moorland and lea,
Now not a breath stirs the shadowy ashes,
Far, far away falls the sigh of the sea.
Yet ev'ry patriot pulse in my body
Knocks at the door of my passionate heart,
While Rhuddlan Marsh in thy battle-field bloody,
Curs'd of the Cymry, again I take part.

Out of the gloom leap the loud crashing targes,
Through the spear forest the battle-axe breaks,
Arrows fly hissing to thundering charges
E'en to its marges the red morass quakes !
O'er the wild tumult, the wail of the wounded,
Hark ! the clear voice of Caradoc is rolled : "
Into yon breach ! or betrayed and surrounded
On Rhuddlan Marsh let the moon find us cold."

Quick to his call hero hearts are up-leaping,
Fierce as their swords hero faces out-flame ;
Strong hero arms the red harvest are reaping,
Gap after gap to their glory they claim !
Then with one voice all our nation kneels praying "
Great is our jeopardy, Lord God of hosts,
Only in Thee our last hope we are staying,
None but Thine Arm can deliver our coasts ! "

Honour and hope kept the vantage till sunset,
Then overpowered our battle gave way ;
Vaunt not, proud foe, your victorious onset
Numbers, not valour, have won you the day !
Oh ! but yon crowd that with Heaven interceded
Grey-headed grandsire, weak women and child
Now from their knees, their petition unheeded,
Flock in white terror far into the wild !

Coom after coom to Eryri's recesses
Echoes the cry of those desolate ones ;
Whilst Mother Wales, as she tears her wild tresses,

Weeps o'er the urns of her mightiest sons !
Beauty's rose dies at Caradoc's disaster,
Terror and panic his battlements climb ;
Whilst his arch-minstrel, lamenting his master,
Makes Morfa Rhuddlan our dirge for all time.

Eryri—either Welsh for eagle or Latin for "to rise"
coom—smut or soot
dirge—a song or lament for the dead
patriot(s)—a person(s) devoted to supporting his country and willing to defend it.

Buckingham Palace
By A. A. Milne

They're changing guard at Buckingham Palace -
Christopher Robin went down with Alice.
Alice is marrying one of the guard.
"A soldier's life is terrible hard,"
Says Alice.

They're changing guard at Buckingham Palace -
Christopher Robin went down with Alice.
We saw a guard in a sentry-box.
"One of the sergeants looks after their socks,"
Says Alice.

They're changing guard at Buckingham Palace -
Christopher Robin went down with Alice.
We looked for the King, but he never came.
"Well, God take care of him, all the same,"
Says Alice.

They're changing guard at Buckingham Palace -
Christopher Robin went down with Alice.
They've great big parties inside the grounds.
"I wouldn't be King for a hundred pounds,"
Says Alice.

They're changing guard at Buckingham Palace
Christopher Robin went down with Alice.
A face looked out, but it wasn't the King's.
"He's much too busy a-signing things,"
Says Alice.

They're changing guard at Buckingham Palace
Christopher Robin went down with Alice.
"Do you think the King knows all about me?"
"Sure to, dear, but it's time for tea,"
Says Alice.

Revolution
By Thomasin Schkrohowsky

We wanted something to
Believe in,
Somewhere to
Begin again.
The glorified pride of a
Fearless soul
Follows the tide of
Freedom's
Anthem, the underline fight
Like lyrics
In the complex chorus
Of spirits
United under one flag
That flies, Unstoppable, within
The Eden
Of a single,
        Unified
          Nation.

Paw Paw
By Annabel Payne

Pawpaw Smiles of sunshine
Warm rays of love,
Tough as cowhide,
Gentle as a dove.
Born 73 years ago,
Between 3 brothers, he grew.
The army called and he enlisted
So they didn't have to.
Hard times often came
On American troops.
He bravely fought
So we didn't have to.
He plays with great-grandkids
Under free skies of blue,
He defended our liberty
And forever, I will, too.

The Music, The Song, The Faith
By Alitsa Setian

There is a struggle in the mountains
I stand firm
My people were almost annihilated
We stand firm
1915, Anguish filled every heart
But the song, the faith,
Held my ancestors together
Enemies did not keep us from proceeding ahead
Our music and faith strengthens us still
With them, nothing can stop us
Hope is never lost,
Beauty and splendor never defeated

The ancestral music pushes me on.
Hope surges through me,
I lift up my instrument
Its melody catches every heart
A stirring of love for my country, my people
The music, the song.

We are not finished
The battle is yet to be won,
But the music is there
It strengthens us all,
The melody and the beat
Keep time to the song!
Love, Wisdom, Hope, all set in motion
A failure does not stop us
We are held together by the faith,
The song
We are the Armenians.

Beethoven In Central Park
By Alfred Noyes

(After a glimpse of a certain monument in New York, during the Victory Celebration)

The thousand-windowed towers were all alight.
  Throngs of all nations filled that glittering way;
And, rich with dreams of the approaching day,
Flags of all nations trampled down the night.
No clouds, at sunset, die in airs as bright.
  No clouds, at dawn, awake in winds as gay;
  For Freedom rose in that august array,
Crowned with the stars and weaponed for the right.

Then, in a place of whispering leaves and gloom,
  I saw, too dark, too dumb for bronze or stone,
  One tragic head that bowed against the sky;
O, in a hush too deep for any tomb
  I saw Beethoven, dreadfully alone
    With his own grief, and his own majesty.

---

gay—happy

Marshland
By Emily Pauline Johnson

A thin wet sky, that yellows at the rim,
And meets with sun-lost lip the marsh's brim.

The pools low lying, dank with moss and mould,
Glint through their mildews like large cups of gold.

Among the wild rice in the still lagoon,
In monotone the lizard shrills his tune.

The wild goose, homing, seeks a sheltering,
Where rushes grow, and oozing lichens cling.

Late cranes with heavy wing, and lazy flight,
Sail up the silence with the nearing night.

And like a spirit, swathed in some soft veil,
Steals twilight and its shadows o'er the swale.

Hushed lie the sedges, and the vapours creep,
Thick, grey and humid, while the marshes sleep.

---

mould—another spelling of mold
monotone—a sound that is unchanging in pitch
swathed—wrapped in layers
sedges—a class of plant that is long and grass like

Oh, My Brother, I Weep For You
By Akiko Yosano

Oh, my brother, I weep for you.
Do not give your life.
Last-born among us,
You are the most belovéd of our parents.
Did they make you grasp the sword
And teach you to kill?
Did they raise you to the age of twenty-four,
Telling you to kill and die?

Heir to our family name,
You will be master of this store,

Old and honoured, in Sakai, and therefore,
Brother, do not give your life.
For you, what does it matter
Whether Lu-Shun Fortress falls or not?
The code of merchant houses
Says nothing about this.

Brother, do not give your life.
His Majesty the Emperor
Goes not himself into the battle.
Could he, with such deeply noble heart,
Think it an honour for men
To spill one another's blood
And die like beasts?

Oh, my brother, in that battle
Do not give your life.
Think of mother, who lost father just last autumn.
How much lonelier is her grief at home
Since you were drafted.
Even as we hear about peace in this great Imperial Reign,
Her hair turns whiter by the day.

And do you ever think of your young bride,
Who crouches weeping behind the shop curtains
In her gentle loveliness?
Or have you forgotten her?
The two of you were together not ten months before parting.
What must she feel in her young girl's heart?
Who else has she to rely on in this world?
Brother, do not give your life.

To the Poet Before Battle
By Ivor Gurney
Now, youth, the hour of thy dread passion comes;
Thy lovely things must all be laid away;
And thou, as others, must face the riven day
Unstirred by rattle of the rolling drums,
Or bugles' strident cry. When mere noise numbs
The sense of being, the sick soul doth sway,
Remember thy great craft's honour, that they may say
Nothing in shame of poets. Then the crumbs
Of praise the little versemen joyed to take
Shall be forgotten; then they must know we are,
For all our skill in words, equal in might
And strong of mettle as those we honoured; make
The name of poet terrible in just war,
And like a crown of honour upon the fight.

strident—harsh and loud
versemen—a person who writes in verse

Joining the Colours
By Katharine Tynan
There they go marching all in step so gay!
Smooth-cheeked and golden, food for shells and guns.
Blithely they go as to a wedding day,
The mothers' sons.

The drab street stares to see them row on row
On the high tram-tops, singing like the lark.
Too careless-gay for courage, singing they go
Into the dark.

With tin whistles, mouth-organs, any noise,
They pipe the way to glory and the grave;
Foolish and young, the gay and golden boys
Love cannot save.

High heart! High courage! The poor girls they kissed
Run with them : they shall kiss no more, alas!
Out of the mist they stepped-into the mist
Singing they pass.

gay—happy

September

Freedom is a fragile thing and it's never more than one generation away from extinction. It is not ours by way of inheritance; it must be fought for and defended constantly by each generation, for it comes only once to a people. And those in world history who have known freedom and then lost it have never known it again.
-Ronald Regan

Father Abe
By Francis William Lauderdale Adams

(*Song of the American Sons of Labour.*)
THE SONG.

"O we knew so well, dear Father,
When we answered to your call,
And the Southern Moloch stricken
Shook and tottered to his fall -

"O we knew so well you loved us,
And our hearts beat back to yours
With the rapturous adoration
That through all the years endures!

"Mothers, sisters bade us hasten
Sweethearts, wives with babe at breast;
For the Union, faith and freedom,
For our hero of the West!

"And we wrung forth victory blood-stained
From the desperate hands of Crime,
And our Cause blazed out Man's beacon

Through the endless future time!

"And forgiven, forever we bade it
Cease, that envy, hatred, strife,
As he willed, our murdered Father
That had sealed his love with life!

"O dear Father, was it thus, then?
Did we this but in a dream?
Is it real, hideous present?
Does our suffering only seem?

"Bend and listen, look and tell us!
Are these joyless toilers We?
Slaves more wretched, patient, piteous
Than the slaves we fought to free!

"Are these weak, worn girls and women
Those whose mothers yet can tell
How they kissed and clasped men god-like
With fierce faces fronting hell?

"Bend and listen, look and tell us!
Is this silent waste, possessed
By bloat thieves and their task-masters,
Thy free, thy fair, thy fearless West?

"Are these Eastern mobs of wage-slaves,
Are these cringing debauchees,
Sons of those who slung their rifles -
Shook the old Flag to the breeze?"

---

rapturous—expressing or feeling full of ecstatic delight; extreme joy
piteous—causing or deserving pity

Patriot Parade
By Elijah Wackler

The Patriots march on the field so green
With guns and drums to the river of blood,

The battle began
George Washington leading the band,

Off Revere went to warn of the coming days,

To Lexington and Concord
Then Bunker Hill,

Let the battle still rage
Till' we get what we want,

"No taxation, without representation!"
Is what they all said.

So let's have a Tea Party
In Paris (Pah-rhee)
On September 3rd, 1783
King George came to his senses
After their loss in Yorktown
He finally granted that America be free!

So hurray to the Patriots
Of the American Revolution
Let's all solute them on our Day of Independence!

---

patriot(s)—a person(s) devoted to supporting his country and willing to defend it.

Old Ironside
By Oliver Wendell Holmes Sr.

Ay, tear her tattered ensign down!
  Long has it waved on high,
And many an eye has danced to see
  That banner in the sky;
Beneath it rung the battle shout,
  And burst the cannon's roar;—
The meteor of the ocean air
  Shall sweep the clouds no more!

Her deck, once red with heroes' blood
  Where knelt the vanquished foe,
When winds were hurrying o'er the flood
  And waves were white below,
No more shall feel the victor's tread,
  Or know the conquered knee;—
The harpies of the shore shall pluck
  The eagle of the sea!

O, better that her shattered hulk
  Should sink beneath the wave;
Her thunders shook the mighty deep,
  And there should be her grave;
Nail to the mast her holy flag,
  Set every thread-bare sail,
And give her to the god of storms,—
  The lightning and the gale!

---

tatter(ed)—when cloth is torn irregularly
vanquish—defeated

Unsung
By Annabel Payne

This exciting tale begins
In the Revolutionary era.
I sing the unsung song
Of the brave Lydia Darragh.
Born a Quaker, she was never suspected.
She was popular, wealthy, loyal, respected.
Her husband and sons rose to fight unjust power, Knowing God is righteous, and if not, they'd be cowards.
One day, a redcoat asked with British pride,
"Madam, we ask for a meeting inside.
" Lydia said, "Of course, but my children and I stay." They agreed, but upstairs she was sent away.
When the troops began to talk,
Lydia spied on them like a hawk.
She soon left with a secret message bag,
Undeterred when a solider began to nag.
"Sir, I've simply come to get some flour!"
She safely reported to Patriot powers.
I admire Lydia Darragh and how she behaved
For the land of the free and the home of the brave!

Lydia Darragh—a Quaker from Philadelphia who was a spy during the American Revolution for the Patriot side.
Quaker—a religion group who believed in pacifism and believed in spiritual equality of men and women.
patriot(s)—a person(s) devoted to supporting his country and willing to defend it.

The Jew
By Isaac Rosenberg

Moses, from whose loins I sprung,
Lit by a lamp in his blood
Ten immutable rules, a moon
For mutable lampless men.

The blonde, the bronze, the ruddy,
With the same heaving blood,
Keep tide to the moon of Moses.
Then why do they sneer at me?

---

loins—the space between the hip bone and the false ribs; the area where your reproductive organs are.

Defence of Fort M'Henry
"The Star-Spangled Banner"
By Frances Scott Keys

O! say can you see, by the dawn's early light,
  What so proudly we hail'd at the twilight's last gleaming,
Whose broad stripes and bright stars through the perilous fight,
  O'er the ramparts we watch'd, were so gallantly streaming?
    And the rockets' red glare, the bombs bursting in air,
    Gave proof through the night that our flag was still there —
      O! say, does that star-spangled banner yet wave
      O'er the land of the free, and the home of the brave?

On the shore, dimly seen through the mists of the deep,
  Where the foe's haughty host in dread silence reposes,
What is that which the breeze o'er the towering steep,
  As it fitfully blows, half conceals, half discloses?
    Now it catches the gleam of the morning's first beam,
    In full glory reflected now shines on the stream —
      'Tis the star-spangled banner, O! long may it wave
      O'er the land of the free, and the home of the brave.

And where is that band who so vauntingly swore
  That the havock of war and the battle's confusion
A home and a country should leave us no more?
  Their blood has wash'd out their foul foot-steps' pollution,

No refuge could save the hireling and slave,
From the terror of flight or the gloom of the grave;
And the star-spangled banner in triumph doth wave
O'er the land of the free, and the home of the brave.

O! thus be it ever when freemen shall stand
Between their lov'd home, and the war's desolation,
Blest with vict'ry and peace, may the heav'n-rescued land
Praise the power that hath made and preserv'd us a nation!
Then conquer we must, when our cause it is just,
And this be our motto — "In God is our trust!"
And the star-spangled banner in triumph shall wave
O'er the land of the free, and the home of the brave.

---

ramparts—a castle or cities defensive wall
hireling—a person who does low level/menial work

England
By Sir Henry John Newbolt

Praise thou with praise unending,
The Master of the Wine;
To all their portions sending
Himself he mingled thine:

The sea-born flush of morning,
The sea-born hush of night,
The East wind comfort scorning,
And the North wind driving right:

The world for gain and giving,
The game for man and boy,
The life that joys in living,
The faith that lives in joy.

The Best School of All
By Henry Newbolt

It's good to see the school we knew,
The land of youth and dream.
To greet again the rule we knew
Before we took the stream:
Though long we've missed the sight of her,
Our hearts may not forget;
We've lost the old delight of her,
We keep her honour yet.

We'll honour yet the school we knew,
The best school of all:
We'll honour yet the rule we knew,
Till the last bell call.
For working days or holidays,
And glad or melancholy days,
They were great days and jolly days
At the best school of all.

The stars and sounding vanities
That half the crowd bewitch,
What are they but inanities
To him that treads the pitch?
And where's the welth I'm wondering,
Could buy the cheers that roll
When the last charge goes thundering
Towards the twilight goal?

Then men that tanned the hide of us,
Our daily foes and friends,
They shall not lose their pride of us,
Howe'er the journey ends.
Their voice to us who sing of it,
No more its message bears,
But the round world shall ring of it,
And all we are be theirs.

To speak of fame a venture is,
There's little here can bide,
But we may face the centuries,

And dare the deepending tide:
for though the dust that's part of us,
To dust again be gone,
Yet here shall beat the heart of us--
The school we handed on!

We'll honour yet the school we knew,
The best school of all:
We'll honour yet the rule we knew,
Till the last bell call.
For working days or holidays,
And glad or melancholy days,
They were great days and jolly days
At the best school of all.

---

melancholy—feeling of sadness for no apparent reason
inanities—nonsensical action or remark; silliness

A War Song To Englishmen
By William Blake

Prepare, prepare the iron helm of war,
Bring forth the lots, cast in the spacious orb;
Th' Angel of Fate turns them with mighty hands,
And casts them out upon the darken'd earth!
Prepare, prepare!

Prepare your hearts for Death's cold hand! prepare
Your souls for flight, your bodies for the earth;
Prepare your arms for glorious victory;
Prepare your eyes to meet a holy God!
Prepare, prepare!

Whose fatal scroll is that? Methinks 'tis mine!
Why sinks my heart, why faltereth my tongue?
Had I three lives, I'd die in such a cause,
And rise, with ghosts, over the well-fought field.
Prepare, prepare!

The arrows of Almighty God are drawn!
Angels of Death stand in the louring heavens!
Thousands of souls must seek the realms of light,
And walk together on the clouds of heaven!
Prepare, prepare!

Soldiers, prepare! Our cause is Heaven's cause;
Soldiers, prepare! Be worthy of our cause:
Prepare to meet our fathers in the sky:
Prepare, O troops, that are to fall to-day!
Prepare, prepare!

Alfred shall smile, and make his harp rejoice;
The Norman William, and the learned Clerk,
And Lion Heart, and black-brow'd Edward, with
His loyal queen, shall rise, and welcome us!
Prepare, prepare!

The Mocking Bird
By Timothy Thomas Fortune

Have you e'er heard, at early morn,
The feathered poet sing his song,
Clear as a huntsman's clarion horn,
Yet softer, sweeter, and as strong?

Have you e'er felt his magic power
Soothe, as a balm, your troubled breast,
Change into mirth the gloomy hour,
Cradle th' enchanted sense to rest?

Have you e'er heard in native bowers
The mocking bird's angelic lay,
In Summer's home, the "Land of Flowers,"
Where cooling streams refresh the way?

I've roamed the woods from morn till night
In that delicious Summer clime—
For there my eyes first saw the light,
There kissed I first the cheek of Time!

I've heard the feathered poet sing—
Electrify the peace around—
Make the wild echoes gladsome ring—
With melody's divinest sound.

The wild flowers all about in bloom—
The nodding pine—the winding stream—
The orange blossoms' sweet perfume—
Ah! was it not a blissful dream?

---

balm—an ointment to place on the skin or wound to aid in healing

At The Melting Of The Snow
By Andrew Barton "Banjo" Paterson
(Australia's winter ends in August/September)

There's a sunny Southern land,
And it's there that I would be
Where the big hills stand,
In the South Countrie!
When the wattles bloom again,
Then it's time for us to go
To the old Monaro country
At the melting of the snow.

To the East or to the West,
Or wherever you may be,
You will find no place
Like the South Countrie.
For the skies are blue above,
And the grass is green below,
In the old Monaro country
At the melting of the snow.

Now the team is in the plough,
And the thrushes start to sing,
And the pigeons on the bough
Sit a-welcoming the Spring.
So come, my comrades all,
Let us saddle up and go
To the old Monaro country
At the melting of the snow.

---

comrade—another person who belongs to or participates in the same group or organization like the military, a club or a society.

The Rose of Freedom
By Ella Baker

The rose petals soft,
Smells of sweet dew.
The flower petals velvet,
And red like the sunset.
The flower chosen,
For our nation.
For the Soldiers,
who gave us freedom.
For the flag of rights,
That waves of privilege.
The rose is special to our hearts.
We honor the dead with the rose.
Chosen for honor and devotion,
Chosen for love, life, and liberty.

Meadowlark
By Melissa Crowther

The meadowlark opens with clear notes
Followed by a melisma of beauty.

The sun shines on the hardened Wyoming ground
Just as brightly as the feathers on his breast.

He is resilient
Like this land.

He is hopeful
Like a settler's heart.

He is free
Like this nation.

The meadowlark hops among the sage,
A remnant of a past, uninhabited land,

Waiting to be discovered.
For a moment I am lost,

But the jaunty fellow's call pulls me back.
My gaze has broken

And like that song with wings,
I rejoice in my freedom!

---

melisma—music notes sung to a single syllable of text
jaunty—self-confident, cheerful and lively

The Country of Malawi
By Amelie Chindongo

Malawi is our country
We love it very much
With such helpful heroes
For us, they did march

Sometimes fires burn in the heat
The smoke can really poke
But not for crazy people
Who talk to crazy folk
But this story of Malawi is
merrily foretold
We pray that God will help us
In the times of drizzling cold

The Spacious Firmament on High
By Joseph Addison

The Spacious Firmament on high,
With all the blue Ethereal Sky,
And spangled Heav'ns, a Shining Frame,
Their great Original proclaim:
Th' unwearied Sun, from day to day,
Does his Creator's Pow'r display,
And publishes to every Land
The Work of an Almighty Hand.

Soon as the Evening Shades prevail,
The Moon takes up the wondrous Tale,
And nightly to the list'ning Earth
Repeats the Story of her Birth:
Whilst all the Stars that round her burn,
And all the Planets, in their turn,
Confirm the Tidings as they rowl,
And spread the Truth from Pole to Pole.

What though, in solemn Silence, all
Move round the dark terrestrial Ball?
What tho' nor real Voice nor Sound
Amid their radiant Orbs be found?
In Reason's Ear they all rejoice,
And utter forth a glorious Voice,
For ever singing, as they shine,
The Hand that made us is Divine.

---

firmament—the sky or the heavens

October

"Freedom consists not in doing what we like, but in having the right to do what we ought."

-Pope John Paul II

The New Colossus
By Emma Lazarus

Not like the brazen giant of Greek fame,
With conquering limbs astride from land to land;
Here at our sea-washed, sunset gates shall stand
A mighty woman with a torch, whose flame
Is the imprisoned lightning, and her name
Mother of Exiles. From her beacon-hand
Glows world-wide welcome; her mild eyes command
The air-bridged harbor that twin cities frame.
"Keep, ancient lands, your storied pomp!" cries she
With silent lips. "Give me your tired, your poor,
Your huddled masses yearning to breathe free,
The wretched refuse of your teeming shore.
Send these, the homeless, tempest-tost to me,
I lift my lamp beside the golden door!"

---

pomp—elaborate ceremony meant for show that are ostentatious and boastful.

Colossus—it's referring to "The Colossus of Rhodes" an antient statue of the Greek sun-god Helios located on the island of Rhodes.

Autumn
By H. P. Nichols

Here's the purple aster,
And the golden-rod,
And the blue fringed gentian,
By the meadow sod.

And the scarlet cardinal
And the yellow sunflower
In some sheltered nook.

Maple boughs are covered
With their foliage red,
And the withered elm leaves
On the ground lie dead.

And within the orchard,
Heavy-laden trees
Shower down the apples,
With each passing breeze.

So by these we know thee,
Lovely autumn time,
With thy deep blue heavens,
And thy snowy rime.

And we gladly greet thee,
With thy colors gay,
Though thou tell'st us summer
Hence hath fled away.

---

bough—the larger branches of a tree

Victory
By Madison Julius Cawein

Though dead the flower,
That, from her tower,
Love flung you in some perfect hour:
Though quenched the light,
That, on the height,
Faith built, a beacon in the fight:
Though gone the star,
That, seen afar,
Hope lit to guide you through the war:
Yet draw your sword,
And shout your word,
And plunge into the battling horde!
Give Fate the lie!
And, live or die,
Yours, yours shall be the victory!

The Troop Ship
By Isaac Rosenberg

Grotesque and queerly huddled
Contortionists to twist
The sleepy soul to a sleep,
We lie all sorts of ways
And cannot sleep.
The wet wind is so cold,
And the lurching men so careless,
That, should you drop to a doze,
Wind's fumble or men's feet
Is on your face.

---

queer(ly)—strange
contortionists—a performer who twists their body into strange shapes.

Dead Man's Dump
By Isaac Rosenberg
GRAPHIC POEM

The plunging limbers over the shattered track
Racketed with their rusty freight,
Stuck out like many crowns of thorns,
And the rusty stakes like sceptres old
To stay the flood of brutish men
Upon our brothers dear.

The wheels lurched over sprawled dead
But pained them not, though their bones crunched,
Their shut mouths made no moan.
They lie there huddled, friend and foeman,
Man born of man, and born of woman,
And shells go crying over them
From night till night and now.

Earth has waited for them,
All the time of their growth
Fretting for their decay:
Now she has them at last!
In the strength of their strength
Suspended—stopped and held.

What fierce imaginings their dark souls lit?
Earth! have they gone into you!
Somewhere they must have gone,
And flung on your hard back
Is their soul's sack
Emptied of God-ancestralled essences.
Who hurled them out? Who hurled?

None saw their spirits' shadow shake the grass,
Or stood aside for the half used life to pass
Out of those doomed nostrils and the doomed mouth,
When the swift iron burning bee
Drained the wild honey of their youth.

What of us who, flung on the shrieking pyre,
Walk, our usual thoughts untouched,

Our lucky limbs as on ichor fed,
Immortal seeming ever?
Perhaps when the flames beat loud on us,
A fear may choke in our veins
And the startled blood may stop.

The air is loud with death,
The dark air spurts with fire,
The explosions ceaseless are.
Timelessly now, some minutes past,
Those dead strode time with vigorous life,
Till the shrapnel called 'An end!'
But not to all. In bleeding pangs
Some borne on stretchers dreamed of home,
Dear things, war-blotted from their hearts.

Maniac Earth! howling and flying, your bowel
Seared by the jagged fire, the iron love,
The impetuous storm of savage love.
Dark Earth! dark Heavens! swinging in chemic smoke,
What dead are born when you kiss each soundless soul
With lightning and thunder from your mined heart,
Which man's self dug, and his blind fingers loosed?

A man's brains splattered on
A stretcher-bearer's face;
His shook shoulders slipped their load,
But when they bent to look again
The drowning soul was sunk too deep
For human tenderness.

They left this dead with the older dead,
Stretched at the cross roads.

Burnt black by strange decay
Their sinister faces lie,
The lid over each eye,
The grass and coloured clay
More motion have than they,
Joined to the great sunk silences.

Here is one not long dead;

His dark hearing caught our far wheels,
And the choked soul stretched weak hands
To reach the living word the far wheels said,
The blood-dazed intelligence beating for light,
Crying through the suspense of the far torturing wheels
Swift for the end to break
Or the wheels to break,
Cried as the tide of the world broke over his sight.

Will they come? Will they ever come?
Even as the mixed hoofs of the mules,
The quivering-bellied mules,
And the rushing wheels all mixed
With his tortured upturned sight.
So we crashed round the bend,
We heard his weak scream,
We heard his very last sound,
And our wheels grazed his dead face.

---

sceptres—a decorative and ornamental staff carried by rulers for ceremonies.
impetuous—acting without contemplating the consequences; forcful and rapid movement

The Charge of the Light Brigade
By Alfred Lord Tennyson

I
Half a league, half a league,
Half a league onward,
All in the valley of Death
  Rode the six hundred.
"Forward, the Light Brigade!
Charge for the guns!" he said.
Into the valley of Death
  Rode the six hundred.

II
"Forward, the Light Brigade!"
Was there a man dismayed?
Not though the soldier knew
  Someone had blundered.
  Theirs not to make reply,
  Theirs not to reason why,
  Theirs but to do and die.
  Into the valley of Death
  Rode the six hundred.

III
Cannon to right of them,
Cannon to left of them,
Cannon in front of them
  Volleyed and thundered;
Stormed at with shot and shell,
Boldly they rode and well,
Into the jaws of Death,
Into the mouth of hell
  Rode the six hundred.

IV
Flashed all their sabres bare,
Flashed as they turned in air
Sabring the gunners there,
Charging an army, while
  All the world wondered.
Plunged in the battery-smoke

Right through the line they broke;
Cossack and Russian
Reeled from the sabre stroke
  Shattered and sundered.
Then they rode back, but not
  Not the six hundred.

V

Cannon to right of them,
Cannon to left of them,
Cannon behind them
  Volleyed and thundered;
Stormed at with shot and shell,
While horse and hero fell.
They that had fought so well
Came through the jaws of Death,
Back from the mouth of hell,
All that was left of them,
  Left of six hundred.

VI

When can their glory fade?
O the wild charge they made!
  All the world wondered.
Honour the charge they made!
Honour the Light Brigade,
  Noble six hundred!

Dulce Et Decorum Est
By Wilfred Owen
GRAPHIC

Bent double, like old beggars under sacks,
Knock-kneed, coughing like hags, we cursed through sludge,
Till on the haunting flares we turned our backs,
And towards our distant rest began to trudge.
Men marched asleep. Many had lost their boots,
But limped on, blood-shod. All went lame; all blind;
Drunk with fatigue; deaf even to the hoots
Of gas-shells dropping softly behind.

Gas! GAS! Quick, boys!—An ecstasy of fumbling
Fitting the clumsy helmets just in time,
But someone still was yelling out and stumbling
And flound'ring like a man in fire or lime.—
Dim through the misty panes and thick green light,
As under a green sea, I saw him drowning.

In all my dreams before my helpless sight,
He plunges at me, guttering, choking, drowning.

If in some smothering dreams, you too could pace
Behind the wagon that we flung him in,
And watch the white eyes writhing in his face,
His hanging face, like a devil's sick of sin;
If you could hear, at every jolt, the blood
Come gargling from the froth-corrupted lungs,
Obscene as cancer, bitter as the cud
Of vile, incurable sores on innocent tongues,—
My friend, you would not tell with such high zest
To children ardent for some desperate glory,
The old Lie: *Dulce et decorum est*
Pro patria mori.

Dulce et decorum est Pro patria mori—a Latin phrase meaning "It is sweet and fitting to die for the homeland."

The Anxious Dead
By John Alexander Mc Crea

O guns, fall silent till the dead men hear
Above their heads the legions pressing on:
(These fought their fight in time of bitter fear,
And died not knowing how the day had gone.)

O flashing muzzles, pause, and let them see
The coming dawn that streaks the sky afar;
Then let your mighty chorus witness be
To them, and Caesar, that we still make war.

Tell them, O guns, that we have heard their call,
That we have sworn, and will not turn aside,
That we will onward till we win or fall,
That we will keep the faith for which they died.

Bid them be patient, and some day, anon,
They shall feel earth enwrapt in silence deep;
Shall greet, in wonderment, the quiet dawn,
And in content may turn them to their sleep.

Halloween
By Robert Burns

Upon that night, when fairies light
On Cassilis Downans dance,
Or owre the lays, in splendid blaze,
On sprightly coursers prance;
Or for Colean the route is ta'en,
Beneath the moon's pale beams;
There, up the cove, to stray and rove,
Among the rocks and streams
To sport that night.
Among the bonny winding banks,
Where Doon rins, wimplin' clear,
Where Bruce ance ruled the martial ranks,
And shook his Carrick spear,
Some merry, friendly, country-folks,
Together did convene,
To burn their nits, and pou their stocks,

And haud their Halloween
Fu' blithe that night.
The lasses feat, and cleanly neat,
Mair braw than when they're fine;
Their faces blithe, fu' sweetly kythe,
Hearts leal, and warm, and kin';
The lads sae trig, wi' wooer-babs,
Weel knotted on their garten,
Some unco blate, and some wi' gabs,
Gar lasses' hearts gang startin'
Whiles fast at night.
Then, first and foremost, through the kail,
Their stocks maun a' be sought ance;
They steek their een, and graip and wale,
For muckle anes and straught anes.
Poor hav'rel Will fell aff the drift,
And wander'd through the bow-kail,
And pou't, for want o' better shift,
A runt was like a sow-tail,
Sae bow't that night.
Then, staught or crooked, yird or nane,
They roar and cry a' throu'ther;
The very wee things, todlin', rin,
Wi' stocks out owre their shouther;
And gif the custoc's sweet or sour.
Wi' joctelegs they taste them;
Syne cozily, aboon the door,
Wi cannie care, they've placed them
To lie that night.
The lasses staw frae 'mang them a'
To pou their stalks of corn:
But Rab slips out, and jinks about,
Behint the muckle thorn:
He grippet Nelly hard and fast;
Loud skirl'd a' the lasses;
But her tap-pickle maist was lost,
When kitlin' in the fause-house
Wi' him that night.
The auld guidwife's well-hoordit nits,
Are round and round divided,
And monie lads' and lasses' fates
Are there that night decided:

Some kindle coothie, side by side,
And burn thegither trimly;
Some start awa, wi' saucy pride,
And jump out-owre the chimlie
Fu' high that night.
Jean slips in twa wi' tentie ee;
Wha 'twas she wadna tell;
But this is Jock, and this is me,
She says in to hersel:
He bleezed owre her, and she owre him,
As they wad never mair part;
Till, fuff! he started up the lum,
And Jean had e'en a sair heart
To see't that night.
Poor Willie, wi' his bow-kail runt,
Was brunt wi' primsie Mallie;
And Mallie, nae doubt, took the drunt,
To be compared to Willie;
Mall's nit lap out wi' pridefu' fling,
And her ain fit it brunt it;
While Willie lap, and swore by jing,
'Twas just the way he wanted
To be that night.
Nell had the fause-house in her min',
She pits hersel and Rob in;
In loving bleeze they sweetly join,
Till white in ase they're sobbin';
Nell's heart was dancin' at the view,
She whisper'd Rob to leuk for't:
Rob, stowlins, prie'd her bonny mou',
Fu' cozie in the neuk for't,
Unseen that night.
But Merran sat behint their backs,
Her thoughts on Andrew Bell;
She lea'es them gashin' at their cracks,
And slips out by hersel:
She through the yard the nearest taks,
And to the kiln goes then,
And darklins graipit for the bauks,
And in the blue-clue throws then,
Right fear't that night.

And aye she win't, and aye she swat,
I wat she made nae jaukin',
Till something held within the pat,
Guid Lord! but she was quakin'!
But whether 'was the deil himsel,
Or whether 'twas a bauk-en',
Or whether it was Andrew Bell,
She didna wait on talkin'
To spier that night.
Wee Jennie to her grannie says,
"Will ye go wi' me, grannie?
I'll eat the apple at the glass
I gat frae Uncle Johnnie:"
She fuff't her pipe wi' sic a lunt,
In wrath she was sae vap'rin',
She notice't na, an aizle brunt
Her braw new worset apron
Out through that night.
"Ye little skelpie-limmer's face!
I daur you try sic sportin',
As seek the foul thief ony place,
For him to spae your fortune.
Nae doubt but ye may get a sight!
Great cause ye hae to fear it;
For mony a ane has gotten a fright,
And lived and died deleeret
On sic a night.
"Ae hairst afore the Sherramoor, —
I mind't as weel's yestreen,
I was a gilpey then, I'm sure
I wasna past fifteen;
The simmer had been cauld and wat,
And stuff was unco green;
And aye a rantin' kirn we gat,
And just on Halloween
It fell that night.
"Our stibble-rig was Rab M'Graen,
A clever sturdy fallow:
His son gat Eppie Sim wi' wean,
That lived in Achmacalla:
He gat hemp-seed, I mind it weel,
And he made unco light o't;

But mony a day was by himsel,
He was sae sairly frighted
That very night."
Then up gat fechtin' Jamie Fleck,
And he swore by his conscience,
That he could saw hemp-seed a peck;
For it was a' but nonsense.
The auld guidman raught down the pock,
And out a hanfu' gied him;
Syne bade him slip frae 'mang the folk,
Some time when nae ane see'd him,
And try't that night.
He marches through amang the stacks,
Though he was something sturtin;
The graip he for a harrow taks.
And haurls it at his curpin;
And every now and then he says,
"Hemp-seed, I saw thee,
And her that is to be my lass,
Come after me, and draw thee
As fast this night."
He whistled up Lord Lennox' march
To keep his courage cheery;
Although his hair began to arch,
He was say fley'd and eerie:
Till presently he hears a squeak,
And then a grane and gruntle;
He by his shouther gae a keek,
And tumbled wi' a wintle
Out-owre that night.
He roar'd a horrid murder-shout,
In dreadfu' desperation!
And young and auld came runnin' out
To hear the sad narration;
He swore 'twas hilchin Jean M'Craw,
Or crouchie Merran Humphie,
Till, stop! she trotted through them
And wha was it but grumphie
Asteer that night!
Meg fain wad to the barn hae gaen,
To win three wechts o' naething;
But for to meet the deil her lane,

She pat but little faith in:
She gies the herd a pickle nits,
And two red-cheekit apples,
To watch, while for the barn she sets,
In hopes to see Tam Kipples
That very nicht.
She turns the key wi cannie thraw,
And owre the threshold ventures;
But first on Sawnie gies a ca'
Syne bauldly in she enters:
A ratton rattled up the wa',
And she cried, Lord, preserve her!
And ran through midden-hole and a',
And pray'd wi' zeal and fervour,
Fu' fast that night;
They hoy't out Will wi' sair advice;
They hecht him some fine braw ane;
It chanced the stack he faddom'd thrice
Was timmer-propt for thrawin';
He taks a swirlie, auld moss-oak,
For some black grousome carlin;
And loot a winze, and drew a stroke,
Till skin in blypes cam haurlin'
Aff's nieves that night.
A wanton widow Leezie was,
As canty as a kittlin;
But, och! that night amang the shaws,
She got a fearfu' settlin'!
She through the whins, and by the cairn,
And owre the hill gaed scrievin,
Whare three lairds' lands met at a burn
To dip her left sark-sleeve in,
Was bent that night.
Whyles owre a linn the burnie plays,
As through the glen it wimpl't;
Whyles round a rocky scaur it strays;
Whyles in a wiel it dimpl't;
Whyles glitter'd to the nightly rays,
Wi' bickering, dancing dazzle;
Whyles cookit underneath the braes,
Below the spreading hazel,
Unseen that night.

Among the brackens, on the brae,
Between her and the moon,
The deil, or else an outler quey,
Gat up and gae a croon:
Poor Leezie's heart maist lap the hool!
Near lav'rock-height she jumpit;
but mist a fit, and in the pool
Out-owre the lugs she plumpit,
Wi' a plunge that night.
In order, on the clean hearth-stane,
The luggies three are ranged,
And every time great care is ta'en',
To see them duly changed:
Auld Uncle John, wha wedlock joys
Sin' Mar's year did desire,
Because he gat the toom dish thrice,
He heaved them on the fire
In wrath that night.
Wi' merry sangs, and friendly cracks,
I wat they didna weary;
And unco tales, and funny jokes,
Their sports were cheap and cheery;
Till butter'd so'ns, wi' fragrant lunt,
Set a' their gabs a-steerin';
Syne, wi' a social glass o' strunt,
They parted aff careerin'
Fu' blythe that night.

---

blithe—cheerful and casual indifference; joyous
kythe—Scottish for make known
coothie—genial; kind; agreeable
worset—a yarn made of tightly twisted; thread made from combed long-staple wool
curpin—buttocks
wintle—rolling or staggering motion
ratton—a rat
winze—Scottish for curse
blypes—Scottish for shred or piece of skin

Ghosts of the New World
By Alfred Noyes

There are no ghosts, you say,
   To haunt her blaze of light;
No shadows in her day,
   No phantoms in her night.
Columbus' tattered sail
Has passed beyond our hail.

What? On that magic coast,
   Where Raleigh fought with fate,
Or where that Devon ghost
   Unbarred the Golden Gate,
No dark, strange, ear-ringed men
Beat in from sea again?

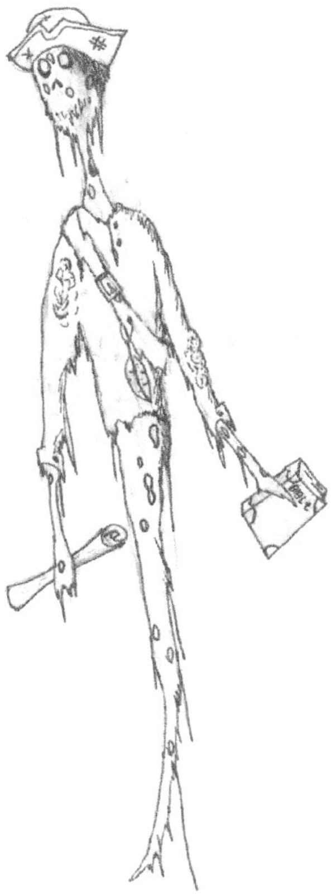

No ghosts in Salem town
   With silver buckled shoon?
No lovely witch to drown
   Or burn beneath the moon?
Not even a whiff of tea,
On Boston's glimmering quay.

O, ghostly Spanish walls,
   Where brown Franciscans glide,
Is there no voice that calls
   Across the Great Divide,
To pilgrims on their way
Along the Santa Fe?

Then let your Pullman cars
   Go roaring to the West,
Till, watched by lonelier stars,
   The cactus lifts its crest.
There, on that painted plain,
One ghost will rise again.

Majestic and forlorn,
   Wreck of a dying race,
The Red Man, half in scorn,
   Shall raise his haughty face,

Inscrutable as the sky,
To watch our ghosts go by.

What? Is earth dreaming still?
   Shall not the night disgorge
The ghosts of Bunker Hill
   The ghosts of Valley Forge,
Or, England's mightiest son,
The ghost of Washington?

No ghosts where Lincoln fell?
   No ghosts for seeing eyes?
I know an old cracked bell
   Shall make ten million rise
When one immortal ghost
Calls to the slumbering host.

---

forlorn—lonely or pitifully sad
disgorge—to pour out

Ode for Trafalgar Day, 1905
By Sir Henry John Newbolt

England! to-day let fire be in thine eyes
   And in thy heart the throb of leaping guns;
Crown in thy streets the deed that never dies,
   And tell their fathers' fame to all thy sons!
Behold! behold! on that unchanging sea
   Where day behind Trafalgar rises pale,
      How dread the storm to be
      Drifts up with ominous breath
   Cloud after towering cloud of billowy sail
      Full charged with thunder and the bolts of death.

Yet when the noon is past, and thy delight,
   More delicate for these good hundred years,
Has drunk the splendour and the sound of fight
   And the sweet sting of long-since vanished fears,
Then, England, come thou down with sterner lips
   From the bright world of thy substantial power,
      Forget thy seas, thy ships,
      And that wide echoing dome

To watch the soul of man in his dark hour
Redeeming yet his dear lost land of home.

What place is this? What under-world of pain
All shadow-barred with glare of swinging fires?
What writhing phantoms of the newly slain?
What cries? What thirst consuming all desires?
This is the field of battle: not for life,
Not for the deeper life that dwells in love,
Not for the savour of strife
Or the far call of fame,
Not for all these the fight: all these above
The soul of this man cherished Duty's name.

His steadfast hope from self has turned away,
For the Cause only must he still contend:
"How goes the day with us? How goes the day?"
He craves not victory, but to make an end.
Therefore not yet thine hour, O Death: but when
The weapons forged against his country's peace
Lie broken round him--then
Give him the kiss supreme;
Then let the tumult of his warfare cease
And the last dawn dispel his anguished dream.

---

ominous—The feeling or impression that something unpleasant is going to happen.

The Ghost, the Gallant, the Gael, and the Goblin
By William Schwenck Dilbert

O'er unreclaimed suburban clays
Some years ago were hobblin'
An elderly ghost of easy ways,
And an influential goblin.
The ghost was a sombre
spectral shape,
A fine old five-act fogy,
The goblin imp, a lithe young ape,
A fine low-comedy bogy.

And as they exercised their joints,
Promoting quick digestion,
They talked on several curious points,
And raised this delicate question:
"Which of us two is Number One
The ghostie, or the goblin?"
And o'er the point they raised in fun
They fairly fell a-squabblin'.

They'd barely speak, and each, in fine,
Grew more and more reflective:
Each thought his own particular line
By chalks the more effective.
At length they settled some one should
By each of them be haunted,
And so arrange that either could
Exert his prowess vaunted.

"The Quaint against the Statuesque"
By competition lawful
The goblin backed the Quaint Grotesque,
The ghost the Grandly Awful.
"Now," said the goblin, "here's my plan
In attitude commanding,
I see a stalwart Englishman
By yonder tailor's standing.

"The very fittest man on earth
My influence to try on

Of gentle, p'r'aps of noble birth,
And dauntless as a lion!
Now wrap yourself within your shroud
Remain in easy hearing
Observe you'll hear him scream aloud
When I begin appearing!

The imp with yell unearthly wild
Threw off his dark enclosure:
His dauntless victim looked and smiled
With singular composure.
For hours he tried to daunt the youth, For days, indeed, but vainly
The stripling smiled! to tell the truth,
The stripling smiled inanely.

For weeks the goblin weird and wild,
That noble stripling haunted;
For weeks the stripling stood and smiled,
Unmoved and all undaunted.
The sombre ghost exclaimed, "Your plan
Has failed you, goblin, plainly:
Now watch yon hardy Hieland man,
So stalwart and ungainly.

"These are the men who chase the roe,
Whose footsteps never falter,
Who bring with them, where'er they go,
A smack of old SIR WALTER.
Of such as he, the men sublime
Who lead their troops victorious,
Enshrined in annals glorious!

"Of such as he the bard has said
'Hech thrawfu' raltie rorkie!
Wi' thecht ta' croonie clapperhead
And fash' wi' unco pawkie!'
He'll faint away when I appear,
Upon his native heather;
Or p'r'aps he'll only scream with fear,
Or p'r'aps the two together."

The spectre showed himself, alone,

To do his ghostly battling,
With curdling groan and dismal moan,
And lots of chains a-rattling!
But no the chiel's stout Gaelic stuff
Withstood all ghostly harrying;
His fingers closed upon the snuff
Which upwards he was carrying.

For days that ghost declined to stir,
A foggy shapeless giant
For weeks that splendid officer
Stared back again defiant.
Just as the Englishman returned
The goblin's vulgar staring,
Just so the Scotchman boldly spurned
The ghost's unmannered scaring.

For several years the ghostly twain
These Britons bold have haunted,
But all their efforts are in vain
Their victims stand undaunted.
This very day the imp, and ghost,
Whose powers the imp derided,
Stand each at his allotted post
The bet is undecided.

---

pawkie—Scottish for mittens

Knights and Ladies
By A. A. Milne

There is in my old picture-book
A page at which I like to look,
Where knights and squires come riding down
The cobbles of some steep old town,
And ladies from beneath the eaves
Flutter their bravest handkerchiefs,
Or, smiling proudly, toss down gages....
But that was in the Middle Ages.
It wouldn't happen now; but still,
Whenever I look up the hill
Where, dark against the green and blue,
The firs come marching, two by two,
I wonder if perhaps I *might*
See suddenly a shining knight
Winding his way from blue to green --
Exactly as it would have been
Those many, many years ago....
Perhaps I might. You never know.

A Death-Bed Adieu
By Thomas Jefferson

Written by Thomas Jefferson to his daughter two days before his death.

"A death-bed Adieu."
Life's visions are vanished, it's dreams are no more.
Dear friends of my bosom, why bathed in tears?
I go to my fathers; I welcome the shore,
which crowns all my hopes, or which buries my cares.
Then farewell my dear, my lov'd daughter, Adieu!
The last pang in life is in parting from you.
Two Seraphs await me, long shrouded in death;
I will bear them your love on my last parting breath.

October
By Ralph Waldo Emerson

October woods wherein
The boy's dream comes to pass,
And Nature squanders on the boy her pomp,
And crowns him with a more than royal crown,
And unimagined splendor waits his steps.
The gazing urchin walks through tents of gold,
Through crimson chambers, porphyry and pearl,
Pavilion on pavilion, garlanded,
Incensed and starred with lights and airs and shapes,
Color and sound, music to eye and ear,
Beyond the best conceit of pomp or power.

---

pomp—elaborate ceremony meant for show that are ostentatious and boastful.

Through Time and Bitter Distance
By Emily Pauline Johnson

Unknown to you, I walk the cheerless shore.
  The cutting blast, the hurl of biting brine
May freeze, and still, and bind the waves at war,
  Ere you will ever know, O! Heart of mine,
That I have sought, reflected in the blue
  Of these sea depths, some shadow of your eyes;
Have hoped the laughing waves would sing of you,
  But this is all my starving sight descries -

I

Far out at sea a sail
  Bends to the freshening breeze,
Yields to the rising gale
  That sweeps the seas;

II

Yields, as a bird wind-tossed,
  To saltish waves that fling
Their spray, whose rime and frost
  Like crystals cling

III

To canvas, mast and spar,
  Till, gleaming like a gem,
She sinks beyond the far
  Horizon's hem.

IV

Lost to my longing sight,
  And nothing left to me
Save an oncoming night, -
  An empty sea.

The Valley of Unrest
By Edgar Allan Poe

Once it smiled a silent dell
Where the people did not dwell;
They had gone unto the wars,
Trusting to the mild-eyed stars,
Nightly, from their azure towers,
To keep watch above the flowers,
In the midst of which all day
The red sun-light lazily lay,
Now each visitor shall confess
The sad valley's restlessness.
Nothing there is motionless,
Nothing save the airs that brood
Over the magic solitude.
Ah, by no wind are stirred those trees
That palpitate like the chill seas
Around the misty Hebrides!
Ah, by no wind those clouds are driven
That rustle through the unquiet Heaven
Unceasingly, from morn till even,
Over the violets there that lie
In myriad types of the human eye,
Over the lilies that wave
And weep above a nameless grave!
They wave:, from out their fragrant tops
Eternal dews come down in drops.
They weep:, from off their delicate stems
Perennial tears descend in gems.

---

azure—a blue hugh like a sky on a clear day
Hebrides—islands off the West coast of Scotland
palpitate—irregular or rapid heart rate

November

"Victory belongs to the most persevering."
-Napoleon Bonaparte

A Child's Thank You
By Sharon K. Michel

"What is war?" My child asked me today.
How can I explain the great price
One such as you had to pay?

Never having lived through the hardship of war,
How do I teach my child the seriousness
Of what you did and fought so hard for?

I answered my innocent child with a painful sigh,
"To keep you safe many soldiers had to fight and die."

"But some came home after winning the war
And we must tell them Thank You so much more!"

My child now knows because of you she's safe today
And will always say thank you in her own special way.

To Always Remember is to Always be Thankful!

On Virtue
By Phillis Wheatley

O Thou bright jewel in my aim I strive
To comprehend thee. Thine own words declare
Wisdom is higher than a fool can reach.
I cease to wonder, and no more attempt
Thine height t'explore, or fathom thy profound.
But, O my soul, sink not into despair,
*Virtue*is near thee, and with gentle hand
Would now embrace thee, hovers o'er thine head.
Fain would the heav'n-born soul with her converse,
Then seek, then court her for her promis'd bliss.
Auspicious queen, thine heav'nly pinions spread,
And lead celestial*Chastity*along;
Lo! now her sacred retinue descends,
Array'd in glory from the orbs above.
Attend me,*Virtue*, thro' my youthful years!
O leave me not to the false joys of time!
But guide my steps to endless life and bliss.
Greatness, or*Goodness*, say what I shall call thee,
To give an higher appellation still,
Teach me a better strain, a nobler lay,
O thou, enthron'd with Cherubs in the realms of day!

---

auspicious—conducive to success

Victory Stuff

By Robert William Service

What d'ye think, lad; what d'ye think,
As the roaring crowds go by?
As the banners flare and the brasses blare
And the great guns rend the sky?
As the women laugh like they'd all gone mad,
And the champagne glasses clink:
Oh, you're grippin' me hand so tightly, lad,
I'm a-wonderin': what d'ye think?

D'ye think o' the boys we used to know,
And how they'd have topped the fun?
Tom and Charlie, and Jack and Joe -
Gone now, every one.

How they'd have cheered as the joy-bells chime,
And they grabbed each girl for a kiss!
And now - they're rottin' in Flanders slime,
And they gave their lives - for *this*.

Or else d'ye think of the many a time
We wished we too was dead,
Up to our knees in the freezin' grime,
With the fires of hell overhead;
When the youth and the strength of us sapped away,
And we cursed in our rage and pain?
And yet - we haven't a word to say. . . .
We're glad. We'd do it again.

I'm scared that they pity us. Come, old boy,
Let's leave them their flags and their fuss.
We'd surely be hatin' to spoil their joy
With the sight of such wrecks as us.
Let's slip away quietly, you and me,
And we'll talk of our chums out there:
You with your eyes that'll never see,
Me that's wheeled in a chair.

Hope
By Joseph Addison

Our lives, discoloured with our present woes,
May still grow white and shine with happier hours.
So the pure limped stream, when foul with stains
Of rushing torrents and descending rains,
Works itself clear, and as it runs refines,
till by degrees the floating mirror shines;
Reflects each flower that on the border grows,
And a new heaven in it's fair bosom shows.

Country At War
By Robert von Ranke Graves

And what of home, how goes it, boys,
While we die here in stench and noise?
"The hill stands up and hedges wind
Over the crest and drop behind;
Here swallows dip and wild things go
On peaceful errands to and fro
Across the sloping meadow floor,
And make no guess at blasting war.
In woods that fledge the round hill-shoulder
Leaves shoot and open, fall and moulder,
And shoot again. Meadows yet show
Alternate white of drifted snow
And daisies. Children play at shop,
Warm days, on the flat boulder-top,
With wildflower coinage, and the wares
Are bits of glass and unripe pears.
Crows perch upon the backs of sheep,
The wheat goes yellow: women reap,
Autumn winds ruffle brook and pond,
Flutter the hedge and fly beyond.
So the first things of nature run,
And stand not still for any one,
Contemptuous of the distant cry
Wherewith you harrow earth and sky.
And high French clouds, praying to be
Back, back in peace beyond the sea,
Where nature with accustomed round
Sweeps and garnishes the ground
With kindly beauty, warm or cold,
Alternate seasons never old:
Heathen, how furiously you rage,
Cursing this blood and brimstone age,
How furiously against your will
You kill and kill again, and kill:
All thought of peace behind you cast,
Till like small boys with fear aghast,
Each cries for God to understand,
'I could not help it, it was my hand.'"

The Land We Love
By Abram Joseph Ryan

Land of the gentle and brave!
Our love is as wide as thy woe;
It deepens beside every grave
Where the heart of a hero lies low.

Land of the sunniest skies!
Our love glows the more for thy gloom;
Our hearts, by the saddest of ties,
Cling closest to thee in thy doom.

Land where the desolate weep
In a sorrow no voice may console!
Our tears are but streams, making deep
The ocean of love in our soul.

Land where the victor's flag waves,
Where only the dead are free!
Each link of the chain that enslaves
But binds us to them and to thee.

Land where the Sign of the Cross
Its shadow hath everywhere shed!
We measure our love by thy loss,
Thy loss by the graves of our dead!

Going to America
Isabel Urso

Her name is America, her feet are in the sea
And she's standing there and waiting,
Waiting there for me.
Cities appear within her eyes,
And laws to guide the passer-byes.
She once was young, now she's growing old.
She once was silver, now she's turning gold.
Her name is America, her feet are in the sea,
She's staring at the ocean,
Waiting there for me.

Niagara
By Joseph Rodman Drake

I.
Roar, raging torrent! and thou, mighty river,
Pour thy white foam on the valley below;
Frown, ye dark mountains! and shadow for ever
The deep rocky bed where the wild rapids flow.
The green sunny glade, and the smooth flowing fountain,
Brighten the home of the coward and slave;
The flood and the forest, the rock and the mountain,
Rear on their bosoms the free and the brave.

II.
Nurslings of nature, I mark your bold bearing,
Pride in each aspect and strength in each form,
Hearts of warm impulse, and souls of high daring,
Born in the battle and rear'd in the storm.
The red levin flash and the thunder's dread rattle,
The rock-riven wave and the war trumpet's breath,
The din of the tempest, the yell of the battle,
Nerve your steeled bosoms to danger and death.

III.
High on the brow of the Alps' snowy towers
The mountain Swiss measures his rock-breasted moors,
O'er his lone cottage the avalanche lowers,
Round its rude portal the spring-torrent pours.
Sweet is his sleep amid peril and danger,
Warm is his greeting to kindred and friends,
Open his hand to the poor and the stranger,
Stern on his foeman his sabre descends.

IV.
Lo! where the tempest the dark waters sunder
Slumbers the sailor boy, reckless and brave,
Warm'd by the lighting and lulled by the thunder,
Fann'd by the whirlwind and rock'd on the wave;
Wildly the winter wind howls round his pillow,
Cold on his bosom the spray showers fall;
Creaks the strained mast at the rush of the billow,
Peaceful he slumbers, regardless of all.

V.

Mark how the cheek of the warrior flushes,
As the battle drum beats and the war torches glare;
Like a blast of the north to the onset he rushes,
And his wide-waving falchion gleams brightly in air.
Around him the death-shot of foemen are flying,
At his feet friends and comrades are yielding their breath;
He strikes to the groans of the wounded and dying,
But the war cry he strikes with is, 'conquest or death!'

VI.

Then pour thy broad wave like a flood from the heavens,
Each son that thou rearest, in the battle's wild shock,
When the death-speaking note of the trumpet is given,
Will charge like thy torrent or stand like thy rock.
Let his roof be the cloud and the rock be his pillow,
Let him stride the rough mountain, or toss on the foam,
He will strike fast and well on the field or the billow,
In triumph and glory, for God and his home!

---

bosom—a woman's chest
comrade—another person who belongs to or participates in the same group or organization like the military, a club or a society.

Bide A Wee!
By William Arthur Dunkerley
Also known as John Oxenham)

Though the times be dark and dreary,
Though the way be long,
Keep your spirits bright and cheery,--
--"Bide a wee, and dinna weary!"
Is a heartsome song.

A Yorkshire Bite
By John Hartley

Bless all them bonny lasses,
I' Yorksher born an bred!
Ther beauty nooan surpasses,
Complete i'th' heart an th' heead.
An th' lads, - tho aw've seen monny lands,
Ther equal aw ne'er met;
For honest hearts an willin hands,
They nivver can be bet.
Aw nivver hold mi heead soa heigh,
Or feel sich true delight,
As when fowk point me aght an say,
"Thear gooas a Yorksher Bite."

My Country
By Dorothea Mckellar

The love of field and coppice
Of green and shaded lanes,
Of ordered woods and gardens
Is running in your veins.
Strong love of grey-blue distance,
Brown streams and soft, dim skies
I know, but cannot share it,
My love is otherwise.

I love a sunburnt country,
A land of sweeping plains,
Of ragged mountain ranges,
Of droughts and flooding rains.
I love her far horizons,
I love her jewel-sea,
Her beauty and her terror
The wide brown land for me!

The stark white ring-barked forests,
All tragic to the moon,
The sapphire-misted mountains,
The hot gold hush of noon,
Green tangle of the brushes
Where lithe lianas coil,
And orchids deck the tree-tops,
And ferns the warm dark soil.

Core of my heart, my country!
Her pitiless blue sky,
When, sick at heart, around us
We see the cattle die
But then the grey clouds gather,
And we can bless again
The drumming of an army,
The steady soaking rain.

Core of my heart, my country!
Land of the rainbow gold,
For flood and fire and famine
She pays us back threefold.
Over the thirsty paddocks,
Watch, after many days,
The filmy veil of greenness
That thickens as we gaze …

An opal-hearted country,
A wilful, lavish land
All you who have not loved her,
You will not understand
though Earth holds many splendours,
Wherever I may die,
I know to what brown country
My homing thoughts will fly.

---

coppice—an area of bushes and trees cleared or cut back;
paddocks—a small field where horses and exercise or are kept

Canada's Resources
By John McIntyre

Small Scotland nobly held its own
Against the might of England's throne,
And shall this land with its vast bounds
Shrink with fear ere the trumpet sounds.

While British blood doth course each vein,
Proudly this heritage maintain,
With fertile acres by the billions,
Future homes for two hundred millions.

Each son could have a fertile farm,
Brave men who ne'er will feel alarm,
And they have both the nerve and skill
To work land with a right good will.

And she has got within her shores
Renowned mines of many ores,
While her furnaces and forges
Iron in useful shape disgorges.

Her mighty forests they do yield
Lumber, her cities for to build,
But her wealth is not in these alone,
She has great quarries too of stone.

Industry it here doth bloom,
And skilful webs come from each loom,
One of great nations under sun,
A mightier race it yet will run.

For with the Anglo-Saxon race
No other people can keep pace,
Here they have room for to expand
Into a nation mighty grand.

With great railroads and canals,
And care in legislative halls,
A mighty future she will gain,
And highest rank she will obtain.

Canada hopes it will be told,
That she hath patriots brave and bold,
To guide her helm shall be extolled,
As loving country more than gold.

---

patriot(s)—a person(s) devoted to supporting his country and willing to defend it.

A Monument for the Soldier
By James Whitcomb Riley

A monument for the Soldiers!
  And what will ye build it of?
Can ye build it of marble, or brass, or bronze,
  Outlasting the Soldiers' love?
Can ye glorify it with legends
  As grand as their blood hath writ
From the inmost shrine of this land of thine
  To the outermost verge of it?

And the answer came: We would build it
  Out of our hopes made sure,
And out of our purest prayers and tears,
  And out of our faith secure:
We would build it out of the great white truths
  Their death hath sanctified,
And the sculptured forms of the men in arms,
  And their faces ere they died.

And what heroic figures
  Can the sculptor carve in stone?
Can the marble breast be made to bleed,
  And the marble lips to moan?
Can the marble brow be fevered?
  And the marble eyes be graved
To look their last, as the flag floats past,
  On the country they have saved?

And the answer came: The figures
  Shall all be fair and brave,
And, as befitting, as pure and white

As the stars above their grave!
The marble lips, and breast and brow
Whereon the laurel lies,
Bequeath us right to guard the flight
Of the old flag in the skies!

A monument for the Soldiers!
Built of a people's love,
And blazoned and decked and panoplied
With the hearts ye build it oft
And see that ye build it stately,
In pillar and niche and gate,
And high in pose as the souls of those
It would commemorate!

---

befitting—appropriate for a situation
bequeath—leave something to a person

After the Battle
By Thomas Moore

Night closed around the conqueror's way,
And lightnings showed the distant hill,
Where those who lost that dreadful day,
Stood few and faint, but fearless still.
The soldier's hope, the patriot's zeal,
For ever dimmed, for ever crost--
Oh! who shall say what heroes feel,
When all but life and honor's lost?

The last sad hour of freedom's dream,
And valor's task, moved slowly by,
While mute they watcht, till morning's beam
Should rise and give them light to die.
There's yet a world, where souls are free,
Where tyrants taint not nature's bliss;--
If death that world's bright opening be,
Oh! who would live a slave in this?

---

patriot—a person devoted to supporting his country and willing to defend it.

Pilgrim
By Thomas Moore

Still thus, when twilight gleamed,
Far off his Castle seemed,
   Traced on the sky;
And still, as fancy bore him.
To those dim towers before him,
He gazed, with wishful eye;
   And thought his home was nigh.

"Hall of my Sires!" he said,
"How long, with weary tread,
   "Must I toil on?
"Each eve, as thus I wander,
"Thy towers seem rising yonder,
"But, scarce hath daylight shone,
   "When, like a dream, thou'rt gone!"

So went the Pilgrim still,
Down dale and over hill,
   Day after day;
That glimpse of home, so cheering,
At twilight still appearing,
But still, with morning's ray,
   Melting, like mist, away!

Where rests the Pilgrim now?
Here, by this cypress bough,
   Closed his career;
That dream, of fancy's weaving,
No more his steps deceiving,
Alike past hope and fear,
   The Pilgrim's home is here

A Pot of Tea
By Robert William Service

You make it in your mess-tin by the brazier's rosy gleam;
You watch it cloud, then settle amber clear;
You lift it with your bay'nit, and you sniff the fragrant steam;
The very breath of it is ripe with cheer.
You're awful cold and dirty, and a-cursin' of your lot;
You scoff the blushin' 'alf of it, so rich and rippin' 'ot;
It bucks you up like anythink, just seems to touch the spot:
God bless the man that first discovered Tea!

Since I came out to fight in France, which ain't the other day,
I think I've drunk enough to float a barge;
All kinds of fancy foreign dope, from caffy and doo lay,
To rum they serves you out before a charge.
In back rooms of estaminays I've gurgled pints of cham;
I've swilled down mugs of cider till I've felt a bloomin' dam;
But 'struth! they all ain't in it with the vintage of Assam:
God bless the man that first invented Tea!

I think them lazy lumps o' gods wot kips on asphodel
Swigs nectar that's a flavour of Oolong;
I only wish them sons o' guns a-grillin' down in 'ell
Could 'ave their daily ration of Suchong.
Hurrah! I'm off to battle, which is 'ell and 'eaven too;
And if I don't give some poor bloke a sexton's job to do,
To-night, by Fritz's campfire, won't I 'ave a gorgeous brew
(For fightin' mustn't interfere with Tea).
To-night we'll all be tellin' of the Boches that we slew,
As we drink the giddy victory in Tea.

---

mess-tin—mess kit
brazier—a portable heater with a place to hold coals
caffy—a fairhaired victor
asphodel—a Eurasian lily plant

As I Wander
By Jake Zesiger

As I wander through the pine trees,
I reflect on those who lived here long ago.

Native Americans blessed this region;
I hear their tales in the wind as it blows.

Flying eagles, colored rocks, wild flowers, untamed horses,
Winding rivers, arrowheads, smokey fires, and buffalo grass.

The indigenous American spirit,
Is freedom and hope in the trails that I pass.

Grateful to live in this country,
Which today we all call "Land of the Free!"

American Indians heritage lives on,
Amongst you and me.

Sword Of Freedom
By Ellie Naomi

United together, we stand
In god's kingdom at hand
Hearts born and raised in one nation
Living the same dream, the USA is our station
Indivisible without restraints, we love our country
While it can be dusty, and at times a little rusty
We adore all Americans, whether in the streets or fields
Gifted to us by those who've fought and refuse to yield
Ultimate sacrifices given by those who now watch from the clouds
We will never surrender, we will fight on and make you all proud
We'll continue the never ending fight for liberty and justice for all
We stand for all our rights, it's time to pull your sword of freedom
from the stone
Together we declare independence, let us make it known
To my American brothers and sisters, I say
Together we are the flag waving in the wind on this glorious day

December

"Always forgive your enemies- - nothing annoys them so much."
-Oscar Wilde

Christmas Bells

by Henry Wadsworth Longfellow

I heard the bells on Christmas Day
Their old, familiar carols play,
And wild and sweet
The words repeat
Of peace on earth, good-will to men!

And thought how, as the day had come,
The belfries of all Christendom
Had rolled along
The unbroken song
Of peace on earth, good-will to men!

Till ringing, singing on its way,
The world revolved from night to day,
A voice, a chime,
A chant sublime
Of peace on earth, good-will to men!

Then from each black, accursed mouth
The cannon thundered in the South,
And with the sound
The carols drowned
Of peace on earth, good-will to men!

It was as if an earthquake rent
The hearth-stones of a continent,
And made forlorn

The households born
Of peace on earth, good-will to men!

And in despair I bowed my head;
"There is no peace on earth," I said;
"For hate is strong,
And mocks the song
Of peace on earth, good-will to men!"

Then pealed the bells more loud and deep:
"God is not dead, nor doth He sleep;
The Wrong shall fail,
The Right prevail,
With peace on earth, good-will to men."

Christmas
By H. P. Nichols

"Little children, when rejoicing
In the merry Christmas morn,
'Mid your sports remember ever
'Tis the day that Christ was born.

"When on earth, the blessed Saviour
Said, 'Let children come to me,'
And the little ones he folded
In his arms, how tenderly!"

"But the Saviour is in heaven,
And we cannot see him now;
We cannot receive his blessing,
In his presence cannot bow."

"Listen. In the holy Bible,
Jesus Christ tells every child
That the way to gain his blessing
Is by being good and mild."

"Here on earth you may not see him;
But when this short life is done,

You shall live with him forever
Where there is no setting sun."

"So remember, Christmas morning,
That on earth the Saviour came;
And that still he guards and blesses
Every child who loves his name."

Thoughts
By Myra Viola Wilds

What kind of thoughts now, do you carry
In your travels day by day
Are they bright and lofty visions,
Or neglected, gone astray?

Matters not how great in fancy,
Or what deeds of skill you've wrought;
Man, though high may be his station,
Is no better than his thoughts.

Catch your thoughts and hold them tightly,
Let each one an honor be;
Purge them, scourge them, burnish brightly,
Then in love set each one free.

---

scourge—a whip that is used to inflict pain as a punishment; something that causes trouble or suffering

The Swiss Alps
By Johann Wolfgang von Goethe

Yesterday brown was still thy head, as the locks of my loved one,

Whose sweet image so dear silently beckons afar.
Silver-grey is the early snow to-day on thy summit,

Through the tempestuous night streaming fast over thy brow.
Youth, alas, throughout life as closely to age is united

As, in some changeable dream, yesterday blends with to-day.

---

tempestuous—strong turbulent feelings; confliction emotions; extremely story

Wartime Christmas
By Joyce Kilmer

Led by a star, a golden star,
The youngest star, an olden star,
Here the kings and the shepherds are,
Akneeling on the ground.
What did they come to the inn to see?
God in the Highest, and this is He,
A baby asleep on His mother's knee
And with her kisses crowned.

Now is the earth a dreary place,
A troubled place, a weary place.
Peace has hidden her lovely face
And turned in tears away.
Yet the sun, through the war-cloud, sees
Babies asleep on their mother's knees.
While there are love and home—and these—
There shall be Christmas Day.

Christmas in Australia
By Victor James Daley

O day, the crown and crest of all the year!
Thou comest not to us amid the snows,
But midmost of the reign of the red rose;
Our hearts have not yet lost the ancient cheer
That filled our father's simple hearts when sere
The leaves fell, and the winds of Winter froze
The waters wan, and carols at the close
Of yester-eve sang the Child Christ anear.
And so we hail thee with a greeting high,
And drain to thee a draught of our own wine,
Forgetful not beneath this bluer sky
Of that old mother-land beyond the brine,
Whose gray skies gladden as thou drawest nigh,
O day of God's good-will the seal and sign!

December's Snow
By Arthur Conan Doyle

The bloom is on the May once more,
The chestnut buds have burst anew;
But, darling, all our springs are o'er,
'Tis winter still for me and you.
We plucked Life's blossoms long ago
What's left is but December's snow.

But winter has its joys as fair,
The gentler joys, aloof, apart;
The snow may lie upon our hair
But never, darling, in our heart.
Sweet were the springs of long ago
But sweeter still December's snow.

Yes, long ago, and yet to me
It seems a thing of yesterday;
The shade beneath the willow tree,
The word you looked but feared to say.
Ah! when I learned to love you so
What recked we of December's snow?

But swift the ruthless seasons sped
And swifter still they speed away.
What though they bow the dainty head
And fleck the raven hair with gray?
The boy and girl of long ago
Are laughing through the veil of snow.

---

aloof—not friendly or uninterested; distant

Peace
By Henry Vaughan

My Soul, there is a country
Afar beyond the stars,
Where stands a winged sentry
All skillful in the wars;
There, above noise and danger
Sweet Peace sits, crown'd with smiles,
And One born in a manger
Commands the beauteous files.
He is thy gracious friend
And (O my Soul awake!)
Did in pure love descend,
To die here for thy sake.
If thou canst get but thither,
There grows the flow'r of peace,
The rose that cannot wither,
Thy fortress, and thy ease.
Leave then thy foolish ranges,
For none can thee secure,
But One, who never changes,
Thy God, thy life, thy cure.

The Banner of the Jews
By Emma Lazarus

Wake, Israel, wake! Recall to-day
The glorious Maccabean rage,
The sire heroic, hoary-gray,
His five-fold lion-lineage:
The Wise, the Elect, the Help-of-God,
The Burst-of-Spring, the Avenging Rod.*

From Mizpeh's mountain-ridge they saw
Jerusalem's empty streets, her shrine
Laid waste where Greeks profaned the Law,
With idol and with pagan sign.
Mourners in tattered black were there,
With ashes sprinkled on their hair.

Then from the stony peak there rang
A blast to ope the graves: down poured
The Maccabean clan, who sang
Their battle-anthem to the Lord.
Five heroes lead, and following, see,
Ten thousand rush to victory!

Oh for Jerusalem's trumpet now,
To blow a blast of shattering power,
To wake the sleepers high and low,
And rouse them to the urgent hour!
No hand for vengeance - but to save,
A million naked swords should wave.

Oh deem not dead that martial fire,
Say not the mystic flame is spent!
With Moses' law and David's lyre,
Your ancient strength remains unbent.
Let but an Ezra rise anew,
To lift the BANNER OF THE JEW!

A rag, a mock at first - erelong,
When men have bled and women wept,
To guard its precious folds from wrong,
Even they who shrunk, even they who slept,
Shall leap to bless it, and to save.
Strike! for the brave revere the brave!

Maccabean—a group of Jewish rebel warriors who were brave and stood up to their Greek-Syrian oppressors

The Mountains
By Walter De La Mare

Still, and blanched, and cold, and lone,
The icy hills far off from me
With frosty ulys overgrown
Stand in their sculptured secrecy.

No path of theirs the chamois fleet
Treads, with a nostril to the wind;
O'er their ice-marbled glaciers beat

No wings of eagles in my mind -

Yea, in my mind these mountains rise,
Their perils dyed with evening's rose;
And still my ghost sits at my eyes
And thirsts for their untroubled snows.

---

blanched—being dipped in boiling water

A Psalm of Life
By Henry Wadsworth Longfellow

Tell me not, in mournful numbers,
  Life is but an empty dream!
For the soul is dead that slumbers,
  And things are not what they seem.

Life is real! Life is earnest!
  And the grave is not its goal;
Dust thou art, to dust returnest,
  Was not spoken of the soul.

Not enjoyment, and not sorrow,
  Is our destined end or way;
But to act, that each to-morrow
  Find us farther than to-day.

Art is long, and Time is fleeting,
  And our hearts, though stout and brave,
Still, like muffled drums, are beating
  Funeral marches to the grave.

In the world's broad field of battle,
  In the bivouac of Life,
Be not like dumb, driven cattle!
  Be a hero in the strife!

Trust no Future, howe'er pleasant!
  Let the dead Past bury its dead!
Act,— act in the living Present!
  Heart within, and God o'erhead!

Lives of great men all remind us
  We can make our lives sublime,
And, departing, leave behind us
  Footprints on the sands of time;

Footprints, that perhaps another,
  Sailing o'er life's solemn main,
A forlorn and shipwrecked brother,
  Seeing, shall take heart again.

Let us, then, be up and doing,
  With a heart for any fate;
Still achieving, still pursuing,
  Learn to labor and to wait.

---

bivouac—to camp outside without any tent; to sleep out under the stars; temporary campsite like a soldier or mountaineer would use

Australian Scenery
By Andrew Barton "Banjo" Peterson

The Mountains
A land of sombre, silent hills, where mountain cattle go
By twisted tracks, on sidelings deep, where giant gum trees grow
And the wind replies, in the river oaks, to the song of the stream below.

A land where the hills keep watch and ward, silent and wide awake
As those who sit by a dead campfire, and wait for the dawn to break,
Or those who watched by the Holy Cross for the dead Redeemer's sake.

A land where silence lies so deep that sound itself is dead
And a gaunt grey bird, like a homeless soul, drifts, noiseless, overhead
And the world's great story is left untold, and the message is left unsaid.

The Plains
A land as far as the eye can see, where the waving grasses grow
Or the plains are blackened and burnt and bare, where the false mirages go
Like shifting symbols of hope deferred, land where you never know.

Land of plenty or land of want, where the grey Companions dance,
Feast or famine, or hope or fear, and in all things land of chance,

Where Nature pampers or Nature slays, in her ruthless, red, romance.

And we catch a sound of a fairy's song, as the wind goes whipping by,
Or a scent like incense drifts along from the herbage ripe and dry
Or the dust storms dance on their ballroom floor, where the bones of the cattle lie.

Hope is the Thing with Feathers
By Emily Dickinson

Hope is the thing with feathers
That perches in the soul,
And sings the tune without the words,
And never stops at all,

And sweetest in the gale is heard;
And sore must be the storm
That could abash the little bird
That kept so many warm.

I've heard it in the chillest land,
And on the strangest sea;
Yet, never, in extremity,
It asked a crumb of me.

---

gale—a very strong wind
abash—to make someone feel ashamed or embarrassed; disconcerted

A Carol from Flanders
By Frederick Niven

In Flanders on the Christmas morn
The trenched foemen lay,
the German and the Briton born,
And it was Christmas Day.
The red sun rose on fields accurst,
The gray fog fled away;
But neither cared to fire the first,
For it was Christmas Day!
They called from each to each across
The hideous disarray,
For terrible has been their loss:
"Oh, this is Christmas Day!"
Their rifles all they set aside,
One impulse to obey;
'Twas just the men on either side,
Just men — and Christmas Day.
They dug the graves for all their dead
And over them did pray:
And Englishmen and Germans said:
"How strange a Christmas Day!"
Between the trenches then they met,
Shook hands, and e'en did play
At games on which their hearts were set
On happy Christmas Day.
Not all the emperors and kings,
Financiers and they
Who rule us could prevent these things —
For it was Christmas Day.
Oh ye who read this truthful rime
From Flanders, kneel and say:
God speed the time when every day
Shall be as Christmas Day.

The Cremation of Sam McGee
By Robert William Service

There are strange things done in the midnight sun
By the men who moil for gold;
The Arctic trails have their secret tales
That would make your blood run cold;
The Northern Lights have seen queer sights,
But the queerest they ever did see
Was that night on the marge of Lake Lebarge
I cremated Sam McGee.

Now Sam McGee was from Tennessee, where the cotton blooms and blows.
Why he left his home in the South to roam round the Pole God only knows.
He was always cold, but the land of gold seemed to hold him like a spell;
Though he'd often say in his homely way that he'd "sooner live in hell."

On a Christmas Day we were mushing our way over the Dawson trail.
Talk of your cold! through the parka's fold it stabbed like a driven nail.
If our eyes we'd close, then the lashes froze, till sometimes we couldn't see;
It wasn't much fun, but the only one to whimper was Sam McGee.

And that very night as we lay packed tight in our robes beneath the snow,
And the dogs were fed, and the stars o'erhead were dancing heel and toe,
He turned to me, and, "Cap," says he, "I'll cash in this trip, I guess;
And if I do, I'm asking that you won't refuse my last request."

Well, he seemed so low that I couldn't say no: then he says with a sort of moan:
"It's the cursed cold, and it's got right hold till I'm chilled clean through to the bone.
Yet 'taint being dead, it's my awful dread of the icy grave that pains:
So I want you to swear that, foul or fair, you'll cremate my last remains."

A pal's last need is a thing to heed, so I swore I would not fail;
And we started on at the streak of dawn, but God! he looked ghastly pale.

He crouched on the sleigh, and he raved all day of his home in Tennessee;
And before nightfall a corpse was all that was left of Sam McGee.

There wasn't a breath in that land of death, and I hurried, horror driven,
With a corpse half-hid that I couldn't get rid because of a promise given;
It was lashed to the sleigh, and it seemed to say: "You may tax your brawn and brains,
But you promised true, and it's up to you to cremate those last remains."

Now a promise made is a debt unpaid, and the trail has its own stern code.
In the days to come, though my lips were dumb, in my heart how I cursed that load.
In the long, long night, by the lone firelight, while the huskies, round in a ring,
Howled out their woes to the homeless snows - O God! how I loathed the thing!

And every day that quiet clay seemed to heavy and heavier grow;
And on I went, though the dogs were spent and the grub was getting low;
The trail was bad, and I felt half mad, but I swore I would not give in;
And I'd often sing to the hateful thing, and it hearkened with a grin.

Till I came to the marge of Lake Lebarge, and a derelict there lay;
It was jammed in the ice, but I saw in a trice it was called the "Alice May."
And I looked at it, and I thought a bit, and I looked at my frozen chum:
Then, "Here," said I, with a sudden cry, "is my cre-ma-tor-eum."

Some planks I tore from the cabin floor, and I lit the boiler fire;
Some coal I found that was lying around, and I heaped the fuel higher;
The flames just soared, and the furnace roared - such a blaze you seldom see;
And I burrowed a hole in the glowing coal, and I stuffed in Sam McGee.

Then I made a hike, for I didn't like to hear him sizzle so;
And the heavens scowled, and the huskies howled, and the wind began to blow.
It was icy cold, but the hot sweat rolled down my cheeks, and I don't know why;

And the greasy smoke in an inky cloak went streaking down the sky.

I do not know how long in the snow I wrestled with grisly fear;
But the stars came out and they danced about ere again I ventured near;
I was sick with dread, but I bravely said: "I'll just take a peep inside.
I guess he's cooked, and it's time I looked," ... then the door I opened wide.

And there sat Sam, looking cool and calm, in the heart of the furnace roar;
And he wore a smile you could see a mile, and he said: "Please close that door.
It's fine in here, but I greatly fear you'll let in the cold and storm -
Since I left Plumtree, down in Tennessee, it's the first time I've been warm."

There are strange things done in the midnight sun
By the men who moil for gold;
The Arctic trails have their secret tales
That would make your blood run cold;
The Northern Lights have seen queer sights,
But the queerest they ever did see
Was that night on the marge of Lake Lebarge
I cremated Sam McGee.

---

queer—strange

Goody Santa Clause on a Sleigh Ride
By Katharine Lee Bates

Santa, must I tease in vain, Deer? Let me go and hold the reindeer,
While you clamber down the chimneys. Don't look savage as a Turk!
Why should you have all the glory of the joyous Christmas story,
And poor little Goody Santa Claus have nothing but the work?

It would be so very cozy, you and I, all round and rosy,
Looking like two loving snowballs in our fuzzy Arctic furs,
Tucked in warm and snug together, whisking through the winter weather
Where the tinkle of the sleigh-bells is the only sound that stirs.

You just sit here and grow chubby off the goodies in my cubby
From December to December, till your white beard sweeps your knees;
For you must allow, my Goodman, that you're but a lazy woodman
And rely on me to foster all our fruitful Christmas trees.

While your Saintship waxes holy, year by year, and roly-poly,
Blessed by all the lads and lassies in the limits of the land,
While your toes at home you're toasting, then poor Goody must go posting
Out to plant and prune and garner, where our fir-tree forests stand.

Oh! but when the toil is sorest how I love our fir-tree forest,
Heart of light and heart of beauty in the Northland cold and dim,
All with gifts and candles laden to delight a boy or maiden,
And its dark-green branches ever murmuring the Christmas hymn!

Yet ask young Jack Frost, our neighbor, who but Goody has the labor,
Feeding roots with milk and honey that the bonbons may be sweet!
Who but Goody knows the reason why the playthings bloom in season
And the ripened toys and trinkets rattle gaily to her feet!

From the time the dollies budded, wiry-boned and saw-dust blooded,
With their waxen eyelids winking when the wind the tree-tops plied,
Have I rested for a minute, until now your pack has in it
All the bright, abundant harvest of the merry Christmastide?

Santa, wouldn't it be pleasant to surprise me with a present?
And this ride behind the reindeer is the boon your Goody begs;
Think how hard my extra work is, tending the Thanksgiving turkeys
And our flocks of rainbow chickens — those that lay the Easter eggs.

Home to womankind is suited? Nonsense, Goodman! Let our fruited
Orchards answer for the value of a woman out-of-doors.
Why then bid me chase the thunder, while the roof you're safely under,
All to fashion fire-crackers with the lighting in their cores?

See! I've fetched my snow-flake bonnet, with the sunrise ribbons on it;
I've not worn it since we fled from Fairyland our wedding day;
How we sped through iceberg porches with the Northern Lights for
torches!
You were young and slender, Santa, and we had this very sleigh.

Jump in quick then? That's my bonny. Hey down derry! Nonny nonny!
While I tie your fur cap closer, I will kiss your ruddy chin.
I'm so pleased I fall to singing, just as sleigh-bells take to ringing!
Are the cloud-spun lap-robes ready? Tirra-lirra! Tuck me in.

Off across the starlight Norland, where no plant adorns the moorland
Save the ruby-berried holly and the frolic mistletoe!
Oh, but this is Christmas revel! Off across the frosted level
Where the reindeers' hoofs strike sparkles from the crispy, crackling snow!

There's the Man i' the Moon before us, bound to lead the Christmas chorus
With the music of the sky-waves rippling round his silver shell —
Glimmering boat that leans and tarries with the weight of dreams she carries
To the cots of happy children. Gentle sailor, steer her well!

Now we pass through dusky portals to the drowsy land of mortals;
Snow-enfolded, silent cities stretch about us dim and far.
Oh! how sound the world is sleeping, midnight watch no shepherd keeping,
Though an angel-face shines gladly down from every golden star.

Here's a roof. I'll hold the reindeer. I suppose this weather-vane, Dear,
Some one set here just on purpose for our teams to fasten to.
There's its gilded cock, — the gaby! — wants to crow and tell the baby
We are come. Be careful, Santa! Don't get smothered in the flue.

Back so soon? No chimney-swallow dives but where his mate can follow.
Bend your cold ear, Sweetheart Santa, down to catch my whisper faint:
Would it be so very shocking if your Goody filled a stocking
Just for once? Oh, dear! Forgive me. Frowns do not become a Saint.

I will peep in at the skylights, where the moon sheds tender twilights
Equally down silken chambers and down attics bare and bleak.
Let me show with hailstone candies these two dreaming boys — the dandies
In their frilled and fluted nighties, rosy cheek to rosy cheek!

What! No gift for this poor garret? Take a sunset sash and wear it
O'er the rags, my pale-faced lassie, till thy father smiles again.
He's a poet, but — oh, cruel! he has neither light nor fuel.
Here's a fallen star to write by, and a music-box of rain.

So our sprightly reindeer clamber, with their fairy sleigh of amber,
On from roof to roof , the woven shades of night about us drawn.
On from roof to roof we twinkle, all the silver bells a-tinkle,
Till blooms in yonder blessèd East the rose of Christmas dawn.

Now the pack is fairly rifled, and poor Santa's well-nigh stifled;
Yet you would not let your Goody fill a single baby-sock;
Yes, I know the task takes brain, Dear. I can only hold the reindeer,
And so see me climb down chimney — it would give your nerves a shock.

Wait! There's yet a tiny fellow, smiling lips and curls so yellow
You would think a truant sunbeam played in them all night. He spins
Giant tops, a flies kites higher than the gold cathedral spire
In his creams — the orphan bairnie, trustful little Tatterkins.

Santa, don't pass by the urchin! Shake the pack, and deeply search in
All your pockets. There is always one toy more. I told you so.
Up again? Why, what's the trouble? On your eyelash winks the bubble
Mortals call a tear, I fancy. Holes in stocking, heel and toe?

Goodman, though your speech is crusty now and then there's nothing rusty
In your heart. A child's least sorrow makes your wet eyes glisten, too;
But I'll mend that sock so nearly it shall hold your gifts completely.
Take the reins and let me show you what a woman's wit can do.

Puff! I'm up again, my Deary, flushed a bit and somewhat weary,
With my wedding snow-flake bonnet worse for many a sooty knock;
But be glad you let me wheedle, since, an icicle for needle,
Threaded with the last pale moonbeam, I have darned the laddie's sock.

Then I tucked a paint-box in it ('twas no easy task to win it
From the Artist of the Autumn Leaves) and frost-fruits white and sweet,
With the toys your pocket misses — oh! and kisses upon kisses
To cherish safe from evil paths the motherless small feet.

Chirrup! chirrup! There's a patter of soft footsteps and a clatter
Of child voices. Speed it, reindeer, up the sparkling Arctic Hill!
Merry Christmas, little people! Joy-bells ring in every steeple,
And Goody's gladdest of the glad. I've had my own sweet will.

---

ruddy— a person having a healthy red color
garret—attic or top floor room
bairnie—small child
wheedle—to persuade someone to do something with flattery and coaxing

Poetry Corner

It's now your turn to be the poet.
Use this space to either write your own poetry
or write down other poems that you love.

National Anthems

Included are the national anthems, of the countries, of each poet in this book.

Australia

Advance Australia Fair
By Peter Dodds McCormick

Australians all let us rejoice
For we are young and free
We've golden soil and wealth for toil
Our home is girt by sea

Our land abounds in nature's gifts
Of beauty, rich and rare
In history's page, let every stage
Advance Australia fair!

In joyful strains then let us sing
Advance Australia fair!
Beneath our radiant Southern Cross
We'll toil with hearts and hands

To make this Commonwealth of ours
Renowned of all the lands
For those who've come across the seas
We've boundless plains to share

With courage let us all combine
To advance Australia fair
In joyful strains then let us sing
Advance Australia fair!

Australians all let us rejoice
For we are young and free
We've golden soil and wealth for toil
Our home is girt by sea
Our land abounds in nature's gifts
Of beauty, rich and rare
In history's page, let every stage
Advance Australia fair!
In Joyful Strains then Let Us Sing
Advance Australia fair!

Canada

O Canada
By Robert Stanley Weir

O Canada! Our home and native land!
True patriot love thou dost in us command.
We see thee rising fair, dear land,
The True North, strong and free;
And stand on guard, O Canada,
We stand on guard for thee.
(Refrain)
O Canada! O Canada!
O Canada! We stand on guard for thee,
O Canada! We stand on guard for thee.
O Canada! Where pines and maples grow,
Great prairies spread and lordly rivers flow,
How dear to us thy broad domain,
From East to Western sea!
Thou land of hope for all who toil!
Thou True North, strong and free!
(Refrain)
O Canada! Beneath thy shining skies
May stalwart sons and gentle maidens rise,
To keep thee steadfast through the years
From East to Western sea,
Our own beloved native land,
Our True North, strong and free!
(Refrain)
Ruler Supreme, Who hearest humble prayer,
Hold our dominion within Thy loving care.
Help us to find, O God, in Thee
A lasting, rich reward,
As waiting for the Better Day,
We ever stand on guard.
(Refrain)

England

God Save the King
By Henry Carey
(King or Queen can be substituted when appropriate)

God save our gracious Queen!
Long live our noble Queen!
God save the Queen!
Send her victorious,
Happy and glorious,
Long to reign over us,
God save the Queen.
Thy choicest gifts in store
On her be pleased to pour,
Long may she reign.
May she defend our laws,
And ever give us cause,
To sing with heart and voice,
God save the Queen.

France

The Marseillaise
By Rouget de Lisle

Arise, children of the Fatherland
Our day of glory has arrived
Against us the bloody flag of tyranny
is raised; the bloody flag is raised.
Do you hear, in the countryside
The roar of those ferocious soldiers?
They're coming right into your arms
To cut the throats of your sons, your comrades!
To arms, citizens!
Form your battalions
Let's march, let's march
That their impure blood
Should water our fields.

La Marseillaise
Allons enfants de la Patrie
Le jour de gloire est arrivé!
Contre nous de la tyrannie
L'étendard sanglant est levé
L'étendard sanglant est levé
Entendez-vous dans les campagnes
Mugir ces féroces soldats?
Ils viennent jusque dans vos bras
Égorger nos fils, nos compagnes!
Aux armes, citoyens
Formez vos bataillons
Marchons, marchons!
Qu'un sang impur
Abreuve nos sillons!

Germany

The Song of the Germans

By Joseph Haydn

Unity and justice and freedom
For the German fatherland!
Towards these let us all strive
Brotherly with heart and hand!
Unity and justice and freedom
Are the foundation of happiness;
Flourish in the radiance of this happiness,
Flourish, German fatherland!

Das Deutschlandied
Einigkeit und Recht und Freiheit
Für das deutsche Vaterland!
Danach lasst uns alle streben
Brüderlich mit Herz und Hand!
Einigkeit und Recht und Freiheit
Sind des Glückes Unterpfand;
Blüh' im Glanze dieses Glückes,
Blühe, deutsches Vaterland!

Ireland

The Soldier's Song

By Peadar Kearney & Patrick Heeney

We'll sing song, a soldier's song,
With cheering rousing chorus,
As round our blazing fires we throng,
The starry heavens o'er us;
Impatient for the coming fight,
And as we wait the morning's light,
Here in the silence of the night,
We'll chant a soldier's song.

Chorus:
Soldiers are we
whose lives are pledged to Ireland;
Some have come
from a land beyond the wave.
Sworn to be free,
No more our ancient sire land
Shall shelter the despot or the slave.
Tonight we man the gap of danger
In Erin's cause, come woe or weal
'Mid cannons' roar and rifles peal,
We'll chant a soldier's song

In valley green, on towering crag,
Our fathers fought before us,
And conquered 'neath the same old flag
That's proudly floating o'er us.
We're children of a fighting race,
That never yet has known disgrace,
And as we march, the foe to face,
We'll chant a soldier's song

Chorus

Sons of the Gael! Men of the Pale!
The long watched day is breaking;

The serried ranks of Inisfail
Shall set the Tyrant quaking.
Our camp fires now are burning low;
See in the east a silv'ry glow,
Out yonder waits the Saxon foe,
So chant a soldier's song.

Chorus

Original Gaeilge (Gaelic)
Amhrán na bhFiann

Seo dhibh a chairde duan Oglaigh,
Cathreimeach briomhar ceolmhar,
Ar dtinte cnamh go buacach taid,
'S an speir go min realtogach
Is fonnmhar faobhrach sinn chun gleo
'S go tiunmhar gle roimh thiocht do'n lo
Fe chiunas chaomh na hoiche ar seol:
Seo libh canaidh Amhran na bhFiann

Curfa:

Sinne Firnna Fail
A ta fe gheall ag Eirinn,
buion dar slua
Thar toinn do rainig chugainn,
Fe mhoid bheith saor.
Sean tir ar sinsir feasta
Ni fhagfar fe'n tioran na fe'n trail
Anocht a theam sa bhearna bhaoil,
Le gean ar Ghaeil chun bais no saoil
Le guna screach fe lamhach na bpilear
Seo libh canaidh Amhran na bhFiann.

Cois banta reidhe, ar ardaibh sleibhe,
Ba bhuachach ar sinsir romhainn,
Ag lamhach go trean fe'n sar-bhrat sein
Ta thuas sa ghaoith go seolta
Ba dhuchas riamh d'ar gcine chaidh
Gan iompail siar o imirt air,
'S ag siul mar iad i gcoinne namhad
Seo libh, canaidh Amhran na bhFiann

Curfa

A bhuion nach fann d'fhuil Ghaeil is
Gall,
Sin breacadh lae na saoirse,
Ta sceimhle 's scanradh i gcroithe
namhad,
Roimh ranna laochra ar dtire.
Ar dtinte is treith gan spreach anois,
Sin luisne ghle san speir anoir,
'S an biobha i raon na bpilear agaibh:
Seo libh, canaidh Amhran na bh Fiann.

Curfa

Jamaica

Jamaica, Land We Love
Lyrics By Hugh Sherlock / Composed By Robert Lightbourne

Eternal Father, Blessour Land,
Guard us with thy mighty hand, Keepus
Free from evil powers, Be our light through countless hours,
To our leaders, great defender, Grant true wisdom from above, Justice,
truth be ours forever, Jamaica, land we love,
Jamaica, Jamaica, Jamaica, land we love
Teach us true respect for all, Stir response to duty's call,
Strengthen us the weak to cherish, Give us vision lest we perish,
Knowledge send us Heavenly Father, Grant true wisdom from above,
Justice, truth be ours forever, Jamaica, land we love,
Jamaica, Jamaica, Jamaica, land we love

Japan

His Imperial Majesty's Reign
By Hiromori Hayashi

May your reign
Continue for a thousand, eight thousand generations,
Until the tiny pebbles
Grow into massive boulders
Lush with moss

In Japanese
Kimigayo
君が代は
千代に八千代に
細石の
巌と為りて
苔の生すまで
Kimigayo wa
Chiyo ni yachiyo ni
Sazare-ishi no
Iwao to narite
Koke no musu mad

Malta

The Hymn of Malta

By Robert Samut

Guard her, O Lord, as ever Thou hast guarded!
This Motherland so dear whose name we bear!
Keep her in mind, whom Thou hast made so fair!

May he who rules, for wisdom be regarded!
In master mercy, strength in man increase!
Confirm us all, in unity and peace!

L-Innu Malti

Lil din l-art helwa, l-Omm li tatna isimha,
Hares Mulej, kif dejjem Int harist:
Ftakar li lilha bl-ohla dawl libbist.

Aghti, kbir Alla, id-dehen lil min jahkimha,
Rodd il-hniena lis-sid, sahha 'l-haddiem:
Seddaq il-ghaqda fil-Maltin u s-sliem.

Scotland

Flower of Scotland
By Roy Williamson

O Flower of Scotland
When will we see your like again?
That fought and died for
Your wee bit Hill and Glen
And stood against him
Proud Edward's Army
And sent him homeward tae think again
The Hills are bare now
And Autumn leaves lie thick and still
O'er land that is lost now
Which those so dearly held
That stood against him
Proud Edward's Army
And sent him homeward tae think again
Those days are past now
And in the past they must remain
But we can still rise now
And be the nation again
That stood against him
Proud Edward's Army
And sent him homeward tae think again
The Hills are bare now
And Autumn leaves lie thick and still
O'er land that is lost now
That though so dearly held
O Flower of Scotland
When will we see your like again?
That fought and died for
Your wee bit Hill and Glen
And stood against him
Proud Edward's Army
And sent him homeward tae think again

South Africa

Lord Bless Africa
By Enoch Sontonga

May her glory be lifted high,
Hear our petitions
Lord bless us, your children.
Lord we ask You to protect our nation,
Intervene and end all conflicts,
Protect us, protect our nation,
Protect South Africa, South Africa.
Out of the blue of our heavens,
From the depths of our seas,
Over everlasting mountains,
Where the echoing crags resound,
Sounds the call to come together,
And united we shall stand,
Let us live and strive for freedom
In South Africa our land.

Nkosi sikelel' Afrika
Maluphakanyisw' uphondo lwayo
Yizwa imithandazo yethu
Nkosi sikelela thina lusapho lwayo
Morena boloka setjhaba sa heso
O fedise dintwa le matshwenyeho
O se boloke (Ntate) o se boloke setjhaba sa heso
Setjhaba sa South Afrika (South Afrika)
Uit die blou van onse hemel
Uit die diepte van ons see
Oor ons ewige gebergtes
Waar die kranse antwoord gee
Sounds the call to come together
And united we shall stand
Let us live and strive for freedom
In South Africa our land

United States

The Star-Spangled Banner
By Frances Scott Keys

O! say can you see, by the dawn's early light,
What so proudly we hail'd at the twilight's last gleaming,
Whose broad stripes and bright stars through the perilous fight,
O'er the ramparts we watch'd, were so gallantly streaming?
And the rockets' red glare, the bombs bursting in air,
Gave proof through the night that our flag was still there —
O! say, does that star-spangled banner yet wave
O'er the land of the free, and the home of the brave?

On the shore, dimly seen through the mists of the deep,
Where the foe's haughty host in dread silence reposes,
What is that which the breeze o'er the towering steep,
As it fitfully blows, half conceals, half discloses?
Now it catches the gleam of the morning's first beam,
In full glory reflected now shines on the stream —
'Tis the star-spangled banner, O! long may it wave
O'er the land of the free, and the home of the brave.

And where is that band who so vauntingly swore
That the havock of war and the battle's confusion
A home and a country should leave us no more?
Their blood has wash'd out their foul foot-steps' pollution,
No refuge could save the hireling and slave,
From the terror of flight or the gloom of the grave;
And the star-spangled banner in triumph doth wave
O'er the land of the free, and the home of the brave.

O! thus be it ever when freemen shall stand
Between their lov'd home, and the war's desolation,
Blest with vict'ry and peace, may the heav'n-rescued land
Praise the power that hath made and preserv'd us a nation!
Then conquer we must, when our cause it is just,
And this be our motto — "In God is our trust!"
And the star-spangled banner in triumph shall wave
O'er the land of the free, and the home of the brave.

Wales

Land of my Fathers
By James James

Verse 1
The land of my fathers is dear to me,
Old land where the minstrels are honoured and free;
Its warring defenders so gallant and brave,
For freedom their life's blood they gave.

Chorus
Home, home, true I am to home,
While seas secure the land so pure,
O may the old language endure.

Verse 2
Old land of the mountains, the Eden of bards,
Each gorge and each valley a loveliness guards;
Through love of my country, charmed voices will be
Its streams, and its rivers, to me.

Verse 3
Though foemen have trampled my land 'neath their feet,
The language of Cambria still knows no retreat;
The muse is not vanquished by traitor's fell hand,
Nor silenced the harp of my land.

Original Welsh
Hen Wlad Fy Nhadau

Verse 1
Mae hen wlad fy nhadau yn annwyl i mi,
Gwlad beirdd a chantorion, enwogion o fri;
Ei gwrol ryfelwyr, gwladgarwyr tra mâd,
Tros ryddid gollasant eu gwaed.
Chorus:
Gwlad, Gwlad, pleidiol wyf i'm gwlad,
Tra môr yn fur i'r bur hoff bau,
O bydded i'r heniaith barhau.

Verse 2

Hen Gymru fynyddig, paradwys y bardd;
Pob dyffryn, pob clogwyn, i'm golwg sydd hardd,
Trwy deimlad gwladgarol, mor swynol yw si,
Ei nentydd, afonydd, i mi.

Verse 3

Os treisiodd y gelyn fy ngwlad dan ei droed,
Mae hen iaith y Cymry mor fyw ag erioed,
Ni luddiwyd yr awen gan erchyll law brad,
Na thelyn berseiniol fy ngwlad.

Tales of Bravery

Bravery comes in many forms and one way that people remember these individuals are through legends. A legend is a story that is considered to be historical but may not be 100% authentic. This is different from a tale that is steeped in imaginative fiction, even if it is based on a small sliver of reality. Examples of Tales would be Americas Paul Bunyan, Irelands Banshee, Germany's Hansel and Gretel, Australia's Bunyip, and Africa's One-Handed Girl. Tales make one think and teach a moral but based on far less act, if any at all. You are about to read a few tales of people who lived and left a permanent mark on history and the lives of others.

Vincent and the Handful of Sand

(Australia)

Important words to know

Gurindji — An aboriginal tribe from the Northern Territory
kartija — an aboriginal word used by the Gurindji to mean "white man" or "person who is not an aborigine"
didgeridoo — A long tubular instrument native to Northern Australia and invented about 1,500 years ago. One plays it by blowing air between the lips and vibrating them while holding one end of the instrument over one's mouth.

Once upon a time, in a real land on the bottom of the world, there was a magical place covered in beautiful grasslands. To a mother, a precious little boy was born and she named him Vincent. He grew up listening to stories of how their people lived free and in peace. The land let cool water flow from the river. The land providing everything his people needed to stay healthy. The land lived as one with the Gurindji and all the animals. His people had lived this way for tens of thousands of years.

But this isn't the life that little Vincent grew up in. A shadow had come over the land. Animals and water were scarce, Gurindji worked from morning to night until they could no longer hunt for their own food. Why you might ask? Forty years ago, the long shadow (a man) had visited on top of a four-legged animal. Vincent's people had never seen such a thing and thought it was from another world. They called him kartiya. The shadow left and time had passed until it became a forgotten memory.

Five year-cycles had passed and the shadow named kartiya returned. Large animals called cattle were placed on their land. The Gurindji we forced to work the land with no say as to how it was treated. They put up fences that cut off their access to hunting grounds, water and sacred sites. The kartiya didn't treat then as equals, but thought very little of the Gurindji. This was the world that Vincent grew up in. While wallaby roamed free, Vincent was doing work for the kartiya. Vincent longed for the life his ancestors talked of. How could this have happened? The kartiya had the Gurindji land given to him, nobody asked for permission because their land was just taken. Not only did they lose their land, but they also lost their freedom.

Vincent grew up and held onto the stories of his people he learned to play the didgeridoo. All he knew was work and servitude. Vincent knew that this was not how his people were meant to live. They were meant to live with the land and not destroy it. He knew that his people deserved to be treated with respect and kindness. For decades, his people were being paid in meager rations, had to walk long distances to get water and had no shelters to live in. Vincent had had enough and decided that he would talk to the kartiya. Time after time the kartiya would promise to treat them better but he never did.

One day Vincent was putting a yolk on a donkey and he got hurt badly. He spent time in a hospital and was visited by three men who said they would help him if he and his people would strike. Vincent saw a big opportunity and he did not want it to go to waste.

Vincent returned to his people and stood as tall and strong as he could. He gathered the workers of Wave Hill Station; over 200 men, women and children walked away from their jobs. The kartiya tried to stop them but Vincent would not back down. A police officer tried to stop them but Vincent would not back down. With all their possessions in their hands, and children at their heels, they walked 16 kilometers with no water.

Parched, they stopped and tried digging for water but to great disappointment they found none. Thirsty and a little scared they all continued on to Libanungku, the only Gurindji land the kartiya didn't own. Vincent led the people with nothing but hope in their hearts. After eighty years, the people were ready to do anything for their freedom.

Vincent and the people sat in protest and would not move. Vincent encouraged the people to stay and after two long weeks a group of union men came to help them. Weeks turned to months and months turned to years. The workers sat in protest to make their needs known. Vincent went to the big city of lights and spoke to many important people. Vincent, the soft-spoken man, made his voice heard. He did not take no for an answer. He did not let people discourage him and continued fighting for what he believed in.

Time did not matter to Vincent. The land of his people was taken and he wanted to see his people living freely on the land of his ancestors. Vincent made many kartija friends to include Gough Whitlam. It was an exciting time when Gough Whitlam became Prime Minister of Australia. On a special day the Prime Minister met with Vincent and many other people. Gough Whitlam bent over and picked up a big handful of Gurindji sand and poured it into Vincent Lingiari's hand. Vincent smiled as an overwhelming feeling of satisfaction of pride filled his soul. He had saved the land of his ancestors. He had done what men before thought impossible to do.

Hear the song "From Little Things Big Things Grow" about Vincent Lingiari written by Paul Kelly & The Messengers

A Man with Bare Feet

(United States)

A long time ago, when people traveled on wooden wheels or horse's backs, there was a boy born to a farmer who was fighting alongside George Washington during the Revolutionary war. When that father returned to his home in Leominister, Massachusetts, he taught his son everything that he knew about farming. The boy grew up to be a man who loved animals, almost as much as he loved apples. His name was John Chapman and he was a thin kind man who wished no ill on anyone or anything. He loved apples so much he didn't want to do anything but plant apple trees. How much did he love apples you ask? He wanted to plant apple trees so badly that he started to collect apple seeds from local people who pressed apples for cider so he could plant more.

One day he started to hear lots of talk about people moving West and getting land. Even though John lived on a very lovely farm with a fine collection of apple trees he started to dream about going West to find his own land. But he could not bear the idea of leaving behind his beautiful orchard. Then he learned that if he were to plant an orchard of 50 trees, just about any place out West, he would have a claim on the land and own it. "Wow," thought John, "how many apples could I plant with unlimited space"? So, John felt inspired and decided that he too would start his own adventure going West.

With nothing but a pot, a sack of seeds, and the clothes on his back he left his home and started walking with his bare feet. That's right, he had no shoes. He walked all over the country and planted apple orchards in Pennsylvania, Ohio, Indiana, Ontario, Canada and even a little part of what people now call West Virginia. Everywhere he went he was welcomed and liked.

Now, John had some ideas that people found mighty peculiar. He did not eat animals, he would not get married and he would not graft any apple trees. He planted all trees from a seed because he could not bring himself to cut into a tree to make a graft. He felt in his soul that it hurt the tree. He followed the teachings of the Swedenborg faith and he took it very seriously. One chilly night he started a fire hoping to warm himself but at the site of mosquitos being burned by the fire he scrambled to put the fire out to save any other mosquitoes from a fiery demise.

John traveled over 100,000 square miles in his lifetime and was proud of his 1200 acres of land adorned with apple trees. John died on March 11, 1845 and I can just imagine what his heaven looks like. Fields and fields of snowy white trees adorned with apple blossoms. It wasn't until after his passing that people started to call him by a new name. Can you guess what it was? That's right, Johnny Apple Seed. His story grew and grew until almost every folk person heard his story, and now you are one of them too.

Now don't be sad if you never got to meet Johnny Apple Seed yourself. There is still a little of Johnny Appleseed still live today. In Savanna, Ohio. You can visit one of his apple trees that were planted long ago. So long ago in fact, that it is 150 years old. So will you keep Johnny's dreams alive and plant an apple tree? I'm sure he smiles every time an apple tree is planted.

---

adorned—to make more appealing or attractive with decoration or objects.
graft—a twig entered into a small cut in a trees trunk called a slit and then fastened in place so the tree will heal to it creating a new branch.
Swedenborg—a Christian religious group started by Emanuel Swedenborg
demise—death

Facing Apartheid

(South Africa)

I open my eyes and looked up at the thatched roof and reaches out to touches the dry mud walls. It's time for me to get up and look after the sheep and cows. I, Rolihlahla, have been a Xhosa herd boy since I was 5 years old with royal Thembu lineage. While looking after animals in the fields, I practiced using my sling to catch bird and I learned what plants and roots were edible. My favorite was drinking fresh warm milk right from the utter of a cow.

Every African boy learned to fight with sticks and that is exactly what I did. I was pretty good and I loved playing with other boys I pretended that I was a fierce warrior with my stick and shield. Have you ever pretended you were a great warrior? I would move my feet really fast and parry, strike and jab. I stop to take a breath and look out towards the small village of Qunu on the African plains. It is my home, the kraal of my mothers.

I was pretty smart for my age and our village would pick only one child to send to school. I was really curious and wanted to learn as much as I could. I was so excited when I found out that I would be the one to go to school. "No one in my family had ever attended school ... On the first day of school my teacher, Miss Mdingane, gave each of us an English name. This was the custom among Africans in those days and was undoubtedly due to the British bias of our education. That day, Miss Mdingane told me that my new name was Nelson. Why this particular name, I have no idea."(-Mandela, 1994). The name Nelson sure sounded funny compared to Rolihlahla. Overtime, I got used to my name being Nelson Mandela.

At age nine my father left this life and my mother gave guardianship of me to The Chief Jongintaba Dalindyebo and his wife Noengland. They were very nice and treated me just like their own children and raised me alongside Justice their son and Namafu their daughter. It was very different growing up in the "Great Palace." Justice and I did everything together to include going to school and participating the Ulwaluko ritual of becoming a man. Justice and I even went to the Methodist College in Fort Beaufort along with most Thembu royalty.

While attending college I became very interested in native African culture and history, long distance running, boxing, and gardening. I then went for my BA degree at the University of Fort Hare where I studied English, politic, anthropology and more. I also did ballroom dancing, participated in drama and taught bible classes in the community.

I found that I had some of my father's rebellious spirit in me. I lead a boycott about the quality of food served to the students and I was given the choice to either stop the boycott or be expelled from school. I stood my ground and chose to be expelled from school. Justice and I returned home only to be told that a marriage had been arranged for us. Neither of us were excited about this and we decided to run away. Life was not easy and I did not have a lot of money. I went to the University of the Witwatersrand and I was the only black person and learned what it felt like to be treated poorly because of the color of my skin. I started to try many different political groups and supported the groups I found to be the most important

Then one day something big happened, something that affected all South Africans. The monarchy had put into place a law that required people of different cultures to be separated. I was appalled but not at all shocked! Africans were not allowed to go to a beach with Europeans. Indians could not be on the beaches with Africans. This affected all areas of life, not just the beaches. They called this new law apartheid. "A nation should not be judged by how it treats its highest citizens, but its lowest ones." My rebellious side was ignited once again and I was ready to fight for the rights of South Africans.

I spoke out against apartheid and rallied with other Africans. I believed that we had to win this battle for ourselves. Many people joined the cause and I could not believe how large the movement became. I was determined to have my voice heard even though it was against the law, I even went to jail with a hundred other men because of this.

Once I got out of jail I became targeted by the government and had to be very careful. I would have to wear disguises and hide just so I could continue the movement. During this time I traveled to other countries and saw people of all cultures speaking with each other and I wanted this for South Africa. "For to be free is not merely to cast off one's chains, but to live in a way that respects and enhances the freedoms of others." I returned to my homeland determined to cleans it of its oppressive segregation but I was captured and once again put into jail.

South Africa was thrown into a frenzy and cried out for my release but weeks, months, and years passed as I sat in a secluded Robben Island jail. My children became adults and my mother passed away. I spent my days smashing rocks or sitting in my small jail cell hour after hour. I found enjoyment in educating other prisoners. "Education is the most powerful weapon which you can use to change the world."

Outside of the prison South Africa was crumbling and my heart ached for my people. They rallied and my people never gave up. I wanted to let the people know that I was thinking of them and encourage them to continue the fight. I would write small notes of encouragement with other prisoners who were released from prison. 27 years passed and the fire inside me had not been vanquished. "A winner is a dreamer who never gives up." I would not give up on my people.

In 1989 a new president was put in place and apartheid was made a thing of the past. He did away with barbaric punishments and in 1990 he released me from prison. Hundreds of people joined to see my release and my heart leapt to see both African and White people joined together when I walked out hand in hand with my wife. "I greet you all in the name of peace, democracy and freedom for all. I stand here before you not as a prophet, but as a humble servant of you, the people. Your tireless and heroic sacrifices have made it possible for me to be here today. I therefore place the remaining years of my life in your hands."

Would you believe that I became the President of South Africa in 1994. There was still a lot of change to be made but I was proud to lead the country to peace and equality. "What counts in life is not the mere fact that we have lived. It is what difference we have made to the lives of others."

Thembu—Xhosa people under the Thembu Kingdom
ulwaluko ritual–a boys coming of age ritual
lineage—the descendants from an ancestor
kraal—a community or village of huts in Africa
apartheid—a South African system put in place to segregate races.

Laura Secord

(Canada)

This is a poem written about the heroic act of Laura Secord. As a young woman she overheard American soldiers talking about the advance into Canada on June 21, 1813. Her husband was recovering from war injurie in October

Laura Secord
By Agnes Maule Machar

Softly the spell of moonlight fell
  On the swift river's flow,
On the gray crags of Queenston Heights,
  And the green waves below.

Alone the whip-poor-will's sad cry
  Blent with the murmuring pines,
Save where the sentry paced his rounds
  Along th' invading lines.

But in one lowly cottage home
  Were trouble and dismay ;
Two anxious watchers could not sleep
  For tidings heard that day ;

Brave James Secord, with troubled heart,
  And weary crippled frame,
That bore the scars of Queenston Heights,
  Back to his cottage came ;

For he had learned a dark design
  Fitzgibbon to surprise,
As with a handful of brave men
  At Beaver Dam he lies.

‘And Boerstler, with eight hundred men,
Is moving from the shore
To steal upon our outpost there,
Guarded by scarce two score !

‘Then, wiping out, as well he may,
That gallant little band,
The foe will sweep his onward way
O’er the defenceless land.

‘Then noble Brock had died in vain—
If but Fitzgibbon knew !’—
And the poor cripple’s heart is fain
To press the journey through.

But Laura, bending o’er her babes,
Said, smiling through her tears :
‘These are not times for brave men’s wives
To yield to craven fears.

‘*You* cannot go to warn our men,
Or slip the outposts through ;
But if perchance they let *me* pass,
This errand I will do.’

She soothed his anxious doubts and fears :
She knew the forest way ;
She put her trust in Him who hears
His children when they pray !

Soon as the rosy flush of dawn
Glowed through the purple air,
She rose to household tasks—and kissed
Her babes with whispered prayer.

To milk her grazing cow she went ;
The sentry at the lines
Forgot to watch, as both were lost
Amid the sheltering pines.

The rising sun's first golden rays
  Gleamed through the forest dim,
And through its leafy arches rang
  The birds' sweet morning hymn.

The fragrant odour of the pines,
  The carols gay and sweet,
Gave courage to the fluttering heart,
  And strength to faltering feet.

And on she pressed, with steadfast tread,
  Her solitary way,
O'er tangled brake and sodden swamp
  Through all the sultry day.

Though, for the morning songs of birds
  She heard the wolf's hoarse cry,
And saw the rattlesnake glide forth,
  As swift she hurried by.

Nor dark morass nor rushing stream
  Could balk the steadfast will,
Nor pleading voice of anxious friends
  Where stood St. David's Mill.

The British sentry heard her tale,
  And cheered her on her way ;
But bade her 'ware the Indian scouts
  Who in the covert lay.

Anon, as cracked a rotten bough
  Beneath her wary feet,
She heard their war-whoop through the gloom,
  Their steps advancing fleet ;

But quickly to the questioning chief
  She told her érrand grave

How she had walked the livelong day
  Fitzgibbon's men to save !

The redskin heard, and kindly gazed
  Upon the pale-faced squaw ;
Her faithful courage touched his heart,
  Her weary look he saw.

'Me go with you' was all he said,
  And through the forest gray
He led her safe to Beaver Dam,
  Where brave Fitzgibbon lay.

With throbbing heart she told her tale ;
  They heard with anxious heed,
Who knew how grave the crisis was.
  How urgent was the need !

Then there was riding far and near,
  And mustering to and fro
Of troops and Indians from the rear
  To meet the coming foe ;

And such the bold, determined stand
  Those few brave soldiers made—
So fiercely fought the Indian band
  From forest ambuscade,—

That Boerstler in the first surprise
  Surrendered in despair,
To force so small it scarce could serve
  To keep the prisoners there !

While the brave weary messenger
  In dreamless slumber lay,
And woke to find her gallant friends
  Were masters of the fray.

*   *   *   *   *

If e'er Canadian courage fail,
  Or loyalty grow cold,
Or nerveless grow Canadian hearts,
  Then be the story told—

How British gallantry and skill
  There played their noblest part,
Yet scarce had won if there had failed
  One woman's dauntless heart !

How Robin Hood Came to Be an Outlaw

Excerpt from Howard Pyle's The Merry Adventures of Robin Hood
(England)

IN MERRY ENGLAND in the time of old, when good King Henry the Second ruled the land, there lived within the green glades of Sherwood Forest, near Nottingham Town, a famous outlaw whose name was Robin Hood. No archer ever lived that could speed a gray goose shaft with such skill and cunning as his, nor were there ever such yeomen as the sevenscore merry men that roamed with him through the greenwood shades. Right merrily they dwelled within the depths of Sherwood Forest, suffering neither care nor want, but passing the time in merry games of archery or bouts of cudgel play, living upon the King's venison, washed down with draughts of ale of October brewing.

Not only Robin himself but all the band were outlaws and dwelled apart from other men, yet they were beloved by the country people round about, for no one ever came to jolly Robin for help in time of need and went away again with an empty fist.

And now I will tell how it came about that Robin Hood fell afoul of the law.

When Robin was a youth of eighteen, stout of sinew and bold of heart, the Sheriff of Nottingham proclaimed a shooting match and offered a prize of a butt of ale to whosoever should shoot the best shaft in Nottinghamshire. "Now," quoth Robin, "will I go too, for fain would I draw a string for the bright eyes of my lass and a butt of good October brewing." So up he got and took his good stout yew bow and a score or more of broad clothyard arrows, and started off from Locksley Town through Sherwood Forest to Nottingham.

It was at the dawn of day in the merry Maytime, when hedgerows are green and flowers bedeck the meadows; daisies pied and yellow cuckoo buds and fair primroses all along the briery hedges; when apple buds blossom and sweet birds sing, the lark at dawn of day, the throstle cock and cuckoo; when lads and lasses look upon each other with sweet thoughts; when busy housewives spread their linen to bleach upon the bright green grass. Sweet was the greenwood as he walked along its paths, and bright the green and rustling leaves, amid which the little birds sang with might and main: and blithely Robin whistled as he trudged along, thinking of Maid Marian and her bright eyes, for at such times a youth's thoughts are wont to turn pleasantly upon the lass that he loves the best.

As thus he walked along with a brisk step and a merry whistle, he came suddenly upon some foresters seated beneath a great oak tree. Fifteen there were in all, making themselves merry with feasting and drinking as they sat around a huge pasty, to which each man helped himself, thrusting his hands into the pie, and washing down that which they ate with great horns of ale which they drew all foaming from a barrel that stood nigh. Each man was clad in Lincoln green, and a fine show they made, seated upon the sward beneath that fair, spreading tree. Then one of them, with his mouth full, called out to Robin, "Hulloa, where goest thou, little lad, with thy one-penny bow and thy farthing shafts?"

Then Robin grew angry, for no stripling likes to be taunted with his green years.

"Now," quoth he, "my bow and eke mine arrows are as good as shine; and moreover, I go to the shooting match at Nottingham Town, which same has been proclaimed by our good Sheriff of Nottinghamshire; there I will shoot with other stout yeomen, for a prize has been offered of a fine butt of ale."

Then one who held a horn of ale in his hand said, "Ho! listen to the lad! Why, boy, thy mother's milk is yet scarce dry upon thy lips, and yet thou pratest of standing up with good stout men at Nottingham butts, thou who art scarce able to draw one string of a two-stone bow."

"I'll hold the best of you twenty marks," quoth bold Robin, "that I hit the clout at threescore rods, by the good help of Our Lady fair."

At this all laughed aloud, and one said, "Well boasted, thou fair infant, well boasted! And well thou knowest that no target is nigh to make good thy wager."

And another cried, "He will be taking ale with his milk next."

At this Robin grew right mad. "Hark ye," said he, "yonder, at the glade's end, I see a herd of deer, even more than threescore rods distant. I'll hold you twenty marks that, by leave of Our Lady, I cause the best hart among them to die."

"Now done!" cried he who had spoken first. "And here are twenty marks. I wager that thou causest no beast to die, with or without the aid of Our Lady."

Then Robin took his good yew bow in his hand, and placing the tip at his instep, he strung it right deftly; then he nocked a broad clothyard arrow and, raising the bow, drew the gray goose feather to his ear; the next moment the bowstring rang and the arrow sped down the glade as a sparrowhawk skims in a northern wind. High leaped the noblest hart of all the herd, only to fall dead, reddening the green path with his heart's blood.

"Ha!" cried Robin, "how likest thou that shot, good fellow? I wot the wager were mine, an it were three hundred pounds."

Then all the foresters were filled with rage, and he who had spoken the first and had lost the wager was more angry than all.

"Nay," cried he, "the wager is none of thine, and get thee gone, straightway, or, by all the saints of heaven, I'll baste thy sides until thou wilt ne'er be able to walk again." "Knowest thou not," said another, "that thou hast killed the King's deer, and, by the laws of our gracious lord and sovereign King Harry, thine ears should be shaven close to thy head?"

"Catch him!" cried a third.

"Nay," said a fourth, "let him e'en go because of his tender years."

Never a word said Robin Hood, but he looked at the foresters with a grim face; then, turning on his heel, strode away from them down the forest glade. But his heart was bitterly angry, for his blood was hot and youthful and prone to boil.

Now, well would it have been for him who had first spoken had he left Robin Hood alone; but his anger was hot, both because the youth had gotten the better of him and because of the deep draughts of ale that he had been quaffing. So, of a sudden, without any warning, he sprang to his feet, and seized upon his bow and fitted it to a shaft. "Ay," cried he, "and I'll hurry thee anon." And he sent the arrow whistling after Robin.

It was well for Robin Hood that that same forester's head was spinning with ale, or else he would never have taken another step. As it was, the arrow whistled within three inches of his head. Then he turned around and quickly drew his own bow, and sent an arrow back in return.

"Ye said I was no archer," cried he aloud, "but say so now again!"

The shaft flew straight; the archer fell forward with a cry, and lay on his face upon the ground, his arrows rattling about him from out of his quiver, the gray goose shaft wet with his; heart's blood. Then, before the others could gather their wits about them, Robin Hood was gone into the depths of the greenwood. Some started after him, but not with much heart, for each feared to suffer the death of his fellow; so presently they all came and lifted the dead man up and bore him away to Nottingham Town.

Meanwhile Robin Hood ran through the greenwood. Gone was all the joy and brightness from everything, for his heart was sick within him, and it was borne in upon his soul that he had slain a man.

"Alas!" cried he, "thou hast found me an archer that will make thy wife to wring! I would that thou hadst ne'er said one word to me, or that I had never passed thy way, or e'en that my right forefinger had been stricken off ere that this had happened! In haste I smote, but grieve I sore at leisure!"

And then, even in his trouble, he remembered the old saw that "What is done is done; and the egg cracked cannot be cured."

And so he came to dwell in the greenwood that was to be his home for many a year to come, never again to see the happy days with the lads and lasses of sweet Locksley Town; for he was outlawed, not only because he had killed a man, but also because he had poached upon the King's deer, and two hundred pounds were set upon his head, as a reward for whoever would bring him to the court of the King.

Now the Sheriff of Nottingham swore that he himself would bring this knave Robin Hood to justice, and for two reasons: first, because he wanted the two hundred pounds, and next, because the forester that Robin Hood had killed was of kin to him.

But Robin Hood lay hidden in Sherwood Forest for one year, and in that time there gathered around him many others like himself, cast out from other folk for this cause and for that. Some had shot deer in hungry wintertime, when they could get no other food, and had been seen in the act by the foresters, but had escaped, thus saving their ears; some had been turned out of their inheritance, that their farms might be added to the King's lands in Sherwood Forest; some had been despoiled by a great baron or a rich abbot or a powerful esquire—all, for one cause or another, had come to Sherwood to escape wrong and oppression.

So, in all that year, fivescore or more good stout yeomen gathered about Robin Hood, and chose him to be their leader and chief. Then they vowed that even as they themselves had been despoiled they would despoil their oppressors, whether baron, abbot, knight, or squire, and that from each they would take that which had been wrung from the poor by unjust taxes, or land rents, or in wrongful fines. But to the poor folk they would give a helping hand in need and trouble, and would return to them that which had been unjustly taken from them. Besides this, they swore never to harm a child nor to wrong a woman, be she maid, wife, or widow; so that, after a while, when the people began to find that no harm was meant to them, but that money or food came in time of want to many a poor family, they came to praise Robin and his merry men, and to tell many tales of him and of his doings in Sherwood Forest, for they felt him to be one of themselves.

Up rose Robin Hood one merry morn when all the birds were singing blithely among the leaves, and up rose all his merry men, each fellow washing his head and hands in the cold brown brook that leaped laughing from stone to stone. Then said Robin, "For fourteen days have we seen no sport, so now I will go abroad to seek adventures forthwith. But tarry ye, my merry men all, here in the greenwood; only see that ye mind well my call. Three blasts upon the bugle horn I will blow in my hour of need; then come quickly, for I shall want your aid."

So saying, he strode away through the leafy forest glades until he had come to the verge of Sherwood. There he wandered for a long time, through highway and byway, through dingly dell and forest skirts. Now he met a fair buxom lass in a shady lane, and each gave the other a merry word and passed their way; now he saw a fair lady upon an ambling pad, to whom he doffed his cap, and who bowed sedately in return to the fair youth; now he saw a fat monk on a pannier-laden ass; now a gallant knight, with spear and shield and armor that flashed brightly in the sunlight; now a page clad in crimson; and now a stout burgher from good Nottingham Town, pacing along with serious footsteps; all these sights he saw, but adventure found he none. At last he took a road by the forest skirts, a bypath that dipped toward a broad, pebbly stream spanned by a narrow bridge made of a log of wood. As he drew nigh this bridge he saw a tall stranger coming from the other side. Thereupon Robin quickened his pace, as did the stranger likewise, each thinking to cross first.

"Now stand thou back," quoth Robin, "and let the better man cross first."

"Nay," answered the stranger, "then stand back shine own self, for the better man, I wet, am I."

"That will we presently see," quoth Robin, "and meanwhile stand thou where thou art, or else, by the bright brow of Saint AElfrida, I will show thee right good Nottingham play with a clothyard shaft betwixt thy ribs."

"Now," quoth the stranger, "I will tan thy hide till it be as many colors as a beggar's cloak, if thou darest so much as touch a string of that same bow that thou holdest in thy hands."

"Thou pratest like an ass," said Robin, "for I could send this shaft clean through thy proud heart before a curtal friar could say grace over a roast goose at Michaelmastide."

"And thou pratest like a coward," answered the stranger, "for thou standest there with a good yew bow to shoot at my heart, while I have nought in my hand but a plain blackthorn staff wherewith to meet thee."

"Now," quoth Robin, "by the faith of my heart, never have I had a coward's name in all my life before. I will lay by my trusty bow and eke my arrows, and if thou darest abide my coming, I will go and cut a cudgel to test thy manhood withal."

"Ay, marry, that will I abide thy coming, and joyously, too," quoth the stranger; whereupon he leaned sturdily upon his staff to await Robin.

Then Robin Hood stepped quickly to the coverside and cut a good staff of ground oak, straight, without new, and six feet in length, and came back trimming away the tender stems from it, while the stranger waited for him, leaning upon his staff, and whistling as he gazed round about. Robin observed him furtively as he trimmed his staff, measuring him from top to toe from out the corner of his eye, and thought that he had never seen a lustier or a stouter man. Tall was Robin, but taller was the stranger by a head and a neck, for he was seven feet in height. Broad was Robin across the shoulders, but broader was the stranger by twice the breadth of a palm, while he measured at least an ell around the waist.

"Nevertheless," said Robin to himself, "I will baste thy hide right merrily, my good fellow;" then, aloud, "Lo, here is my good staff, lusty and tough. Now wait my coming, an thou darest, and meet me an thou fearest not. Then we will fight until one or the other of us tumble into the stream by dint of blows."

"Marry, that meeteth my whole heart!" cried the stranger, twirling his staff above his head, betwixt his fingers and thumb, until it whistled again.

Never did the Knights of Arthur's Round Table meet in a stouter fight than did these two. In a moment Robin stepped quickly upon the bridge where the stranger stood; first he made a feint, and then delivered a blow at the stranger's head that, had it met its mark, would have tumbled him speedily into the water. But the stranger turned the blow right deftly and in return gave one as stout, which Robin also turned as the stranger had done. So they stood, each in his place, neither moving a finger's-breadth back, for one good hour, and many blows were given and received by each in that time, till here and there were sore bones and bumps, yet neither thought of crying "Enough," nor seemed likely to fall from off the bridge. Now and then they stopped to rest, and each thought that he never had seen in all his life before such a hand at quarterstaff. At last Robin gave the stranger a blow upon the ribs that made his jacket smoke like a damp straw thatch in the sun. So shrewd was the stroke that the stranger came within a hair's-breadth of falling off the bridge, but he regained himself right quickly and, by a dexterous blow, gave Robin a crack on the crown that caused the blood to flow. Then Robin grew mad with anger and smote with all his might at the other. But the stranger warded the blow and once again thwacked Robin, and this time so fairly that he fell heels over head into the water, as the queen pin falls in a game of bowls.

"And where art thou now, my good lad?" shouted the stranger, roaring with laughter.

"Oh, in the flood and floating adown with the tide," cried Robin, nor could he forbear laughing himself at his sorry plight. Then, gaining his feet, he waded to the bank, the little fish speeding hither and thither, all frightened at his splashing.

"Give me thy hand," cried he, when he had reached the bank. "I must needs own thou art a brave and a sturdy soul and, withal, a good stout stroke with the cudgels. By this and by that, my head hummeth like to a hive of bees on a hot June day."

Then he clapped his horn to his lips and winded a blast that went echoing sweetly down the forest paths. "Ay, marry," quoth he again, "thou art a tall lad, and eke a brave one, for ne'er, I bow, is there a man betwixt here and Canterbury Town could do the like to me that thou hast done."

"And thou," quoth the stranger, laughing, "takest thy cudgeling like a brave heart and a stout yeoman."

But now the distant twigs and branches rustled with the coming of men, and suddenly a score or two of good stout yeomen, all clad in Lincoln green, burst from out the covert, with merry Will Stutely at their head.

"Good master," cried Will, "how is this? Truly thou art all wet from head to foot, and that to the very skin."

"Why, marry," answered jolly Robin, "yon stout fellow hath tumbled me neck and crop into the water and hath given me a drubbing beside."

"Then shall he not go without a ducking and eke a drubbing himself!" cried Will Stutely. "Have at him, lads!"

Then Will and a score of yeomen leaped upon the stranger, but though they sprang quickly they found him ready and felt him strike right and left with his stout staff, so that, though he went down with press of numbers, some of them rubbed cracked crowns before he was overcome.

"Nay, forbear!" cried Robin, laughing until his sore sides ached again. "He is a right good man and true, and no harm shall befall him. Now hark ye, good youth, wilt thou stay with me and be one of my band? Three suits of Lincoln green shalt thou have each year, beside forty marks in fee, and share with us whatsoever good shall befall us. Thou shalt eat sweet venison and quaff the stoutest ale, and mine own good right-hand man shalt thou be, for never did I see such a cudgel player in all my life before. Speak! Wilt thou be one of my good merry men?"

"That know I not," quoth the stranger surlily, for he was angry at being so tumbled about. "If ye handle yew bow and apple shaft no better than ye do oaken cudgel, I wot ye are not fit to be called yeomen in my country; but if there be any man here that can shoot a better shaft than I, then will I bethink me of joining with you."

"Now by my faith," said Robin, "thou art a right saucy varlet, sirrah; yet I will stoop to thee as I never stooped to man before. Good Stutely, cut thou a fair white piece of bark four fingers in breadth, and set it fourscore yards distant on yonder oak. Now, stranger, hit that fairly with a gray goose shaft and call thyself an archer."

"Ay, marry, that will I," answered he. "Give me a good stout bow and a fair broad arrow, and if I hit it not, strip me and beat me blue with bowstrings."

Then he chose the stoutest bow among them all, next to Robin's own, and a straight gray goose shaft, well-feathered and smooth, and stepping to the mark—while all the band, sitting or lying upon the greensward, watched to see him shoot—he drew the arrow to his cheek and loosed the shaft right deftly, sending it so straight down the path that it clove the mark in the very center. "Aha!" cried he, "mend thou that if thou canst;" while even the yeomen clapped their hands at so fair a shot.

"That is a keen shot indeed," quoth Robin. "Mend it I cannot, but mar it I may, perhaps."

Then taking up his own good stout bow and nocking an arrow with care, he shot with his very greatest skill. Straight flew the arrow, and so true that it lit fairly upon the stranger's shaft and split it into splinters. Then all the yeomen leaped to their feet and shouted for joy that their master had shot so well.

"Now by the lusty yew bow of good Saint Withold," cried the stranger, "that is a shot indeed, and never saw I the like in all my life before! Now truly will I be thy man henceforth and for aye. Good Adam Bell(1) was a fair shot, but never shot he so!"

(1) Adam Bell, Clym o' the Clough, and William of Cloudesly were three noted north-country bowmen whose names have been celebrated in many ballads of the olden time.

"Then have I gained a right good man this day," quoth jolly Robin. "What name goest thou by, good fellow?"

"Men call me John Little whence I came," answered the stranger.

Then Will Stutely, who loved a good jest, spoke up. "Nay, fair little stranger," said he, "I like not thy name and fain would I have it otherwise. Little art thou indeed, and small of bone and sinew, therefore shalt thou be christened Little John, and I will be thy godfather."

Then Robin Hood and all his band laughed aloud until the stranger began to grow angry.

"An thou make a jest of me," quoth he to Will Stutely, "thou wilt have sore bones and little pay, and that in short season."

"Nay, good friend," said Robin Hood, "bottle thine anger, for the name fitteth thee well. Little John shall thou be called henceforth, and Little John shall it be. So come, my merry men, we will prepare a christening feast for this fair infant."

So turning their backs upon the stream, they plunged into the forest once more, through which they traced their steps till they reached the spot where they dwelled in the depths of the woodland. There had they built huts of bark and branches of trees, and made couches of sweet rushes spread over with skins of fallow deer. Here stood a great oak tree with branches spreading broadly around, beneath which was a seat of green moss where Robin Hood was wont to sit at feast and at merrymaking with his stout men about him. Here they found the rest of the band, some of whom had come in with a brace of fat does. Then they all built great fires and after a time roasted the does and broached a barrel of humming ale. Then when the

feast was ready they all sat down, but Robin placed Little John at his right hand, for he was henceforth to be the second in the band.
Then when the feast was done Will Stutely spoke up. "It is now time, I ween, to christen our bonny babe, is it not so, merry boys?" And "Aye! Aye!" cried all, laughing till the woods echoed with their mirth.
"Then seven sponsors shall we have," quoth Will Stutely, and hunting among all the band, he chose the seven stoutest men of them all.
"Now by Saint Dunstan," cried Little John, springing to his feet, "more than one of you shall rue it an you lay finger upon me."
But without a word they all ran upon him at once, seizing him by his legs and arms and holding him tightly in spite of his struggles, and they bore him forth while all stood around to see the sport. Then one came forward who had been chosen to play the priest because he had a bald crown, and in his hand he carried a brimming pot of ale. "Now, who bringeth this babe?" asked he right soberly.
"That do I," answered Will Stutely.
"And what name callest thou him?"
"Little John call I him."
"Now Little John," quoth the mock priest, "thou hast not lived heretofore, but only got thee along through the world, but henceforth thou wilt live indeed. When thou livedst not thou wast called John Little, but now that thou dost live indeed, Little John shalt thou be called, so christen I thee." And at these last words he emptied the pot of ale upon Little John's head. Then all shouted with laughter as they saw the good brown ale stream over Little John's beard and trickle from his nose and chin, while his eyes blinked with the smart of it. At first he was of a mind to be angry but found he could not, because the others were so merry; so he, too, laughed with the rest. Then Robin took this sweet, pretty babe, clothed him all anew from top to toe in Lincoln green, and gave him a good stout bow, and so made him a member of the merry band.
And thus it was that Robin Hood became outlawed; thus a band of merry companions gathered about him, and thus he gained his right-hand man, Little John; and so the prologue ends.

Maewyn and the Clover

(Ireland)

He opened his eyes when he felt a strange rocking feeling. The room he was in was very dark. "Maewyn Succat, Get Up!" shouts a voice from above. Maewyn stood up and staggered as he made his way to a set of stairs. Grabbing a length of rope, he pulled his way up the steps. As he immerged from the dark hole the brightness of the sun caused him to squint. Eyes squeezed shut he notices a damp breeze and a strange sound. Once his eyes were open, he came to realize that he was not on land but on a ship. Someone grabbed his hand and placed a mop into it. Maewyn looked up and saw a dirty, drab pirate looking straight at him. "Mop, boy!" he snarled at him.

Maewyn spent the entire day mopping and scrubbing. Then off in the distance he saw something. "Land Ho!" a pirate called from above. Once on land, 16-year-old Maewyn's hands were tied and then he was sold as a slave. He spent the next six years in prison and tending to sheep and pigs. He spent much of his spare time on his knees in prayer and hope was all he had.

A dream so vivid, Maewyn could see himself escaping his captors and stowing away on a boat to Britain. Maewyn took this as a sign and did just as he saw in his dream. Once at sea all he could think about was his family. Curled up in a ball, he stayed hidden until he heard the calls of hundreds of seagulls. With a peak from under his covering he could see that the boat was docked and he made his quick escape. "Hey! Who are you?" Maewyn heard a man scream as he ran down the gangplank.

With soar feet, Maewyn journeyed many days until he felt the warm embrace of his mother. Time went by and Maewyn had another vision. He saw the people of Ireland asking him to come back and teach them about God. Even though Maewyn was now an adult he did not feel prepared to follow such a large calling. He prayed and pondered fervently and he felt his next step was to study in a French monastery. He had made the decision to dedicate his life to teaching God's word. Reading, studying, and praying led to a special day. Dressed in gilded robes, he walked across the cold grey stone floor and knelt down to complete his consecration as bishop. The Pope has given his consent for Maewyn, now Patrick, to travel to Ireland to share God's word.

Patrick disembarked the boat and knelt down to run his hands through the thick carpet of clover. He picked a single clover and placed it on his lips. With a gentle kiss to the three delicate leaves, he stood up and asked where he could find the High King. With his gentle nature and with much respect, he gained permission from King Lóegaire to teach Christianity.

Patrick wandered all about pagan Ireland. Unfortunately, not all of the inhabitants wanted to hear Patrick's message. Chieftains would imprison him but he would always win his freedom back. Druids were also a great challenge. Once on the hill of Tara, a significant religious Pagan site, Patrick struggled with explaining the existence of God. In frustration he knelt down to brush his hand through the clover and as he did he watched their little heads spring back up. He gently plucked one from the ground and while looking at this he had an epiphany. With this little clover in his hand, he explained the Father, the Son and the Holy Ghost.

After 20 years of Patrick took it upon himself to spread Christianity throughout Ireland, he was able to establish churches, monasteries, schools and baptize those who became believers in Christ.

Now you may be asking yourself, did it really happen that way? Did a little green clover convert the Pagans of Ireland? Well, we will never know. But what we do know is that Christianity still flourishes to this day and we have Saint Patrick to thank for it.

The Brave Scot

(Scotland)

William Wallace is known throughout Scotland, and the world, for standing up to the English to claim freedom for his country. The stories are larger than life and full of battle like the one at Sterling Bridge. Unfortunately, William Wallace lost his life while leading his countrymen to freedom. But to this day, Scots embrace his zeal and pride for their country. This poem

The Summary History of Sir William Wallace
By William Topaz McGonagall

Sir William Wallace of Ellerslie,
I'm told he went to the High School in Dundee,
For to learn to read and write,
And after that he learned to fight,
While at the High School in Dundee,
The Provost's son with him disagree,
Because Wallace did wear a dirk,
He despised him like an ignorant stirk,
Which with indignation he keenly felt,
And told him it would become him better in his belt.

Then Wallace's blood began to boil,
Just like the serpent in its coil,
Before it leaps upon its prey;
And unto him he thus did say:
'Proud saucy cur, come cease your prate,
for no longer shall I wait,
For to hear you insult me,
At the High School in Dundee;
For such insolence makes my heart to smart,
And I'll plunge my dagger in you heart,'

Then his heart's blood did quickly flow,
And poor Wallace did not know where to go;
And he stood by him until dead.
Then far from him he quickly fled,
Lamenting greatly the deed he had done,

the murdering of the Provost's son.

The scene shifts to where he was fishing on day,
Where three English soldiers met him by the way,
And they asked him fo give them some fish,
And from them they would make a delicious dish,
then Wallace gave them share of his fish,
For to satisfy their wish;
But they seemed dissatisfied with the share they got,
So they were resolved to have all the lot.

Then Wallace he thought it was time to look out,
When they were resolved to have all his trout;
So he swung his fishing-rod with great force round his head ,
And struck on of them a blow that killed him dead;
So he instantly seized the fallen man's sword,
And the other two fled without uttering a word.

Sir William Wallace of Ellerslie,
You were a warrior of great renown,
And might have worn Scotland's crown;
Had it not been for Monteith, the base traitor knave,
That brought you to a premature grave;
Yes! you were sold for English gold,
And brought like asheep from the fold,
To die upon a shameful scaffold high,
Amidst the derisive shouts of your enemies standing by.

But you met your doom like a warrior bold,
Bidding defiance to them that had you sold,
And bared your neck for the headsman's stroke;
And cried, 'Marion, dear, my heart is broke;
My lovely dear I come to thee,
Oh! I am longing thee to see!'
But the headsman was as stolid as the rock,
And the axe fell heavily on the block,
And the scaffold did shake with the terrible shock,
As the body of noble Wallace fell,
Who had fought for Scotland so well.

The Crowned Prince of Wales

(Wales)

I have but a short time to tell of my tale. I am the mighty Owain Glyndwr. My father descends from the Princes of Powrys and my mother is of the Deheubarth family. We lived comfortably in Sycharth house of Glyndyfrdwy near the border of Wales and England. We are a family of influence. I had land, servants and enjoyed entertaining. Poets are my favorite form of entertainment and were a great excuse to have a party. I was happy in my grand house. I had a beautiful wife and 11 children; 6 strong (cryf) boys and 5 lovely (hyfryd) girls. One would say that my life as perfect but not everything was as wonderful as they seemed.

A detestable Marcher Lord of England placed claim upon my land. I paid my taxes and was a good citizen, but this was to much. King Henry IV is a greedy king who wants to rule all of Wales. The Marcher Lord Reginald Grey knew that the king would side with him and when I went before the king my plea was pushed aside and I lost my home and land. My way of life was stripped away. Of course, I was not the first to be wronged by the king.

I met with many other Welsh men and rallied them to go to battle with me to fight for our land and freedom. I wanted to see a Welsh flag flying atop every Welsh castle. A flame of excitement and pride grew in their hearts as they began to chant "Owain Glyndwr, the Prince of Wales. Owain Glyndwr, the Prince of Wales." So I took to it and formed an army and where do you think we went first? Ruthin, where Lord Reginald Grey lived. We approached Rithin during a fair, for the soldiers were engaging in frivolity, so a battle was the last thing they would be expecting.

We burnt down the town, and collected all the gold, riches, and horses we could get our hands on. With this grand success the Welsh were hungry for more and we went after the other towns ruled by the Marcher Lords. We felt invincible. But in Shrewsbury, one of our Welsh brothers, Goronwy ap Tudur, were captured and what they did was unthinkable. I'll just say that King Henry IV used his body as a symbol against rebellion in more than one city.

I, we, could not let the king intimidate us. With a heavy heart, my Welsh brothers and I struck back with a vengeance. In June 1401, we advanced to Northern Wales and came upon Ceredigion and Powys where we engaged the enemy. We were outnumbered 2 to1, the English had horses and us on foot, but the odds did not squelch our fury. At the Pumlumon Mountains, on our own familiar terrain, we won the battle of Hyddgen using our keen Welsh archery skills.

The news of our victory spread across the land and Welshmen came from near and far to join me in claiming our land. We had our own culture and language; the people were ready to fight for it. Our success had infuriated the King, and a new set of oppressive laws were put into place. We were no longer allowed to own weapons or castles. We were not allowed to assemble for meetings unless an English Lord was present. We could not marry an English citizen and we could not hold important possessions of employment. Needless to say, I ignored these new laws.

For a year, my men and I pushed on and we won the battle of Bryn Glas. We had heavy casualties, but following this battle we were able to capture many castles to include Kidwelly and Harlech. By 1403 I ruled Wales. The Welsh Flag was dominating the Welsh castles. Owain Glyndwr had the King of England shaking in his boots. I created the first Welsh Parliament in Machynlleth. I was proud and lead a precession into the town and again the people shouted "Owain Glyndwr, the Prince of Wales. Owain Glyndwr, the Prince of Wales." It seemed as if we had succeeded, we were an independent country.

Then in 1405 we engaged in the battle of Pwll Meltn in the South of Wales and my son Gruffydd, along with 1500 others, lost their lives. This shook the Welsh and they started to question my leadership. With or newly weakened zeal the English moved in and started to reclaim our castles. It looked as though all was lost. Then I received a letter from Charles VI, the king of France. He was willing to help Wales. Unfortunately, even with support of the French, the English continued to rip through my motherland and claim the land as their own. It's the winter 1407 now and I had truly lost everything.

My army was gone and I no longer have my home, Harlech Castle. King Henry IV had my wife and children arrested and imprisoned and I haven't seen them since. Now I am dressed like a shepard and wander about the country like a vagabond. I can see Sycharth from where I stand. King Henry IV has burned my first home to the ground and I have nowhere to go. I hope you will tell my tale to others for I fear that I must wander in hiding for the rest of my days.

Planning a Robert Burns Night

What is a Burns Night?

A Burns Night is an evening of honoring the writings and life of Robert Burns. He is a Scottish poet and song writer. The celebration is held on or near his birthday which is January 25th. A Burns Night, also referred to as a Burns Supper, is meant to be a night of fun and humor. It can be as casual or formal as you would like. At the same time, there are certain things that are typically expected if you are wanting to create an authentic Scottish experience. To help with your planning you can download a free printable at www.littlerabbittrails.com/robertburns

When planning your Burns Night, you are going to need the following.

- Haggis & side dishes (and other optional dishes)
- Scottish music
- A drink for toasting
- Poetry of Robert Burns
- Tartan for decorating

Don't worry, I am going to give you all the information you will need. You can also get the Burns Night printable at **www.littlerabbittrails.com/robertburns** with the required poetry & song as well as menu, games, invitations, decorations, and more to get you started. You can also find all the Recipes starting on page 362.

The Haggis

Besides the poetry, food is the thing that everyone will be coming for. The first thing you will want to plan is haggis. Now haggis is a dish from the old world that is still enjoyed in Scotland today. Unfortunately, the traditional dish cannot be found in the United States because sheep lung, and all other forms of lung, have been banned for use in food since 1971. So, this part will be easier in a country where you can go to a store and pick up a haggis. For those in countries you cannot just purchase it, you can make dish that is as close as you can get. You will be able to find a recipe for both traditional and Mock Haggis at the end of this chapter.

A Haggis is a combination of sheep trimmings, onion, suet, spices and oats all cooked in a sheep's stomach. Don't worry, if you have to make it yourself you will not have to go out looking for a sheep's stomach. Think of it as a fat sausage with a slight grainier texture. This was my experience when I had it in Scotland. The Scottish Grocer (**www.scottishgrocer.com**) sells everything from haggis casings to cans of haggis to cooked haggis and Burns supper kids. If cooking the Scottish dish isn't your cup of tea, you could mail order a haggis from Scottish Gourmet USA. The Scottish Grocer sells food safe casings if you want to cook your own haggis more traditionally. Do I have to serve Haggis? Besides it being a traditional Scottish dish, Robert Burns wrote an entire poem dedicated to it. So, do you know how you are going to get your haggis?

Now, let's move onto serving the full meal. Now remember you can do all or part of this meal. I am sharing with you what a full Burns Night would be. If you are not up to the full meal then do the parts you would like (not skimping on the haggis of course). But this may also be a fun time to do an etiquette dinner and go over the manners expected at a multi course dinner with your children or group.

The Soup

The first course of the meal will be a soup. Good soups to choose from would be cock-a-leekie soup or a Scotch Broth. The cock-a-leekie soup is a cock-a-leekie soup is made with chicken, onion, rice, and herbs. Scotch Broth is made with lamb shanks, onion, barley, and a collection of vegetables to include turnip or rutabaga, cabbage, and potato to name a few.

The Sides

Now that you have chosen your soup let's move onto the sides. there are two sides that any good Scott would serve with their haggis and that would be neeps and tatties. Don't worry, that isn't anything super strange. Neeps are mashed turnips or swede and tatties are mashed potatoes. They can be served side by side or you can get fancy and do a stack with haggis, then neeps and topped with tatties all layered in a mold. You will also want to serve a green veggie like green beans with your meal.

The Sauce

Over the years the addition of a whisky sauce has been added to the haggis meal. This is relatively modern. In the past whisky would have not been something the common person would always have on hand. But a sauce will for sure add a nice depth to the dish. If you are not one who has alcohol in your house, like me, than you can still make the sauce and replace the whisky with white grape juice or you could just omit it.

The Dessert

Moving on to the dessert. This does not need to be fancy. It could be as simple as picking up some shortbread cookies or go all out and make a clootie dumpling. If you opt for the dumpling, make sure you plan out your time because this Scottish treat will take about 5 hours to make.

The Drink

Next you will need to choose your drink for toasting. Again, traditionally this would be done with scotch but it is your house and you can choose what you would want to use. Maybe juice is a treat in your house. Or you can pick up some sparkling apple cider to accompany your meal. Make it special for your family or group.

The Celebration Begins

Remember this is a celebration and meant to be fun, not stuffy and stiff. Your night will be filled with food, drinking, laughter, good company, poetry and the sound of bagpipes…that's right, BAGPIPES! How could one have a Scottish themed event and think that bagpipes would not be involved. It would just be unheard of.

Now if you happen to be lucky and know someone who plays the bagpipes you can have the person play the bagpipes as your guests arrive. Your guests will not be able to help but smile. The next best alternative will be play recorded music. On Spotify, Amazon Music and other music streaming services you will find great pipe play lists to include Bagpipes of Scotland. You can also find great folk music to play white poetry isn't being read by searching "Burns Night" music or Robert Burns. Music is always a welcome addition to any gathering of friends. And don't forget to play his most popular song Auld Lang Syne.

Another way you could kick off the night is start with some traditional folk music. Once your guests have all arrived and it is time for the festivities to begin, you could turn on some fun and upbeat pipe music to get everyone's attention.

The Chairman's Welcome
Typically, the host will welcome all of their guests and share why they love Robert Burns so much. If this is your first time holding a Burns Night you could also share your excitement for trying something new and the opportunity to eat and share poetry together. Of course, the host could also ask someone else to do the welcome. Maybe even one of your children if you're are doing this with a co-op or your poetry tea time group.

The Selkirk Grace
This is a grace that Burns himself gave at the Earl of Selkirk on Saint Mary's Island. Depending on your religious beliefs you can either read it as the prayer for the meal or you can read it more as an informative prayer before or after you pray over the food.

The Selkirk Grace

Some Folk hae meat that canna eat,
And some can eat that want it;
But we hae meat, and we can eat,
So let the Lord be Thanket!

<u>*In Simple English*</u>
The Selkirk Grace

Some have meat and cannot eat,
Some cannot eat that want it;
But we have meat and we can eat,
So let the Lord be thankit.

Pipping in the Haggis

The Haggis is the center feature of the night, besides Burns of course. If you have a piper, he/she will lead a procession into the room followed by a person carrying the haggis and another person holding the toasting drink you have chosen. If you don't have the piper just rock your Bluetooth speaker. The most recognized song is *Scotland the Brave* but other songs can be used. It is common for the guests to clap or tap their feet to the beat of the bagpipe song. The haggis can be paraded around for all to see before bringing it to its place. The haggis will be placed at the head of dining table or on its own table. It should be someplace where everyone will be able to see the performance of Address to the Haggis. Glasses will be poured to be prepared for the next part.

The Address to the Haggis

Once your haggis has joined you at the table that is when a guest will perform *To a Haggis*. This person needs to be chosen well ahead of time and be an outgoing and humorous individual. This performance should be entertaining and lively. Look for others performing it online to get a feel for how it should be presented. Besides the haggis you will need a knife for the performer. At the end of the poem the performer will raise their glass and make a toast to the haggis.

The Toasting

Toasting is a big part of the Burns Night. As the host, you will get to decide when the toasting will take place. You have a few options. You can do it before you eat but after the address to the haggis and get the majority of the formality over. You could have a different toast between each meal to spread out the fun and break up the meal. Another option is to save it for after the meal, especially if you want to encourage people to stay for a while after the meal for dancing and singing.

I think my personal favorite would be between courses. This would make sure you squeeze in as much fun as you can throughout the meal and prevents from too many guests sneaking out at the end before you have fad your fun.

Below are the customary toasts that will happen during your Burns Supper.

The Immortal Memory Toast
Either the chairman (host), or a designated person, will give a toast to Robert Burns and his art. If you don't happen to have a burning love for the Scottish bard, you could even do a short bio to introduce your guests to the legacy he created. You could also share a favorite poem. Maybe a poem that has inspired you or that your guests may relate to. Whatever you choose to do make sure it emphasizes that he is the reason you are gathering and keep it to a length that will not bore your guests. At the end of the toast everyone is to stand and dink to Burns the Scottish Bard. You could say something like "Now let us all stand and shout out our praises to the bard of Scotland, Hear, Hear!"

The Toast to the Lassies
This is a toast that can lean towards being humorous. This is a chance to lighten up the party again. Burns admired woman and the toast to the lassies is meant to either shower compliment upon the ladies at the table or for mild comical jabs. Now it's not meant to be a full-on roast but meant to be kept light hearted and fun. You don't want to hurt someone's feelings during the party. If this fells to risk to you, then pick some lines of one of Burns' love poems, like "A Fond Kiss" and dedicate them to the ladies at the table. This toast should be done by a man (or a boy if it's a homeschooling group).

The Toast to the Ladies
Once the toast to the lassies is over a girl/woman can respond with a toast to the ladies and it too can be either romantic or comical. The purpose of the toasts to the lassie and ladies are meant to liven things up and get people laughing.

The Works by Burns
With this you can either take turns reading his poems or you can have people perform a song of his. To make sure your event is enjoyable you may want to ask each of your guests, or couples, to bring a poem to read to everyone. This way everyone feels included and you don't have to dictate everything. But please keep in mind that some people really do not like performing so don't make it a requirement to perform. An alternative would be to have a few small books full of his poetry and to pass them around the table and let everyone read one poem. Suggested poems are included in the printable.

Auld Lang Syne
You will end the evening with singing Robert Burns' most famous song Auld Lang Syne. Not everyone knows all of the words to the song so make sure to print out the words and you can even make it themed to match your Burns Night. A printable version of the song is available in the free printable.

Inviting Your Guests

Choosing the Dress Attire

When planning any event, you must choose what the attire will be. You will want to encourage people to wear a tartan. A tartan is plaid cloth that is related to or represents Scottish clans. Even if there is no Scottish heritage within your group tartans will add a festive feel for your night. You will also need to choose if it will be casual with shirt and jeans or a fancy black tie event. With the uniqueness of this night in areas that don't traditionally celebrates Burns Night you will want to also describe what the expected attire would intel. Casual, Semi-Dress, black tie or any in-between.

When choosing what tartan to wear, you have a few options.

- You can learn about your own heritage and wear your own tartan. Try visiting https://clan.com/families to see if your family has a tartan. If not, it will even share some more popular tartans.
- Woman can choose to wear the same tartan as their date or wear their own family tartan to represent their own heritage.
- If you don't have any Scottish heritage then you can have fun with it. Maybe even look up the background of different tartans or just choose one you like.

Casual: Anything with tartan or Scottish accessories. For men that could be a tartan patterned shirt, tie, socks or hat. For woman that could be a skirt, shirt, scarf, tartan sash held in place with a Celtic pin, hair accessories, purse…for both man and woman anything can go. Another option would be Scottish heritage pins and clips.

Kilt attire (Semi-Dress or Business Casual): You can encourage people to wear a kilt or something that represents a kilt. Kilts are pricy and people will not be buying one on a whim. But guests may be able to rent kilts from a costume shop. Or they could purchase some cotton tartan cloth and fashion their own mock kilt. Since the night is during winter another option would be a kilt with a tweed jacket and/or vest along with a kilt.

A common accessory with any kilt (Casual or formal) is a sporran. This has been the kilts pocket since the time of the medieval highlands. This was used to hold ammunition and rations. But today it can hold your wallet and keys and possibly a flask. The sporran can be anywhere from plain leather to a much more decorative with fur and metal studs.

Black Tie/ Formal Highland Dress: If you are thinking of going all out, then people will need to be looking into renting a full formal tux. Below you will find Kilt rental/hire shops that will mail your kilt rental directly to your door. For woman

Discover Your Tartan

Everyone's Tartan

The tartan for everyone is names Scotland Forever tartan is a newer tartan but specifically design to be worn by anyone. It is named after the infamous battle cry at waterloo "Scotland Forever." If you love purple, you will love this tartan.

For Australia

Most tartans have been designed for group or organizations. Some are inspired by Australia itself.
https://www.tartanregister.gov.uk/qResults?searchString=australia

For Scotland

Being the originator of the tartan, you will find tartans for many surnames. Keep in mind that
https://clan.com/families

For Wales

Welsh tartans are a very new thing. The first registered Welsh tartan was in 2000. You can try searching your name at the link below and see if there is a tartan for your welsh name.
https://www.welsh-tartan.com/tartan-finder

Tartans by World Districts (US, Africa, Asia, South America…)

Discover tartans that have been designed for different parts of the world. Tartans for parts of South America, No Scottish history required.
https://www.scotclans.com/scottish-clans/tartan-pattern-book/district-tartans/

Does it Really Matter?

When it comes down to it, you can wear any tartan that fits your fancy. There is no unwritten rule that forbids you from wearing another family or clan tartan. As a matter of fact, wearing the tartan of another family is a sign of respect. So, head out to your local mall and see how many different tartans you can find. Maybe one will catch your eye.

Kilt Rental Companies

USA: *Kilt Rental USA* is pretty amazing. You pick out what you want online and they ship it right to you.
Scottsdale Arizona / PHONE: 480-460-0907
https://www.kiltrentalusa.com

Canada: *William Glen & Sons* lets you select the individual items you want or have full outfits you can rent. They do have a shipping option for those who don't live locally.
Toronto, Ontario / PHONE: 416-782-5227
www.williamglen.ca

Australia: Australia World Kilt Hire running since 2002 has their site set up so you can measure yourself at home and place your rental order all online. If you prefer to be fitted in person you can also set up an appointment online to be fitted at one of the Australian City capitals.
Locations in each Capital City / PHONE: 0419 464 723
www.kilthire.net.au

Britain: Harris Kilt Company is a newer company opening in 2017 but their team has a collective 100 years' experience so they are not new to the business. They not only mail deliver in Ireland but they also service customers in the UK, U.S., The Isle of Man, and New Zealand.
Belfast, Northern Ireland / PHONE: (+44) 00754 550 275
www.harriskilts.com

South Africa: *Staghorn Scottish Outfitting & Kilt Hire* has been the preeminent kilt-making and kilt hire company for almost 30 years. They service South Africa, but also Zimbabwe, Botswana, Namibia, Angola, Malawi, Kenya, Mauritius and the Seychelles. They actually run their own delivery service to securely deliver your rental to you.
Cape Town, South Africa / PHONE: +27 (0)21 761 4853
www. scottishoutfitting.com

Decorating
Decorating for your Burns Night can really make your event feel special. The best part is it doesn't have to break the bank to make it festive. Some tartan from your local cloth store can help set the mood.

Simple things you may have around from other holiday or just around the house are garland, candles, tartan ribbon, cloth napkins, pinecones, old books, tartan or solid table cloth vases and more. Your table will be set similar to a holiday dinner like Christmas. Again, you can make this as simple or as fancy as you would like. Other thing that may be a fun addition would be little Scottish flags, pictures of Robert Burns, Poems printed out and placed on the table or put up on the walls of the room, tartan pendants on a string, little kilts around the bottles of drinks (if going casual), streamers matching your color theme, balloons, and so on. All of this and more can be found in the free printable.

The Table
To keep the costs down you can measure the length of your table and purchase a length of cloth to use as a wide runner or simple table cloth. If you can sew a straight line then you can make a hem along all side so you can use it again in the future. No sewing skills? Then you can cut the edges with pinking shears (but this will not guarantee that the edges wont fray) or you can use a liquid stitch or cloth adhesive.

To add a touch of elegance you can drink from stemmed glass wear and tie little bows at the base of the stems. You can

Below is a way you can set the table places.
From bottom to top
Plate
A Robert Burns Quiz
Cloth or paper napkin
Silverware tied together with some tartan ribbon.

The quiz can be a fun way for people to test their Burns IQ or learn more about him. You can even give a prize to the winner. If you plan on doing that let people know so they don't help each other with the quiz.

Political Leaders, the Perfect Cuppa & Other Tidbits

Tea had become a staple of the upper class. Not only was tea enjoyed casually but it was used to entertain guests and dignitaries. Below you will find how presidents and leaders enjoyed their teas and more.

Queen Victoria of England would always have two tea cups when she took tea. She would pour her tea from one cup to another to help cool the tea. She had been enjoying tea since at least the age of 13.

George Washington (first US President) placed his first order for tea in 1757for six pounds of "the best" Hyson and Green tea. Other teas he had ordered were Bohea, Gunpowder, Congo, Imperial and Young Hyson. The Washington's were so fond of tea that they were not without any tea ware, from fine china to drink from to tea chests to hold their precious tea. Tea was not missed in summer or winter. In the summer, they had tea at sunset and in the winter, they would enjoy a cup by candle light.

Thomas Jefferson (Second US President) His original tea of choice was Beohea but Hyson became his staple till 1816. He loved tea so much he had a special polygonal-shaped room specifically for taking tea. Guests were served tea in this room often after dinner. This room was adorned with the portraits and buts of famous leaders throughout time. He would go through 20 pounds of tea a year. In this tea room Thomas Jefferson even worked on and wrote the Declaration of Independence in 1776.

Dolley Todd, wife of James Madison (fourth US President), loved her silver tea set and would invite guests over for tea and spoil them with desserts such as Layered cake, seed cake, and ice cream.

Quincy Adams (6th US President) and his wife would would hold levees bi-weekly on Wednesdays and would serve tea with coffee, jellies, cakes, ice cream, cordials and more.

Martin Van Buren (8th US President) lived during a time when tea was becoming a little more involved. Things like sea food, honey cakes, game pasties and olykacks were served with china tea for high tea. People would also hold a cube of sugar between their teeth and sucked the tea through the sugar as they drank.

John Taylor's (10th US President) wife Julia claimed that her remarkable recovery from an illness was because she drank black tea. Years later she had a stroke and a doctor offered her a strong drink but she refused and only said the word "tea." This was the last word she ever said.

James Buchanan (15th US President) had the Washington D.C. Botanical Gardens built initially to test the ability of growing imported tea trees.

Abraham Lincoln (16th US President) once said to a clerk "Colonel, my wife tells me we are out of tea. Put up a pound of the best."

Rutherford B. Hayes' (19th US President) wife Lucy would had daily afternoon tea consisting of bread, butter, cold meats and tea.

James Garfield (20th US President) enjoyed himself some tea, but he had some very unique ways he liked to drink it. Try one of his favorites. In the recipe section you will find two of his favorites, Spice Tea and Garfield Herbal Tea.

Queen Elizabeth II of England has tea promptly at 5 o'clock every day. She enjoys sipping on a cup of Assam or Earl Grey tea and only uses loose leaf tea. First the tea if poured into the cup, followed by the milk and no sugar. If you happen to host the queen at a tea, make sure to serve cucumber, egg or smoked salmon finger sandwiches; and don't forget to cut off the crust. And for dessert, serve up some ginger cakes

Gerald Ford (38th US President) was known to prepare his own breakfast. He enjoyed having a grapefruit, English Muffin and a cup of tea.

Prince Charles - Darjeeling Tea with honey and milk

Ronald Reagan (40th US President) and his wife Nancy enjoyed holding teas at the White House in the red, yellow, and green rooms. Once they had tea with Prince Charles and Princess Diana in the Yellow room. A British pottery company had made a Reagan caricature tea pot.

Princess Diana – Emperor Rose Congou, a blend of black teas from India and china that would be have rose petals layered over it five times.

George Bush (41st US President) and his wife Barbara both love to drink Green Tea.

Meghan Markle (Wife of Prince Harry) opts for herbal teas like mint tea. At home tea may be accompanied by her Chocolate Chip Ginger Banana Bread.

Kate Middleton, Duchess of Cambridge (wife of Prince William of England) enjoys a traditional cup of tea with a touch of milk.

Prime Ministers of Australia have been printed on a tea towel for decades and gets an update every time a new prime minister takes charge. Check out this fun tea towel at Rodriquez.com/au How fun.

Canadian Tea Creation

Have you heard of the London Fog? The story goes that a Mary Loria, who was pregnant, was wanting to avoid drinking coffee. She asked the barista to make her a cup of steamed milk with Earl Grey and a dash of vanilla. No doubt, people hard her ordering this when she would go for her soul warming cup and people started to order it. It started to spread and popular coffee shops like Starbucks and Second Cup made them part of their menu. Its popularity has now spread to other areas like New York and San Francesco have their own twists on the frothy cup of delight. Learn how to make a London Fog in the recipe section.

Recipes

Teas to Try

London Fog

Serves 4 small cups or 2 large cups

INGREDIENTS

- 2 cups (250ml) boiling water
- 2 Earl Grey Tea Bags (double the bags of tea if you like a strong taste)
- 2 cups (1 pint) milk
- 2-4 Tbsp Sweetener of choice (honey, sugar, pure maple syrup, stevia…)
- ½ tsp vanilla extract

INSTRUCTIONS

1. Add boiling water and tea bags to a tea pot to steep for 3-5 minutes.
2. Heat the milk on the stove unit hot.
3. Froth the milk with a frother, hand blender, in a blender or shaking vigorously in a jar for 30 seconds.
4. Add your vanilla (1/8 tsp for a small cup or ¼ tsp for a large cup)
5. Add ½-1 Tbsp sweetener to each cup
6. Fill each cup half way with the tea and the other with half of the frothed milk. Top with extra froth

Veriations

- Herbal London Fog – Use a lavender tea bag in the place of the Earl Grey.
- Orange London Fog – Use an orange tea in the place of the Earl Grey for a cream and orange flavor.

-

Spice Tea

Serves 12

INGREDIENTS

- water, sugar, black tea, allspice, mint leaves, orange juice, and lemon juice.
-

INSTRUCTIONS

1. Boil together 1 cup (125ml) water and 1 cup (250g) sugar until sugar is dissolved.
2. In a tea ball, maybe 2, add 2 tsp black tea, ½ tsp allspice, and 2 fresh mint leaves (or ½ dried mint leaves) and steep covered for 10 minutes.
3. Mix your tea with 2 more quarts boiling water, ¾ cup (177ml) orange juice and 6-8 Tbsp fresh lemon juice. If you want it piping hot then return to a boil and serve.

Garfield Herbal Tea

Servings Adjustable

INGREDIENTS

- Catnip, Hot Water, Pennyroyal

INSTRUCTIONS

1. Add 1 cup of water per guest into your tea kettle and bring to a boil
2. Put ½ tsp herbs, per cup you are preparing, into a tea ball and steep in your hot water for 10-20 minutes. Pour contents into your tea pot and serve.

Scones, Buns, Breads and Jam

Orange Scones $

Did you know that Queen Elizabeth of England loves herself an orange scone. How oranges arrived in England is not entirely known. Some say they came from Portugal; others say Asia but what we do know is that the first oranges in Europe were bitter and used as medicine and tasted nothing like the sweet oranges we enjoy today. The Seville orange is the bitter orange that was originally enjoyed by the royal family. The capital city of Spain, Seville, would pack up oranges and ship a crate to the royal palace as far back as Queen Victoria. These oranges were used to make the marmalade that brits love to eat. **(GF** *(if you use a cup 2 cup gf flour)***, NF)**

Servings

INGREDIENTS

- 4 cups (500g) flour
- 4 tsp baking powder
- 1 tsp salt
- 5 Tbsp sugar
- 10.5 Tbsp (150g) cold butter
- 4 Tbsp orange zest
- 8 Tbsp orange juice
- ½ cup ¼ pint) milk + 1 Tbsp for egg wash
- 1 tsp vanilla extract
- 3 eggs (2 for the scones, 1 for egg wash)

INSTRUCTIONS

1. Preheat oven to 350°F (180°C)
2. Grease a baking sheet with butter
3. In a large bowl whisk together all dry ingredients until well combined.

4. Cut butter into smaller chunks. Add it to the flour mixture and cut it in with a pastry blender or two knives. Finish incorporating in the butter with your fingertips.
5. Stir in the orange zest and orange juice
6. Whisk together the eggs, milk and vanilla and pour it into the dry ingredients. Mix until well combined.
7. Turn dough out onto a lightly floured area and knead until soft and it holds together. If the dough is to sticky, you either need to add a little more flour or try putting it into the fridge to chill.
8. Roll dough out until it is about 3/4" -1" thick.
9. Cut out circles that are about 2.5" in diameter. Make sure not to twist when cutting them out, do not twist.
10. Place circles on greased baking sheet
11. Whisk together I egg and 2 tablespoons milk. Brush over the top of scones with pastry brush or finger tips.
12. Bake for 15-20 minutes until risen and golden brown.

TIP: You can freeze the rounds and then bake them from frozen and add about 5 minutes to their cooking rime. To do this place scones in single layers with parchment or plastic wrap between layers. And store them in an air tight container. You could use Ziplock bags. Just make sure they are flat while they freeze. Then when you are ready to bake them, place the circles on a greased baking sheet, top them with the egg wash and bake.

Bath Buns of Sally Lunn $

Queen Mary, wife of King George V loved bath buns. Bath England has become famous for their Bath Buns. There are many versions of how this sweet, fluffy, heavenly bun came to be. One is that a young French woman, Solange Luyon, had left France and immigrated to Bath in 1680 where she worked for a baker. She sold baked goods in the streets but in the evening, she would make her own baked goods and the owner of the bakery tried selling her sweet buns. They were a hit. They eventually gained the name Sally Lunn, a simplified version of her French name. Read a poem about this tasty bun in the month of January "Receipt To Make A Sally Lun" On page 57.

Servings 6

INGREDIENTS

- 1 ¼ cup (280 ml) whole milk
- 6 Tbsp (85g) butter (room temperature)
- ¼ cup (50g) sugar
- 3 ¾ cups (450g) flour (or bread flour)
- 7 grams or one packet instant yeast
- 2 eggs (+ 1egg for egg wash)
- Zest of one lemon
- 1 ½ tsp salt
- Optional saffron (2 threads)
- Optional Swedish Peal Sugar for garnish

Optional Glaze: instead of doing the egg wash you can mix 1 Tbsp milk with 2 Tbsp sugar and glaze the buns before baking them. Once the buns are baked you can put a second wash on them and sprinkle with the pearl sugar. Let dry. **To keep the price down you can used smashed sugar cubes to sprinkle on top rather than the pearl sugar.

INSTRUCTIONS

1. If you do not have instant yeast and using active dry yeast then activate your yeast in ¼ cup of the milk slightly warmed and a pinch of sugar.
2. If you are using instant years then heat all the milk in a saucepan making sure not to scold the milk. Once it starts to warm up add the sugar and stir to dissolve and then add the butter and stir till melted.
3. Add the optional saffron to the milk.
4. Remove milk from heat and let it cool to 110°F
5. In a large bowl sift in the flour and add the instant yeast.

6. Add the milk, zest, eggs, and salt. Mix some and then add the activated yeast if you went that route.
7. Mix until it all combined. This will be a very sticky dough but it will start to look smooth.
8. Cover and set in a warm place and let it sit till doubled in size. This will take 60-90 minutes.
9. Turn your dough out onto a lightly floured surface and divide into 6 sections and form each one into a ball and pat down. Cover your buns to let them rise again for 45 minutes. Use something very light like plastic wrap or aluminum foil.
10. About 30 minutes into the second rising, you can preheat your oven to 400°F and make your egg wash by whisking a single egg until it looks light and bubbly.
11. Brush the egg wash onto your buns, once they have finished rising, and bake them for 15 minutes till golden brown.
12. Let them cool and eat when slightly warm or when cooled. You can top them with butter jams or clotted cream.

Irish Soda Bread $

Nothing says Ireland like a good soda bread. Created in the 1830's in response to the famine that swept across Ireland it was made of the most basic and readily available ingredients. It also came with the introduction of sodium bicarbonate. Why does sodium bicarbonate sound familiar? It can be found in your kitchen as baking soda. The soft wheat flour, sour milk, salt and baking soda. The chemical reaction between the soured milk and baking soda took the place of yeast and caused the bread to raise. This peasant's bread was cooked in iron skillets or pots over a fire. If you feel adventurist, you can give that a try but this recipe will use the convenience of an oven. **(GF, EF** *(if you skip the egg wash)*, **NF)**

Servings 6-8

Ingredients

- 4 cups (500g) wheat flour (or white flour if you prefer)
- 1 tsp baking soda
- 1 ½ tsp salt
- 2 cups (1 pint) butter milk
- 1 egg yolk

Optional

- add in 1 cup golden raisins (sultanas) to add a touch of sweetness to your soda bread for tea.
- Add 3 Tbsp sugar

Instructions

1. Preheat your oven to 375° F
2. In a large bowl whisk together the flour, salt, and baking soda until well combined.
3. Stir in the butter milk and mix until a dough begins to form. If you are adding the raisins, you will mix them into the dough now.
4. Turn out your dough onto a lightly floured surface and put flour on your hands. The dough will be sticky. knead it or 40 seconds and then shape into a rounded loaf.
5. Place on a greased baking sheet or cover the baking sheet with a piece of parchment paper, and put your dough on top.
   -If you happen to own a seasoned iron skillet or pot you could grease it and cook your bread in it. If you are using an iron skillet pot do not use the lid while baking.
6. With a serrated knife cut a ½" deep "X" in the top.
7. Lightly whisk your egg yolk, and with a pastry brush or your fingertips, brush the yolk over the doughs surface.

8. Bake for 50-55 minutes. The bread will be done when the bred sounds hollow when thumped on the bottom or when an instant read thermometer reads 190°F (88°C)

Tip: For serving with tea, you could offer it plain or slice into smaller pieces and top with butter and jam. Or put sliced bread into a basket and serve with a few jam choices for guests to top as they please.

Scottish Bannock $

Both Canada and Scotland claim to be the homeland of the bannock or oatcakes. The difference between them are the type of flour that is used. **(GF, EF, NF, DF)**

Servings 4

INGREDIENTS

- ¼ cup (4 Tbsp) whole milk (you can use water)
- 2 Tbsp butter (or coconut oil)
- ½ tsp salt
- 1 cup (39g) coarsely ground rolled oats
  You can make the ground oat flour buy blending oats in a food processor.

INSTRUCTIONS

1. Combined the milk, butter, and salt in a sauce pan and heat over a medium heat until the butter has melted.
2. Add the heated liquid to the oat flour and stir until it forms a dough.
3. Turn out onto a lightly floured surface using oat flour. Put some flour on your hands and knead the dough a few times and then roll out into an 8-inch circle until it is ¼ inch thick.
4. Over medium-low heat a cast iron pan for 5 minutes
5. Cut the circle into 4 wedges and cook for 5 minutes on both side until golden.
6. Serve warm with butter, honey, and jam

Orange Marmalade $

Orange marmalade is a staple in Britain and is even enjoyed by the loveable children's book character Paddington Bear. Depending on how you prepare your marmalade will vary the level of bitterness. Many people do not like marmalade because it has a bitter aftertaste. I personally love marmalade but I am not fond of a strong bitterness. After making it once and being disappointed in the final outcome I wanted to find a method that made a more desirable citrus spread I hope you and your children will find this to be a tasty sweet orange spread for your fresh scones.

(GF, EF, NF, DF)

Yields one jar

Ingredients

- 2 oranges
- 2 cups (500g) granulated sugar
- Juice of half a lemon

Instructions

1. Place a small plate in the freezer.
2. Wash your oranges really well if they are purchased from a store. You want to remove any pesticides or coatings that may have been added to them.
3. With an orange peeler remove the orange part of the peel leaving behind the white pith (this is the bitter part of the peel.
4. Julienne cut the zest (slice thinly) and cut in half any long pieces so they are about 2 inches long.
5. Going back to the oranges, cut off all the white pith and discard.
6. Remove the orange segments, chop them up into chuncks and set them aside in a bowl.
7. In a medium saucepan add the zest and 2.5 cups water and bring it to a boil. Reduce the heat to medium high and let the contents boil on 10 minutes.
8. Drain out the water, making sure not to lose the zest and add a new 2.5 cups of water to the pan. Return to the stove heat and set the time for 10 more minutes and then drain out the water.
9. Repeat step 8 one more time.
10. With the rind still in the pot add the orange slice pieces, sugar, lemon juice and, two cups water. Bring the contents to a boil and then reduce heat to bring it to a simmer.
11. Cook the marmalade for about 40 minutes until it starts to look thicker. Make sure to stir every few minutes to prevent scorching

and burning. To test if it is ready, take the plate out of the freezer and put a dollop of marmalade on it. If it is still quite runny when you tip the plate then you need to keep cooking for about 8-10 minutes. You want the marmalade to stick together and wrinkle when you push it.
12. Put in a jar or bowl and let come to room temperature. Then store in the fridge.

Other variations:

- ***Ginger Orange Marmalade*** *Add 1 tsp finely diced ginger on step 10.*
- ***Cinnamon Orange Marmalade*** *Add a pinch of cinnamon after it is done cooling and before you set it aside to cool.*

Blackberry Jam

Topping any bread, bun, or scone with the sweet tartness of blackberry jam will excite any tastebuds and have people reaching for more. This jam is quick and can be made in 30 minutes. If you don't have pectin you can eliminate it. It will just result in a softer set jam.

(GF, EF, NF, DF)

Servings 40

INGREDIENTS

- 2.2 lbs (1 kg) fresh blackberries
- 1 ½ cups (375g)granulated sugar
- 2 Tbsp pectin (can be eliminated for a softer set jam)
- 1 freshly squeezed lemon juice about 4 Tbsp
-

INSTRUCTIONS

1. Wash the berries and lightly smash the berries in a bowl
2. In a heavy bottomed pot place the smashed berries, sugar, lemon juice, and pectin.
3. On medium-low heat start stir constantly until the sugar is dissolved.
4. Bring the jam to a rolling boil so that when you stir it the bubbles don't disappear. Let cool for 5 minutes checking the bottom of the pan now and then to make sure it is not sticking. Then give a few stirs to loosen it.
5. You will notice the color of the jam darkening and thickening. Cook until it reaches 220°F (105°C). If you dip in a wooden spoon, you will notice that the jam coats the spoon. If you swipe your

finger through the coating (be careful, it will be hot) on the spoon the jam will not run into the cleared space. You can also do the saucer test with a plate that has been in the freezer. Put a small dollop of jam on the frozen plate and wait 30 seconds and then push on the edge of the jam. If it wrinkles then it is ready.

6. Remove any foam that has collected on the surface of the jam.
7. Remove from the heat and let cool for about 10 minutes.
8. Store in your preferred way.

Clotted Cream $

Clotted cream is native to the UK. Australians top their scones with whipped cream, as a variant. And in the US the scone is so sweet on its own that there is no need to add anything to it. Clotted cream is a process but it's simple. Just make sure you are using a cream that is not ultra-pasteurized and that you give yourself plenty of time to complete this 20-hour process. Yep, I said 20 hours. But in the end, you will be left with a nutty, smooth spread that normally would require travel all the way to the UK for this experience. **(GF, EF, NF)**

Yields 2 cups (about 8 servings)

INGREDIENTS

- 4 cups (32oz, 960g) of heavy cream (NOT ultra-pasteurized)

INSTRUCTIONS

1. Preheat your oven to 180° F (80°C)
2. In a 8–9 inch square pan pour in the cream. You will want it to be between 1 ½ –2 inches deep.
3. Now place it in the oven and leave it for 12 hours, and do not stir it.
4. At the end of the 12 hours, remove the baked cream from the oven and let cool until it reaches room temperature.
5. Cover it and place it in the fridge until completely cooled. (This step can be done overnight.)
6. Fold back a small piece in the corner of the pan and carefully drain any leftover liquid hiding underneath your baked cream.
7. Place the clotted cream into a bowl and stir it gently to reveal its creamy smooth texture. If it's too thick, you can add some of the runoff back into it.
8. Pack the clotted cream into a jar or ceramic container that you can cover. It will stay good for up to 14 days.

TIP:*If your oven runs hot, then you may want to check on it at 8 and 10 hours. You don't want the top of your clotted cream to become any darker than a tan color. Also, some ovens are programmed to shut off if left on for too long. If your oven does this you may want to do the baking during the day so you can keep an eye on it.*

Cakes

Irish Apple Cake $
The Irish apple cake is a simple but delicious treat to accompany your tea. I loved desserts with baked fruits. This is a classic that is made in countless ways throughout Ireland. **GF (see Note), NF)**
NOTE: The crumble topping for this cake is made with oats for if you want to try this one with a GF cup-for-cup flour then it can be gluten free.

Servings 10

INGREDIENTS
Topping
- 2 cup (180g_rolled oats
- 6 Tbsp cold butter
- ½ cup (125g) sugar (123g brown sugar for a richer flavor)

Cake
- 8 Tbsp butter (one stick)
- ½ cup (125) granulated sugar
- 2 eggs
- 2 Tbsp cream (milk can be used)
- 1 ¼ cup (185g) flour
- 1 tsp baking powder
- 1 tsp cinnamon
- 1/8 tsp salt
- 3 tart apples, like Granny Smith, peeled and sliced thin

INSTRUCTIONS
1. Butter a 9-inch cake pan and preheat the oven to 350°F (177°C)
2. In a food processor add 1 ½ cups of the rolled oats and process until it's an oat flour.
3. Add the cold butter, sugar, and ½ coats and process until the butter is incorporated. It should be moist and binding to itself. Set aside
4. In a large bowl cream together the sugar and butter until creamy and fluffy with an electric mixer.
5. Add the vanilla and eggs and beat in.
6. In another bowl combined the dry ingredients and then fold them into the dry ingredients.

7. Pour cake batter into the prepared pan
8. Lay apple slices in an even layer on top of the batter in a single layer and top with the oat crumble.
9. Bake for approximately 50 minutes and toothpick comes out clean. Let it cool in the pan on a wire rack before removing.

Optional: Dust with powdered sugar before serving.

Australian Lamington

This is a great little dessert that originated in Australia day. Australians enjoy this cake on Australia day but its so well liked you will find people eating it any tame of the year and you will even find it on restaurant menus. This special treat can be spread out over two days. Also make sure to have your eggs, milk, and butter at room temperature.

Servings 32

INGREDIENTS

Cake

- 1 ¼ cup (185g) flour
- 2 tsp baking powder
- 1//3 cup (40g) cornstarch
- 15 Tbsp (200g) unsalted butter softened
- 1 cup +1 Tbsp (230g) caster sugar (you can use granulated sugar)
- 2 tsp vanilla extract
- 3 eggs
- ½ cup (125ml) whole milk

Chocolate Icing

- 3 2/3 cup (500g) powdered sugar
- 7 oz (200g) 60% or 70% dark chocolate
- 1 Tbsp (15g) unsalted butter
- ½ cup (125ml) milk plus a little extra
- 12 oz (325g) shredded coconut

INSTRUCTIONS

Cake

1. Make sure you have your milk, eggs, and, butter sitting out to come to room temperature.
2. Preheat the oven to 350°F (180°C)
3. Butter 7X11 inch baking pan and line the bottom with parchment paper

4. Put all cake ingredients into a food processor and blend for a few seconds. Or mix in a large bowl with an electric hand mixer on low speed until combined and then increase the speed until you have a thick, smooth, yellow batter.
5. Turn the batter out into the prepared pan. And bake for 30-35 minutes until a toothpick comes out clean.
6. Cool the cake inside the pan for 10 minutes and then remove and place onto a wire rack upside down.
7. Once cool, cut off the edges of the cake to make the sides of the cake flat. Use a long-serrated knife, cut the cake into 32 equal pieces. Place in freezer to chill for 1 hour.
8. Now to make the chocolate icing. Place the butter and chocolate over low heat in a double boiler (bain-marie) with the water simmering below.
9. Add in the powdered sugar and milk and whisk until it has thickened, but still thin enough that it will only leave a thin coating once the cake is dipped. Leave the chocolate on the double boiler over the low heat.
10. Place the shredded coconut onto a plate
11. Using two forks, gently pick up a cake piece and dip it into the icing. Make sure to cover all sides. Lift up and let access icing to drip off.
12. Roll the chocolate covered cake piece in the coconut and place onto a wire rack to dry. You may want to put a pan or parchment paper under the rack to catch any mess.
13. Repeat with the remaining cake pieces
14. Let them sit on the wire rack for 30-60 minutes

NOTE: You can make the cake the day earlier you can let the cake sit out and dry overnight to help reduce the crumbliness when dipping the cake pieces into the icing.

Variations

Raspberry and cream Lamingtons

If you want to take this to the next level then give this a try. You can use any jam for this recipe and make it your own. Or maybe you can use Nutella, marshmallow fluff or some other tasty filling.

INGREDIENTS

- ½ cup (8 Tbsp) raspberry jam warmed
- 1 cup (250ml) whipped cream (whip together 1 cup heavy cream, ½ vanilla extract and 1-2 Tbsp powdered sugar on high

INSTRUCTIONS

1. cut your finished, cooled, and trimmed cake in half lengthwise so you will have a top and bottom layer.
2. With your heated jam, spread it evenly on one half of the cake
3. With the whipped cream, spread a thin layer on the cut side of the other layer.
4. Sandwich the layers together and gently tap down. Remove any filling that pours out the sides.
5. Cut into the mini c pieces and place in the freezer to prep for dipping. Continue with step 8 to finish your Lamingtons.

Decadent Chocolate Cheese Cake

This is a supe rich and yummy chocolate cheese cake and super easy to make gluten free without changing the taste at all. This cake is perfect for a special tea time, or if you want to teach your children a lot about baking. This cake is also a perfect birthday cake for those who love cheesecake. **(GF, NF)**

Yields 1 full sized cheese cake
Servings 10-12
Prep time 40 minutes
Cook Time 60-70 minutes
Cooling Time 6 hours

Equipment

- 8" or 9" springform pan
- Aluminum foil
- A pan larger for the spring form pan to sit in, like a roasting pan. Must be able to hold a few inches of water.

Crust

- Butter or non-stick cooking spray for the pan
- 4 Tbsp butter, melted
- 15 chocolate and cream sandwich cookies, like Oreo cookies. Use gluten free Oreos to make this recipe gluten free.
- 2 Tbsp granulated sugar

Filling

- 10 oz (284g) semisweet chocolate
- 4-8oz (907g) packages of cream cheese at room temperature
- 1 ½ cups (375g) granulated sugar

- ½ cup (4 oz, 118 ml) sour cream / soured cream
- ¼ cup (50g, 1.3 oz) unsweetened cocoa powder
- 4 eggs
- Boiled water (if not added to the recipe)

Ganache topping

- 1/3 cup (60g, 2.1 oz) semisweet high quality chocolate chips or baking chocolate bar.
- 1/3 cup (2.8 oz, 83 ml) heavy whipping cream / double cream

Optional chocolate whipped Cream

- 2 cups (16 oz, 480ml) heavy whipping cream / double cream
- 1/3 cup (35g, 1.2 oz) cocoa powder
- 1/3 cup (35 g, 1.2 oz) powdered sugar / icing sugar
- 1 tsp vanilla extract
- Pinch of salt

INSTRUCTIONS

Crust

1. Preheat your oven to 350° F (180° C) and grease your spring form pan. Wrap the outside of the pan in two layers of aluminum foil. Make sure to seal it tight to avoid water leaking in during the baking process. You can do this by placing two long pieces of foil on the counter and place your springform pan in the center and wrap the foil up and around the edges, not allowing the foil to go into the pan.
2. Place cookies in a food processor with sugar and process until you have a crumbly consistency. Now add the butter and process to combined. The cookie pieces should stick to together when pressed together. If you do not have a food processor, place cookies in a zip lock plastic bag and crush them with a rolling pin or the back of a heavy cup. Then empty the crumbs into a bowl and stir in the sugar and butter till evenly moist.
3. Press the crumbs into the bottom of your greased spring form pan. Make sure to spread it evenly over the bottom and press up the sides of the pan, making sure your bottom corners do not become to thick.
4. Place in the oven and bake for 8 minutes. Once the time is up, remove it from the oven and set aside on a cooling rack and reduce the oven temperature to 325° F (160° C).

Filling

1. Melt the chocolate in a double boiler or in the microwave (being careful not to overcook) until it is smooth. Remove from the heat.
2. In a stand mixer with the paddle attachment or with electric hand mixer, beat together the sugar and cream cheese. Mix on medium speed until you reach a smooth consistency without lumps. Make sure to scrape down the sides of the bowl once or twice to make sure you have incorporated all the cream cheese that may be stuck on the sides or the bottom of the bowl.
3. Switch to a slower speed and mix in the cocoa powder and sour cream until combined. Scrape down the sides of the bowl as needed.
4. Add the melted chocolate to combine.
5. Add the eggs in one at a time keeping it at a slow speed. You do not want to over mix because this will add to much air and cause your finished cheesecake to fall or crack.
6. Pour your filling on top of the crust and spread it out to the edges and make the filling nice and even.
7. Place an into larger pan and carefully add the hot water to the large pan till the water rises about 1 inch (about 2.5 cm).
   DO NOT let the water do over the edge of the foil.
8. Place in the oven and bake for 60-70 minutes. When checking for doneness shake the springform pan a little. The center of the cake with be slightly jiggly but the edges will be well set. Turn off the oven and crack open the oven door. Leave in the over for 1-2 hours to cool.
9. Place in your refrigerator and let it cool for an additional 4 hours. For best results let chill overnight.

Ganache topping (make after cake is cool)

1. Chop up your chocolate till it is in small pieces (the smaller the pieces the faster the stirring will go). Place into a clean dry bowl. *You do not want even a drop of water because that will cause you chocolate to seize and there is no saving it.*
2. Heat your heavy cream until it just starts to simmer and pour it over the chopped-up chocolate. Let it sit for a minute or two.
3. With a rubber spatula stir the two together making sure to completely incorporate. Do not whip.
4. Now you get to decide how you want your ganache to look.
    - Option 1: Poor it into the spring form pan, on top of the cake, and place back in the fridge for 2 hours to set.

- Option 2: Remove the cake from the spring form pan and place on serving dish. (If the ring does not release easily you may need to gently run a thin knife around the edge being careful not to cut or pierce the cake. Once placed on your dish you can pour your ganache on the center of the cake. Then you can use a rubber spatula or knife to spread it out to the edges and let it spill over the sides some. **If the ganache seems as if it is too runny then just let it sit out until it cools some and it will thicken.**

Optional: Chocolate Whipped Cream

TIP: For best results start with very cold cream and you can even chill your bowl.

1. Place ingredients into a clean dry bowl and whip with a stand mixer with the whisk attachment or with a hand mixer with beaters or whist attachment. Mix on high until stiff peaks form. If you whip to long the whipped cream will start to look grainy. So, make sure to stop and check for the stiff peaks once it starts to thicken. It should take about 4-5 minutes depending on the speed of your mixer.
2. Place whip cream into a pastry back with your desired tip or onto a good quality zip lock back and cut off one of the corners large enough to let the whipped cream out.
3. Now it's time to decorate your cake.
    - Option 1: Pipe dollops evenly around the top edge of the cake in 8-10 places. Place a berry, candy, cookie piece or decorative pearl if you want to.
    - Option 2: Pipe it from the center and work your way outwards and then working your way back towards the center. Top with berries, shaved chocolate, or chopped up toffee candy bars like Heath or Score.
    - Option 3: Heap the whipped cream into a mound in the center of the cake and adorn with fresh berries and either sprinkle with powdered sugar or brush with apricot jam that has been heated.

Cookies and Desserts

Canadian Maple Cream Cookie

If you go to Canada, you are likely to run into a maple cream cookie with a maple flavored filling. If you are a lover of everything maple you will want to give these a try. They would also be a great addition to a fall tea time. Traditionally, these would be in the shape of a maple leaf but don't let that stop you. Your guests will not care what shape they are in, only in how they taste.

Servings 18

INGREDIENTS

- 2 cups (250g) flour
- 2 cups (224g) powdered sugar
- ½ tsp salt
- 1 ½ tsp maple or vanilla extract
- 1 ½ cups 337g) unsalted butter cut into cubes and softened
- ¼ cup (4 Tbsp) maple syrup

INSTRUCTIONS

1. Preheat the oven to 325°F and line two cookie sheets with parchment paper or silicone mat.
2. In a food processor add the flour, 1 cup powdered sugar, and salt. Pulse to combined and then add in the butter and maple extract. Process until it becomes moist looking and starts to cling to itself.
3. It won't look like dough quit yet, but you will turn this out onto a floured surface and form it into a ball.
4. Knead the dough for about 60 seconds and then form into a ball.
5. Add more flour to the surface and coat your rolling pin with flour. Roll out the dough until it is ¼ inch thick.
6. Now it's time to cut out your cookies. You can use a knife to cut out squares, a 2" circle cookie cutter, or use any 2' shape you would like.
7. Once you cut out your cookies, collect the left-over dough and roll out again to make more cookies.

8. Put cookies on one of the lined baking sheets and place them into the freezer for at least 15 minutes. Then transfer cookies to the second cookie sheet with enough cookies to cover. Make sure to leave at least ½ inch between every cookie.
9. Bake for 15-18 minutes and edges are slightly golden.
10. Cool on the cookie sheet for 2 minutes and then transfer to a cooling rack till completely cooled.
11. To make the maple filling, in a large bowl beat together ½ cup butter until light and smooth. A little at a time, add the 2 cups powdered sugar until smooth and then beat in the maple syrup on high for 2 minutes.
12. Lay out ½ of the cookies upside down and ad your cream filling wo a piping bag or into a zip lock bag with the corner cut off. Pipe the filling onto all of your prepared cookies and top them with another cookie to make your cute little sandwiches.

Welsh Tea Cakes

As we travel around and try new things why not give the Welsh Tea Cake a try. This is a traditional recipe from the land of wales. My husband's ancestors would have enjoyed these alongside a nice cup of tea. This recipe can be doubled.

Servings 18

INGREDIENTS

- 1 ¼ cups (185g) flour
- ½ cup cold butter
- 1/3 cup + 1 Tbsp sugar (plus some extra)
- 1/8 cup (11g) quick oats
- 1 egg
- 2 Tbsp milk
- ½ cup dried currents

INSTRUCTIONS

1. Preheat the oven to 350°F
2. In a large bowl add the flour and cubed butter and cut in. You can use a pastry blender, wo knives or your fingers. Continue until you have a crumbly texture.
3. Add the oats, sugar, nutmeg, eggs and milk and mix until it is all incorporated.
4. Add the currents and fold them into the dough.
5. Turn dough out onto on to a heavily floured surface and roll out dough until it is ¼. Inch thick.
6. Flour a, round 2 ½ inch cookie cutter and place on a greased cookie sheet and sprinkle with extra sugar.
7. Bake for 12-15 minutes until lightly browned and cook on a wire rack.

Blueberry Flummery

Flummery is a fruit pudding that was popular in the British Ails It was a dessert also used by the Pilgrims that established Plymouth Plantation in 1620. The original flummery would have been made with flour or oats and took a couple days to make. It was a much blander fare and the word flummery took on the meaning of "empty compliments" such as talking or writing that was unsubstantial or nonsense. It became a popular dish in the seventeenth and eighteenth centuries after it took on a fruity and creamy texture. It was very popular in Australia in the 1950's-1970's.

(GF, EF, NF)

Servings 6

INGREDIENTS

- ½ cup (125g) sugar
- 2 Tb Corn Starch
- 1 ½ cup (375ml) water
- 2 ¼ cups (427g) whole blueberries
- 1 Tbsp lemon zest (optional)
- Juice of one lemon (optional)
- 2 cups (1 pint) heavy whipping cream (optional)
- 4 Tbsp powdered sugar (optional)
- 1 tsp vanilla (optional)

INSTRUCTIONS

- In a sauce pan whisk together the sugar and cornstarch
- Add the water and whisk till the sugar and cornstarch dissolve.
- Add the blueberries, lemon zest, and lemon juice.
- On low heat cook the flummery till it starts to bubble.
- Cook until it starts to thicken, about 10-15 minutes.
- Pour into a desert dish of your choice and chill for two hours
- To make the whipped cream pour the heavy whipping cream, sugar and vanilla into a medium bowl and whip with a hand or stand mixer on high until the cream thickens and forms medium to stiff peaks.

Tip: Do not over beat your cream or it will start to get a strange grainy look to it and the consistency will be a bit different. That being said, it you think you beat it to long just stop. It will still be eatable and taste good.

Honey Flummery

George Washington's sister Betty included Honey Flummery as part of a Christmas Brunch she served to George Washington in 1769. This recipe may be similar to the one George Washington enjoyed one Christmas morning. Keep in mind that the first step of the old-world recipe takes two days. So, make plans for that. **(GF, EF, NF)**

Serves 4

INGREDIENTS

- ½ cup (45g) oatmeal
- ¾ cups (177ml) orange juice
- 2 Tbsp granulated sugar
- 5 oz (142ml) heavy cream
- Zest of 2 oranges
- ¼ cup (57ml) clear honey
- 2 Tbsp peach juice (in place of whisky or brandy)
- 5 oz (57ml) whipped cream

INSTRUCTIONS

1. Soak your oatmeal in 3 ½ cups of cold water for 48 hours.
2. Stir the oatmeal and then strain out the oat water into a sauce pan. Get rid of the oats (or feed them to your chickens if you have any).
3. Add the orange juice and sugar to the oat water and bring it to a boil while constantly stirring. Cook for 10 minutes until it is thick.
4. Remove from the heat and set aside to cool until it is lukewarm. Stir in the heavy cream.
5. Pour into dessert glasses and chill for 1 hour.
6. When you are ready to serve sprinkle with the orange zest, pour honey and then peach juice over each one. Top with whipped cream.

Banana Tart

(Flan)

What was your favorite dessert as a child? Princes William and Harry of England loved Banana Flan. This is not a flan like you encounter in Spain. This is more of a tart with a pastry crust, custard and banana on top. This is sure to delight both children and adults. This dessert requires a full-sized tart pan.

Serves 8

INGREDIENTS

Pastry

- 1 ¼ (185) cups flour
- 4 Tbsp sugar
- 1 stick cold unsalted butter (cut into small pieces)
- 1 egg yolk
- 2 Tbsp heavy cream

Filling

- 4 ripe bananas (not over ripe)
- ½ cup (157g) apricot jam
  (Recipe on page 256 in A Year of Poetry Tea Time)
- 5 egg yolks
- 1 egg
- 1 ½ cups (.75 pint) milk
- ½ cup (1/4 pint) heavy cream
- ¾ cup (12Tbsp) granulated sugar
- 2 tsp vanilla paste or extract
- ¼ cup (40g) corn starch
- Pinch of salt
- 1 Tbsp butter softened

INSTRUCTIONS

1. In a food processor add the butter, flour and sugar. Pulse until smooth and combined.
2. Add the egg yolk and cream and process it for about 60 seconds.
3. Turn out onto a floured surface and knead it only until it forms a nice dough. Do not over knead. If the butter was not cold enough you may have to chill the dough for to 2 hours.
4. Preheat the oven
5. Roll out the pastry dough on a lightly floured surface until it is big enough to cover your 9-inch tart pan, about ¼ inch thick. Place the

pastry on the pan and press it into the bottom edges. Remove any access that may be hanging over the side and use those pieces to fill in any gaps in the crust. Now go around the pan and press the pastry into the side of the pan and pinch off any extras.

6. Using a fork poke some wholes all over the bottom of the pastry and put it onto the fridge to chill for 30 minutes.
7. After the 30 minutes you will place a piece or parchment down in the pastry and fill the center with ceramic pie weights or beans.
8. Bake on a baking sheet in the oven at 350°F for 30 minutes. Lake the pan out, remove the parchment and weights and then bake for 10-15 more minutes.
9. Place the milk, cream, and butter into a sauce pan and bring it to a boil.
10. In a large bowl add the egg yolks, egg, sugar, vanilla, salt, and corn starch and whisk together.
11. Once the milk hits a boil, and the butter is melted, you can whisk it slowly into the egg mixture and then add it back into the pan and return to the heat.
12. Continue to cook and whisk while you wait for it to thicken.
13. Pour the custard into the shell and chill in the fridge.
14. Bring the apricot jelly to a boil
15. Slice up your ripe banana at a slight angle and about ½ inch thick.
16. Place your banana slices on top of the tart starting with the outer edge, slightly overlapping them. Then continue with another row of bananas inside the first row. Place a few more slices in the center.
17. Give the banana slices a nice pat to set them into the custard a little and remove it from the tart pan.
18. brush generously with the apricot jam.

19.

Whetstone Caramels

These caramels are amazing. A neighbor of mine shared this recipe with me and I was blown away. I am a huge fan of caramel and my favorite place to purchase candies with caramel is See's Candies. This caramel tastes just like their caramel. Eat it plain, dip it in chocolate, or even sprinkle a tiny bit of sea salt on top. This would be a very special treat indeed. The key is to start with a very clean pot and then make sure there is no water left in it. **(GF, EF, NF)**

Yields a 9x13 pan and can be cut into any size caramels you would like.

Ingredients

- 1 10 oz can sweeten condensed milk
- 2 cups (500g) white sugar
- 1 cup (16 Tbsp) butter
- ¼ tsp salt
- ½ cup (164g) corn syrup

EQUIPMENT

Heavy bottom pot sauce pan/pot
Candy Thermometer
9X13 pan
plate
Wooden Spoon
Rubber spatula
Wax paper (if you plan on individually wrapping the caramels)

Preparation: Thoroughly wash and dry the pot you are going to cook in. Making sure no dirt, dust or water are left inside the pot. This can affect the way your caramels turn out.

INSTRUCTIONS

1. Butter the 9X13 baking dish and a plate and set aside
2. Over a medium low heat add all ingredients to the pot. Stir all ingredients until combined.
3. Continue to stir, alternating between a circular and figure-8 pattern. You do not want the sugars to cook to the bottom of the pan. If you see tiny flecks showing up in your caramel but don't become to alarmed. Some will not ruin your caramel, but make

sure that when you're stirring that your spoon is making contact to the bottom of the pot to reduce the specks.

4. Once the caramel starts to bubble place your candy thermometer into the candy, making sure it is not touching the bottom of the pot.
5. Continue stirring and watch the thermometer. The caramel will begin to turn into a light golden brown. Once it hits 142 degrees you will remove it from the heat.
6. Carefully pour the hot caramel into the buttered 9X13 pan BUT don't scrape the bottom of the pan.
7. Scrape out the remaining caramel onto the buttered plate. This is because the candy on the bottom of the pan is hotter and could affect how the rest of the candy sets.
8. Let cool at room temperature. The caramel will set but still be a little soft.
9. Loosen the sides of the caramel with a knife and pull out of the pan with a rubber spatula onto the counter or cutting board.
10. Cut into desired sized pieces and wrap in pieces of wax paper.

Burns Night Recipes

Here you will find the recipes for all of the foods mentioned in the section about planning a Burns Night. I chose these specific recipes because they are as authentic as you are going to get in the U.S. (some ingredients just aren't available there) and they can be made kid friendly.

The Easy Haggis

This haggis is for the person who does not want to go through the process of stuffing the haggis into a casing and cooking it for a long period of time. You can also choose if you want to make it with lamb or just substitute ground beef. Just know that the bee is not traditional and will not have the same taste. Traditionally the meats would be things like a sheep's stomach, liver, tongue, lung & heart. In the US you cannot purchase lung and the other parts are not a typical grocery store find. So, this is as simple of a haggis you will find.

Ingredients

- ½ Tbsp (5g) butter
- 1 onion diced
- ½ tsp freshly ground pepper
- ¾ tsp ground coriander
- ¾ tsp nutmeg
- 1 tsp allspice
- ½ tsp dried thyme or 1 tsp fresh thyme chopped
- ¼ tsp cinnamon
- 1lb (450g) ground lamb (ground beef to cut cost or avoiding lamb)
- ½ lb (225g) chicken liver, fat removed
- 1 cup (240ml) stock
- 4 oz (115g) steel cut oat (also known as pinhead oats)
- salt and pepper

Instructions

Tip, If you have an iron skillet you can cook your haggis on top of the stove and in the oven so you only dirty one dish.

1. Melt the butter in a pan and cook the diced onions over medium heat for five minutes or until soft.
2. Add the spices to the pan and add the ground meat and chicken livers and brown.

3. Once the meat is cooked add the stock. Cover and simmer for about 20 minutes.
4. Preheat the oven to 350 degrees
5. Uncover and add the oatmeal, stirring it in to incorporate it evenly.
6. Cover pan or place meat mixture in an oven safe dish and cover. Cook for 30 minutes
7. Remove the cover and cook for another 10 minutes This will help evaporate any access liquid

Whisky Sauce (non-alcoholic option)

This sauce has been added to the meal to adorn the haggis and is not a must but with elevate to your haggis experience. For those who do not cook with alcohol you can either spend the money on a non-alcoholic whisky or you can just substitute it with some peach juice. It will not have the same flavor but it will add a pleasant creaminess.

Yields about 2 cups

INGREDIENTS

- 4 Tbsp butter
- 6-8 Tbsp whisky, non-alcoholic whisky, or white grape juice
- ¾ cup (.4 pint) +2 Tbsp (200ml) heavy cream
- 7 Tbsp (100ml) chicken stock
- 2 tsp Dijon mustard
- Salt and pepper

INSTRUCTIONS

1. Melt the butter in a sauce pan over medium heat
2. Add the whisky or your chosen substitute
3. IF USING WHISKY, light the whisky with a lighter and let the alcohol burn off.
4. Add the cream, mustard, and chicken stock
5. Continue to cook, stirring to keep it from sticking. It will begin to thicken and reduce.
6. Salt and pepper to taste

Neeps

I just love the Scottish names for things. Neeps are mashed turnips and a must have for your Burns night celebration. Neeps, also called a turnips or seweds, are a root vegetable with a beautiful white and purple skin. The root flesh is very hard and can be eaten raw as well as the turnip greens. When at the store don't get it mixed up with the Rutabaga which is larger.

Servings 4-6

Ingredients

- 1 large neep (turnip, swede)
- 3 Tbsp butter
- Salt and pepper

INSTRUCTIONS

1. Use a paring knife, peel the turnip
2. Cut into thick slices, about 2 cm wide and then cut those slices into cubes.
3. Ad turnips to a pot and cover with water. Add salt and bring to a boil.
4. Simmer for 15 minutes until the turnips are tender. Check with a fork and do not let them over cook.
5. Once cooked, drain the water out and return the turnips to the pot.
6. Mash with te butte and then season with salt and pepper
7. Serve warm

Tatties

Tatties are the mashed potatoes that will be joining your haggis on the plate. Seriously, I may be calling our mashed potatoes "tatties" from now on, it just makes me smile. You will want these tasty tatties cozied up next to your neeps and haggis.

Servings 4

INGREDIENTS

- 1 ¼ lbs (about ½ kg) potatoes peeled and chop into chunks
- ½ tsp salt
- 2 Tbsp butter
- 2 Tbsp milk
- 1/8 tsp nutmeg
- salt and pepper

INSTRUCTIONS

1. placed cut up potatoes into a pot and cover with water. Add a dash of salt and bring water to a boil.
2. Reduce to a simmer, cover with a lid and cook for 20 minutes or until the potatoes can be poked by a fork.
3. Strain the potatoes and place them into a bowl (keep the pot at the stove). Mash them with a potato masher.
4. Add the butter into the cooking pot and melt it over medium heat.
5. Add the nutmeg and stir it about to heat up the nutmeg and to release its aroma. You don't want to butter to bubble.
6. Add your mashed potatoes (tatties) back to the pot and mix it all together well.
7. Salt and pepper to taste.

Cock-a-leekie soup

I love the name of this traditional Scottish soup. Before you look at the ingredients (unless you already took a peek) see if you can figure out what the two main ingredients are. Did you guess right? This is a nice simple soup that doesn't need a manual to make. It does require some watching since you do things to the soup and isn't just left to simmer on its own. Do be prepared to

Ingredients

- Water
- A nice small collection of fresh herbs such as parsley, thyme, rosemary and oregano. A few sprigs of each.
- 2 Tbsp salt
- One whole chicken
- 6 larch leeks chopped
- 1 onion chopped
- 1 cup (230g) rice
- Honey (Optional)
- Salt and petter to taste

Instructions

1. Fill large pot with water and turn your burner on high
2. Add your herbs, salt and whole chicken making sure that you push the chicken down into the water.
3. Once the water comes to a boil reduce the heat until it's only at a simmer. Cover and cook for 1.5 hours. If your chicken is larger than 4 lbs you may have to cook it longer or check for a temp of 165° F/ 64° C
4. 20-30 minutes into the cooking you want to take out any scum and add ½ of your chopped leeks. Return the water to a simmer and recover.

5. After another 30 minutes add the onion, stir and recover.
6. When there is about 15 minutes left add the rest of the leeks and recover and pre heat the oven to 400° F/200° C.
7. Transfer the chicken to a roasting pan and then add the 1 cup of rice to the broth.
8. Brush or drizzle some olive oil on the chicken and season with salt and pepper and place in the oven for 15 minutes.
9. Remove the chicken from the oven and cover the chicken with honey. Turn off the oven and return back to the oven. Let sit in there for about 10 minutes, till it gets a little browned.
10. Remove the chicken and cut the meat off the bones. Cut the loose meat into bite sized pieces. And add it to the broth.

Scotch Broth

Scotch broth is documented to exist back to the 1600's it most likely existed centuries before that. This is one of two soup recipes I have included in this section. This soup is rich and hearty soup that will satisfy any person's belly. If you like a thicker soup then use 6 cups chicken broth and if you like a thinner soup you will want to use 8 cups of broth.

Servings 6

INGREDIENTS

- 1 ½ lbs (.7 kg) lamb shank, shoulder or beef with bones
- 2 Tbsp butter
- 1 medium yellow onion
- 3 cloves garlic
- ½ cup (83 grams) pearl barley
- 1/3 cup (75 kg) dried green split peas
- 3-4 sprigs thyme (1 Tbsp dried thyme)
- 2 bay leaves
- 1 tsp salt
- 6-8 cups (3-4 pints) chicken broth (depending on how thick or thin you like your soup)
- 1 large diced carrot
- 1 turnip peeled and diced
- ½ cup shredded green cabbage
- 1 medium leek, chopped
- Parsley chopped for garnish

INSTRUCTIONS

1. Melt the butter in your pot and sauté the garlic and onions for 6 minutes
2. Add the meat, thyme, split peas, bay leaves, salt, and broth to the pot and bring to a boil. Lower the heat and cover the pot and simmer for 2 hours.
3. Skim off any foam that forms
4. Add the root vegetables and simmer for another hour
5. Take the thyme, bay leaves and meat/bones out of the pot.
6. Shred the meat and return the shredded meat to the pot along with the leeks and cabbage. Simmer for 30 minutes.
7. Serve the soup hot and garnished with chopped parsley.

Clootie Dumpling

This is a traditional dessert to have with your Robert Burns night celebration. Now keep in mind that this is an old-world recipe so it is a bit involved and you want to leave time to make it. You will need a muslin cloth large enough to hold your dumpling

Servings 6-10

INGREDIENTS

- 4 oz (125g) suit
- 8 oz + 1 Tbsp (125g) flour
- 4 ox (125g) oatmeal
- 4 oz (125g) golden raisins (sultanas)
- 4 oz (125g) dried currents
- 3oz (75g) granulated sugar
- 1 tsp baking powder
- 1 tsp ground ginger
- 1 tsp ground cinnamon
- 2 large beaten eggs
- 1 Tbsp golden syrup
  (this can also be called light treacle or use corn syrup)
- ¼ cup milk
- 1 tsp caster sugar/superfine sugar or granulated sugar

INSTRUCTIONS

1. Boil some water in a tea pot
2. In a large bowl add the flour and suet and rub it together until it if fine and crumbly.
3. Mix in the next 7 ingredients until well combined
4. Next mix in the eggs and syrup.

5. Now you will slowly add in the milk until the dough binds to itself and the consistency is firm. Avoid adding to much of the milk. You do not want the dough to be soggy.
6. Put you muslin cloth Your clootie) into a bowl and pour the boiling hot water over it. Remove and once cool enough to tough, ring it out over the bowl. Now spread it out on the counter and sprinkle the cloth with flour.
7. Place your clootie dumpling at the center of the cloth and form into a nice circle. Gather the cloth up and over the dumpling and tie tightly leaving space inside the cloth for the dumpling to expand.
8. Tie another string to the top of the clootie and tie the other string to the handle of the pot to keep the dumpling from sitting on the bottom of the pot. This Is how they did it long ago. You could also place a saucer plate, upside down, onto the bottom of the pot and place the clootie on the place.
9. Cover the clootie with boiling water. Put the lid on the pot and simmer for 3 hours checking now and then to make sure the water has not boiled away. The clootie needs to stay submerged.
10. Once the 3 hours are up, carefully remove your clootie dumpling from the pot and remove the cloth from your dumpling.
11. Sprinkle the dumpling with the sugar.
12. Preheat the oven to 225°F (100°C) and bake for 30 minutes
13. When it is done it will have formed a shiny outer cover.
14. Slice and serve

Shortbread

Shortbread is a staple of Scottish fare and a perfect little treat to serve at either tea or at your Burns Night. It could even be packaged up and used as a nice parting gift to your guests. You may be surprised to know that shortbread was originally a crumbly treat enjoyed by the elite and royals. This is because butter was a luxury at the time.

Servings 18 pieces

INGREDIENTS

- 2 cups (240g) flour
- 2 sticks (239g) unsalted butter at room temperature and cubed
- ½ cup (129g) caster sugar (ground up granulated sugar)
- ½ tsp salt

INSTRUCTIONS

1. Preheat the oven to 350°F and butter a 9X9 or 8X8 square or circle pan.
2. In a food processor, place all ingredients and pulse until it resembles course bread crumbs. The result should be a dough that holds its shape when pinched together. It it seems to still be dry, then pulse some more.
3. Turn contents out into the greased pan and press it evenly in the bottom of the pan. If it does not hold together you will need to return it to the food processor and process it some more.
4. Poke holes all over the shortbread with a fork. Score your shortbread with a knife where you plan on cutting it apart.
5. Bake in the center of the oven and back for 30-35 minutes and a light golden color. Cool and cut apart.

Tea Etiquette

This section is also included in the first book of this series *A Year of Poetry Tea Time*. It will share with you the basic rules of etiquette for a traditional English Tea. If you are interested in learning how to plan a Poetry Tea Time event you will want to get the first book. It is complete with a check list, how to choose your menu, invitations, decor, planning for kids or adults, making sure it goes smoothly and a whole lot more. It has tips for those planning a Poetry Tea Time on a budget all the way to a decked out formal event. You won't want to miss that. Not to mention the huge collection of poetry and different recipes included.

It is time to learn the ins and outs of tea etiquette. There are many different rules and many ways people choose to follow them. Do you eat with your fingers or a fork? Does the clotted cream go on your scone before or after your jam? The following internationally accepted rules of etiquette taught by international etiquette consultant Jamila Musayeva and English Etiquette expert William Hanson will prepare you for any level of formality. Of course, if all else fails, do as your host does and you will be fine.

Afternoon Tea

As we learned in the history of tea, Anna Russell, Duchess of Bedford, popularized the Afternoon Tea. It is traditionally held between 3 and 5 pm. One would dress nicer for afternoon tea. If attending an afternoon tea, you would want to confirm with your host what the expected dress code will be. It can be smart casual (dressed up jeans) to cocktail dresses, depending on the event you are attending.

Food to expect at afternoon tea will include tea sandwiches, scones, and small desserts. If small desserts are not served you may enjoy a cake, such as sponge cake.

The Place Setting

When you sit down to tea you will place the napkin, folded in half, onto your lap, with the folded side towards yourself. When you need to use your napkin you will dab your mouth, not wipe. At your place setting you will have at least a plate, pastry fork, knife, tea cup and saucer, tea spoon, and possibly a tea strainer if your host is using loose-leaf tea (tea that is not in a tea bag). The knife is not for cutting things, rather for spreading.

Pouring the Tea

Typically, the host or hostess will pour the tea unless they have given the honor to someone else. In England this person is referred to as the "Mother." You will be asked "would you like your tea strong or weak." If you want it strong then your tea cup will be filled ¾ full. If you say weak, your cup will be filled half way, leaving room for additional hot water to be added.

Next you will be asked if you would like milk, lemon, or sugar. If you want nothing added to your tea you will just say "plain please" or if in England "blank please." Sugar is always added to the tea first so it can dissolve well. As for the milk, some people argue whether milk should go into the cup before or after the tea. Jamila Musayeva explained that in the past, cups could possibly crack if hot tea were to be poured straight into them. The milk was used to temper the delicate cups. Tea cups no longer have this problem. So, I would suggest doing tea first so the hot tea can dissolve the sugar. Then you can add your milk.

If you will be pouring your own tea, you would place the strainer on your cup and pour the tea through it. Once you place the strainer back on its holder, you will add your sugar. You do not drop your sugar into the center of the cup. That could cause your tea to splash and would be poor manners. Instead, you place it in closer to the edge of the cup. After this you will "stir" your tea by gently moving your spoon back and forth in a 6 o'clock to 12 o'clock motion until the sugar has dissolved. Place your spoon behind your cup, on your saucer once you are done. Now you can add your milk or lemon.

Drinking the Tea

If you are sitting at a high table, like a dining table, then the saucer remains on the table and you only pick up the cup. If you are standing or sitting at a low table, like a coffee table, then you will pick up the saucer with the cup. When drinking you will bring the cup to your mouth and you will tilt the cup towards your mouth. You never tilt your head or lean towards the cup. While you are drinking your tea, never look over the edge of the cup, but look into the cup and maintain your elegance.

How to Hold the Tea Cup

Yes, there is a way to hold the tea cup. You will NOT put your index finger all the way through the tea cups handle. It will meet your thumb just on the other side of the handle and the underside of the handle will rest upon the side of your middle finger. There is no need to lift your pinky finger. This was something that may have been done when tea cups had no handle. An elegant lady holds her pinky in. But of course, if you're holding a tea party at your house and those little girls want to feel fancy and lift up their pinky, then let them have their fun.

Eating Etiquette

The food may be served on a three-tier tray. There will either be one for each person or ones for all guests to share. Sandwiches on the bottom, scones in the middle, and desserts on the top. First you will eat sandwiches. This is to be light and fresh to clear your palate. Will foods be picked up with tongs or the fingers? Observe the table (are there tongs?) and do as your host does. Finger sandwiches are just that, little sandwiches to be eaten with one's fingers. Some might say that you should eat the tea sandwich with a fork and knife; William Hanson says one should eat your finger sandwiches with your fingers. But as I have mentioned before, do as the host does. One should not start eating the scones until everyone else has eaten their sandwiches. If you don't want to eat sandwiches then you will just wait until the other guests finish so everyone starts with the scones at the same time.

The Scone

The word scone is pronounced two different ways depending on where you are in the world. Scone can either rhyme with gone or cone. And now to eating the yummy little scone. A scone is not to be cut in half with a knife, but pulled apart by hand. There should be clotted cream and jam to put on top of your scone. You will first dish up a little clotted cream and jam onto your own plate. Then you will spread them onto the scone with your knife. There is a debate on whether you are supposed to put cream or jam on your scone first. Unless you are having afternoon tea in the English counties of Devon or Cornwall it can be done either way. But for your information, the Queen of England does jam first. If you happen to be served a scone with cheese, then you will have butter and relish to put on it. The scone is also meant to be eaten with your hands. William Hanson does warn to "never sandwich the two together, and eat as a whole." Again, if you're not interested in eating a scone, then wait for everyone else to finish their scone before eating a dessert.

The Dessert

You can expect to have a tart, mini cakes, petit fours, macaron, or biscuits (an English tea cookie), but cupcakes are not an English tea dessert. The dessert will be removed by hand and then placed on your plate. Then you will use the small fork or pastry fork to eat unless it is traditionally eaten with your fingers, like a macaron. When using your fork, it should be "upturned and in the right hand" suggests William Hanson. When using your fork remember, your saucer is only for your tea cup. So, make sure to use your other plate to prepare your scone and for eating your other desserts.

When You Are Done

Once you are done eating and ready to leave the table, you place your napkin neatly on the table to the left of your place setting.

Some other common variations of tea time include:

High Tea

High Tea is held around noon. It originated from when a person would have tea with lunch. This tea is eaten at a normal dining table which sits higher than a coffee table. This is the reason for the term "high" tea. It includes things like meats, cheeses, fruits, bread, and other meal fare.

Royal Tea
Royal Tea is like the afternoon tea, but you also have a glass of champagne.

Cream Tea
Cream Tea is the most basic tea. It includes scones, clotted cream, and jam.

Other Tips:

- Never place your elbows on the table.
- When you are not using a hand, you should rest it in your lap on top of your napkin.
- Never slurp while drinking your tea.
- Keep both legs in front of you when sitting in your chair.
- Do not talk while your fork is in your hand. You are supposed to put your fork down between bites.
- Do not reach across for items on the table, but ask others to hand them to you.
- Don't talk while there is food in your mouth.
- Sit up straight and do not slouch.
- Do not check your cell phone while sitting at the table.
-

If you would like to learn more about etiquette, then check out William Hanson's book
Bluffer's Guide to Etiquette: Instant Wit and Wisdom

Bring Poetry to Life

Bringing Poetry to Life
I believe that learning can be done just about any place, and that there is more to learning than just reading, writing, and arithmetic. Getting out and experiencing life, exploring the world around us and touching the lives of others is part of what makes each individual a unique person. The experiences we share and knowledge we gain by stepping out of our personal bubble is what makes us grow.

Hosting a tea is social and makes the poetry experience fun, but that isn't the end-all. Reading poetry transports us into another's mind and heart, and we experience something new every time. We see and feel what another person has experienced and learn empathy. We experience joy, laughter, peace, and pain. Poetry is a form of literature that all ages can enjoy together. Don't limit your experience to your dining room table. Get out there and bring poetry to life.

Poetry and Historical Sites
Get your kids in the car and head to a local historical site. If it is a civil war location read poetry by soldiers who experienced it first-hand. If you're in a national park, read poetry about the beauty of nature. If you're visiting a president's birth place then read a poem they wrote themselves or that another poet wrote about them. Once we visited the home of Paul Revere and we decided to take the time to read Paul Revere's Ride while sitting in the courtyard right in front of his home. The older kids will never forget it. Ever with plenty. Of other people walking around the children listened intently. We were right there where Paul Revere would have dashed to his horse and take to the roads to warn the citizens of the coming danger.

Besides poems, important speeches are also great to share with children at special locations. Martin Luther King Jr's I had a Dream speech could be read in Georgia, Washington D.C. or Alabama. Lincoln's Gettysburg Address could be read while visiting his birthplace in Kentucky, Ford's Theater, while visiting the Lincoln Monument or on any of the fields of the Civil War. Journal entries, accounts of a person's life, and music from a certain time period are all things that will help engage the senses and emotions of your children while exploring historical sites.

Poetry and Gardens
One of my favorite things to do is read in a garden. It might seem silly, but when you're reading something that highlights or brings attention to your surroundings it creates a memory. For instance, I once took my children to the Chicago Botanical Garden where we only had a few chapters left of *The Secret Garden*. We took a picnic lunch and read for a while on a blanket before going in. Then we went into the English walled garden and read for a while, ending our reading next to a pond. To this day my children will say that has been their favorite reading experience.

This can be done with even more ease when it comes to poetry. You can read maritime themed poetry at the beach, visit a zoo and read poems at the different animal enclosures. Take a walk around a lake and read poems by Henry David Thoreau. Visit a farm and read poems about farm animals, hard work, and life. The possibilities are endless.

Poetry and Service
Retirement and nursing homes are often looking for new things to add to their programming.
There are also many seniors who are rarely visited by family and miss seeing the life and excitement of children. Work on memorizing a poem or reading some poems with great expression. Reach out to a local community home and ask to set up a time to come and perform. If that doesn't work with their schedule you could see if going room to room is a possibility. Do this with just your children or with a poetry-tea-time group. As a confidence building experience, it helps the children learn to speak in front of groups and help children to look past their own needs and see the needs of others. All ages can participate—get some parents involved too.

Poetry and Preschool
What better way to spread the love of poetry than to teach the youngest of minds? Reach out to someone who owns a preschool and set up a time for your kids or group to come by and share poetry. Some possible activities:

- Teach poems with hand actions.
- Teach simple Mother Goose rhymes.
- Memorize a few lines of a longer poem each time you go.
- Choose a different animal poem each time and learn about the animal.

These are all things that little kids will enjoy. Just keep it simple and focus on memorization and making it an active experience – act like the animal, sound like the animal, color a picture of the animal with the poem on the paper and so on.

Get Out and Learn

Check into your local area and find libraries, museums, and historical sites that are dedicated specifically to a poets. One summer we were staying in North Carolina for a while and our friend Michael Jordan (an English Professor at Hillsdale College) asked us if we were planning on visiting the Carl Sandburg house. Sadly, we had never heard of this person who was considered one of the greatest American poets.

We decided to jump at the chance to learn something new. We looked up his poetry and found one poem that was nice and short entitled: "Fog." We worked on memorizing it for a couple days. We made the pilgrimage out to the house on the day they held their bluegrass music festival. We enjoyed music, took the tour, petted the sheep, and then recorded all of the children reciting the poem in front of Sandburg's house. The kids still know the poem to this day, years later.

Make sure to check out the Field Trip section of this book. Not only will you find interesting places to visit but a huge list of Robert Burns Statues all over the world that you may just happen to live near enough to make a special picnic trip to go see.

Poetry Rabbit Trails

Below are hands on activities and learning experiences inspired by the poetry in this book. You will find the poem and poet underlined for each activity. Feel free to do the activity as described or put your own twist on it. The most important thing is that you and your children are enjoying the poetry and that it sparks their love of learning. Learn more about creating an awesome homeschooling environment and learning through classic literature. Learn this and more in my book *Relaxed Homeschooling or visit LittleRabbitTrails.com.*

January

- Learning for teens
  Related to the poem *"Address to Edinburgh"* by Robert Burns on pg.51. Learn about the teachings of the Scottish philosopher Lord Monboddo and develop your own thought on his philosophical teachings. He had thoughts on such things as evolution, linguistics & metaphysics.
- Plan your very own Burns Night. Scotland is crazy for Robert Burns and most everyone will celebrate the writings of Robert Burns by reading "Address to a Haggis" on pg.54 and eating a meal that includes haggis, neeps and tatties. Don't know what those are? Just go to the section towards the end of the book about planning a burns night and you will find everything you need. And go to **www.littlerabbittrails.com/robertburns** to print out your very own Burns Night planner with everything you need to know. You also get printable decorations, invites, games, poems and way more.
- Memorize *"The Rule of Life* By Johann Wolfgang von Goethe" and pick a trait that you want to work on this year.

February

- Read the poem *"On Being Brought from Africa to America"* By Phillis Wheatley on pg. 66 and learn about her life. She enjoyed writing poetry for people who made an impression on her. Write a poem for someone important in your life and mail it to them. Learn how to address an envelope.

- What makes a nation strong? Could the same qualities make a strong family? Read *"A Nation's Strength"* By William Ralph Emerson and make a list of strengths a family should have. Pick a strength your family would like to work on together. Write it and post it someplace you will see it every day.
- Learn how to make butter and make some and read *"The King's Breakfast"* By A. A. Milne.

March

- This is the month that all over the world people remember Saint Patrick. Do you know anything about him? Read the poem *"Ireland"* By Franceis William Lauderdale Adams. Then read Saint Patrick's tory *Maewyn and the Clover* in the chapter titled Tales of Bravery. Make a "stained glass clover with wax paper, green tissue paper and glue. Fold a 2 foot long of waxed paper in half, draw a clover and cut it out. Cover one clover with glue and tissue paper. Adding more glue if needed, place the other wax paper clover on top and let dry. Hang in a window.
- Learn how to draw a Kangaroo with **Art for Kids Hub** on You Tube and then learn about how marsupials have babies. Read the poem *"The Kangaroo"* By Barron Fields
- After reading At the *"Tug-O-War"* By Henry Lawson have your own tug of war. Try it one on one and try it with some other friends or with your family if it is big enough.

April

- Learn where Boston, Massachusetts is and learn where Paul Revere rode to warn people of the coming danger. *"Paul Revere's Ride"* By Henry Wadsworth Longfellow pg. 103
- What are your thoughts about the country you live in? Read *"To My Country"* By Katharine Lee Bates and then write a letter to your own country. If your country could read a letter from you, what would you say?
- Read *"Mrs. Earth"* By Walter De La Mare on pg.115 and choose a simple project to show your love for the planet. Plant a tree, pick up trash at the park, write a song or poem, clean up your favorite beach.

May

- Plant poppies in your yard or in a pot indoors. Read "In Flanders field" By John McCrae on pg.126

- Learn where Sydney, Australia is on a map and do a google search for something performed in the Sydney Opera House. *Read "A Song of Sydney"* By Ethel Castille on pg.135
- Read *"The French Revolution as It Appeared to Enthusiasts at Its Commencement"* By William Wordsworth Learn where France is and learn a little about the French Revolution by watching the TED Ed video titled *"What Caused the French Revolution?–Tom Mullaney"*

June

- Learn how you can send a letter to a active duty military member. Maybe you have a family member or someone from church is deployed (serving in the military away from home). Write them a letter and tell them thank you for protecting your freedom and others. *"Glimpses"* – By Nellie Boyer
- Do you know what a haiku is? Read *"The Summer Grass"* By Matsuo Basho and count how many syllables are in each line. That is all there is to it. The first line has 5 syllables, the second line has 4 syllables and the third lie has 5 syllables. Give it a try. Share your poem in the Little Rabbit trails group on Facebook.
- Read *"To the King's Most Excellent Majesty 1768"* By Phillis Wheatley on pg.157 and then learn the difference between a democracy and a monarchy. Draw out the government structure for whichever you find interesting.

July

- Read *"A Daughter Of The States"* By Madison Julius Cawein on pg. 162 and learn about Britain Queen Boadicea (her husband was King Prasutagus). She led the Iceni tribe in a revolt against the Romans.
- The US expansion to the West was greatly influenced by those who decided to leave the colonies in the East with the hope of establishing a new life on the frontier. Many of these people were called Pioneers. Learn about the Organ trail and map out the path the pioneers used to travel. Read *"Pioneer! O Pioneer!"* By Walt Whitman
- Is the weather nice outside. Pack a picnic and read a bunch of poetry. Talk about what it would have be like if you were sitting there at a picnic and you witnessed a horrible battle. What would you do? Read *"The Picnic Battle"* By Anicka Melville on pg.70

August

- Read *"William Wallace"* By Francis William Lauderdale Adam on pg.179. Do you know about the Battle of Sterling Bridge? Did you know that there were two Scottish armies and that William Wallace wasn't the only leader? Learn about Andrew de Moray who helped win the battle of sterling on the You Tube video "The Battle of Sterling Bridge and the Other William Wallace." Make some swords out of cardboard and have your own battle.
- In the poem *"The Dreamer"* By Walter De La Mare it mentions the word dew. What is dew? Learn about the dew point. What creates dew? Go out early in the morning and take pictures of dew on plants. Look up dew in the glossary and read other poems with the word dew.
- Music is a way for people to express themselves and for others to enjoy listening. You learn about a statue in *"Beethoven In Central Park"* By Alfred Noyes on pg.185. Listen to the song Beethoven's 5th Symphony. Dance to what you hear. If you don't want to dance, then draw a picture as you listen…or do both

September

- Boats are able to float because of something called buoyancy. Learn about Archimedes and how he discovered buoyancy. Try the TED Ed video *"The real story behind Archimedes' Eureka!- Armand D'Angour"* Using aluminum foil, create your own boat and make a boat that can hold a strawberry, grapes, marbles or some other small object. How many can it hold? Read *"Old Ironside"* By Oliver Wendell Holmes Sr. on pg. 192
- Did you know that the Mocking Bird was real? Did you know it was the state bird of Arkansas? Listen to a recording of the mocking bird and learn how to draw it. Enjoy the poem *"The Mocking Bird"* By Timothy Thomas Fortune
- Did you know that the weather on the other side of the world is the opposite of their own? Would it be strange to have Christmas in the Summer? Discover what country is opposite of yours on a globe. What is the weather there right now? Use your imagination and do something that you would do if you were in that other country. Have a snowball fight inside with socks. Have a beach party in your house. You could even chart the differences of your weather over the week. Share what you do on the Little Rabbit Trails Group on FB.

October

- The poem *"The New Colossus"* By Emma Lazarus on pg.205 leaves one wondering what the old colossus is. Learn about the Colossus of Rhodes and see what the inspiration for the Statue of liberty was. The sculpture Frédéric August Bartholdi had taken a trip to Egypt to find inspiration.
- Lean how to make a new apple dessert after reading *"Autumn"* By H. P. Nichols on pg.206.
- Ralph Waldo Emerson wrote the poem *"October."* He was a transcendentalist and he loved nature. Go for an autumn nature walk and look at all the beautiful colors on the trees. Look up a video on how to make an all-natural leaf crown out of leaves. Like "5 min autumn leaf crown" on You Tube.

November

- There are Native Indians in just about every part of the world. Jake Zesiger wrote the poem ***"As I Wander"*** expressing this sentiment. What Native Indians live in your part of the world? Learn more about them and see if there is a way for you to visit a historical site.
- Joseph Rodman Drake's *"Niagara"* on pg.236 talks about the powerful waterfall on the border of New York and Canada. It's time to be a detective and discover if there are any waterfalls in the world that are as tall as Niagara Falls is wide. If there is, where is it located? How many mils would you have to travel to go from Niagara Falls to the other water fall?
- *"A Pot of Tea"* By Robert William Service talks about how much he loves tea. Try a new tea that you have never tasted. Make a treat and have a poetry tea time.

December

- What do you think about? After reading *"Thoughts"* By Myra Viola Wilds on pg,249 think about this last year. What did you like? What do you wish you had done? Write down a few things you think you would like to do this next year. Write it onto a piece of paper and save it to open next year.
- Read *"Goody Santa Clause on a Sleigh Ride"* By Katharine Lee Bates and then draw a Santa Claus like how he is described in the poem. Or try to write your own poem or story about Santa. What do you think Santa looks like? What is your favorite season? *"December's Snow"* By Arthur Conan Doyle compares the

different seasons to winter. Fold a piece of paper in half. Look out one of your windows and draw what you see. Now draw the same scene as it would look during a different season.

Field Trips

Here are some great places you can visit to learn about poets and/or patriotism. Even if you don't live close to any of these locations, try looking up historical sites or poets who came from your area. For 25 poetry field trip locations check out the book A Year of Poetry Tea Time. Also, remember to check for poets in any area where you might be visiting.

International

Robert Burns Statues Around the World

There are so many statues of Robert Burns that you could very likely visit one of them. They range from busts in a public space to large statues in parks. If you happen to visit one including a dog, it is the dog he had on his farm. Also commemorating his time as a farmer, you may see a statue featuring him standing with a plough.

Why am I including this huge list of statues? I want you to know about these statures so if you happen to travel to any of these locations you can plan to go visit one. I have found that my children visiting real places helps bring their learning to life. I have been to 15 of these locations and wish that I would have known about even one of them to take my children to. So to save you from disappointment, I have spent to time to include all of these statue locations.

Australia

- Adelaide, South Australia – outside the State Library of South Australia.
- Ballarat, Victoria – on Sturt Street (corner of Lydiard Street)
- Bendigo, Victoria – bust found in the Bendigo Art Gallery
- Brisbane, Queensland – statue at Centenary Place.
- Camperdown, Victoria – statue, possibly the oldest existing outside Burns statue. Unfortunately, because of vandalism only the plinth (the base) remains in the botanic park. The statue has been moved to the shire council chambers.
- Canberra, ACT – statue outside the eponymous Burns Centre, National Circuit

- Melbourne, Victoria – Bronze statue in Treasury Gardens, with bronze friezes decorating the plinth. The bronze reliefs show scenes from 3 of his poems. They are *To a mountain daisy* (1786), *Tam O'Shanter* (1790), and *The cotter's Friday night* (1785).
- Sydney, New South Wales – statue of Burns with plough outside the Art Gallery of New South Wales. The plough represents his time as a farmer.

Canada

- Edmonton, Alberta – bronze statue the grounds of the Hotel Macdonald
- Fredericton, New Brunswick – statue on the Green, by the banks of the Saint John River. It can be found across from the Provincial Legislature.
- Halifax, Nova Scotia – statue erected in Victoria Park
- Montreal, Quebec – statue in Dominion Square at the Western entrance.
- Toronto, Ontario – brass statue on a light granite plinth in Allan Gardens.
- Vancouver, British Columbia– statue in Stanley Park.
- Victoria, British Columbia – the statue is in Beacon Hill Park near the southern car park.
- Windsor, Ontario – large bronze bust located on the east side of Jackson Park beside a parking lot.
- Winnipeg, Manitoba – statue is on Kennedy Street in the grounds of the Provincial Legislature.

England

- London – statue in the Victoria Embankment Gardens
- London – memorial bust in Poets' Corner, Westminster Abbey
- Newcastle upon Tyne – statue in Walker Park.

Estonia

- **Tallinn, Estonia** – statue (bust) in Scottish Park (Šoti Park), Uus 31 (street), beside the Old Town.

Ireland

Belfast, Northern Ireland – in the Linen Hall Library you will find a small pedestal and bronze statue in the reception area.

New Zealand

- Auckland, North Island – a brass statue in The Domain.
- Dunedin, South Island – statue in The Octagon near the St. Paul's Cathedral. One of the city's founding fathers was the poet's nephew Thomas Burns.
- Hokitika, South Island – statue in Cass Square
- Timaru, South Island – statue in Timaru Botanic Gardens

Scotland

- Aberdeen – statue near Union Terrace Gardens
- Alloway – monument a short distance from his birthplace
- Arbroath – in the grounds of Arbroath Library.
- Ayr – statue in Burns Statue Square
- Bathgate – statue of Rabbie Burns in grounds of Partnership Centre.
- Dumfries – at the end of the town centre, opposite Greyfriars Church.
- Dumfries – mausoleum at burial site in St Michaels Churchyard
- Dumfries – Burns House museum
- Dundee – statue in Meadowside
- Edinburgh – monument on Regent Road, Calton Hill. The marble statue that was inside it was moved to the Scottish National Portrait Gallery in Edinburgh.
- Eglinton Country Park – bronze statue found in the Visitor Centre.
- Glasgow – statue in George Square
- Irvine – statue on Irvine Moor
- Kilmarnock – Sicilian marble statue at the Burns Monument Centre.
- Kilmarnock – statue at Kilmarnock Cross
- Leith – statue on Bernard Street
- Mauchline – Burns National Memorial
- Montrose – stone statue
- Paisley – statue in the Fountain Gardens
- Portpatrick – the statue overlooks the bowling greens.
- Stirling – statue outside Albert Halls
- Stirling – a white marble bust of Burns, found inside the Wallace Monument
- Stonehaven - a stone bust of Burns, within the Burns Memorial Garden found at the corner of David Street and Belmont Brae.

United States

- Albany, New York – statue in Washington Park
- Atlanta, Georgia – this location is not a statue but a replica of Burns' birthplace cottage tat is in Scotland. It belongs to the Burns Club Atlanta.
- Barre, Vermont – statue in front of the old Spaulding High School building.
- Boston, Massachusetts – bronze statue in the Back Bay Fens
- Cheyenne, Wyoming – bronze statue erected in Gilchrist Park
- Chicago, Illinois – statue in Garfield Park. The statue was cast in Edinburgh.
- Denver, Colorado – bronze statue in the city park. The sculptor is believed to be William Grant Stevenson who also did the original Kilmarnock statue in Scotland.
- Detroit, Michigan – bronze statue in Cass Park across from the Masonic Temple near downtown.
- Houston, Texas –Bust in the International Sculpture Garden of Hermann Park.
- Jacksonville, Florida – a limestone bust on a large plinth in Confederate Park, The four panels were stolen during World War II, possibly sold as scrap metal. Located near the corner of Main and Phelps Streets.[29]
- Milwaukee, Wisconsin – bronze statue in Burns Square between Prospect and Farwell Avenues on Knapp Street,
- New York City – the statue is in Central Park and has a twin statue in London, England.
- Pittsburgh, Pennsylvania – statue at the Phipps Conservatory & Botanical Gardens.
- Quincy, Massachusetts – statue can be found on Granite Street.
- San Francisco, California – statue is in Golden Gate Park near the Rhododendron Grove, off JFK Drive.
- St. Louis, Missouri – statue on the Danforth Campus of Washington University.

Patriotic Quotes

Here is a collection of great quotes promoting freedom, patriotism and more. I chose these quotes based on their messages, not necessarily geographically. We can learn from people all over the world. So read the quotes for what their message is. Apply them to yourself and your own country.

"I think of a hero as someone who understands the degree of responsibility that comes with his freedom."
—*Bob Dylan*

"It's better to fight for something in life than to die for nothing."
—*General George S. Patton*

"May we never forget our fallen comrades. Freedom isn't free."
—*Sgt. Major Bill Paxton*

"I think patriotism is like charity—it begins at home."
—*Henry James*

"One cannot and must not try to erase the past merely because it does not fit the present."
—*Golda Meir*

"The history of freedom in never really written by chance but by choice."
—*Dwight Eisenhower*

"May we think of freedom, not as the right to do as we please, but as the opportunity to do what is right."
—*Peter Marshall*

"All great change in America begins at the dinner table."
—*Ronald Reagan*

“The government is the strongest of which every man feels a part.”
—Thomas Jefferson

“There is no such thing as society: there are individual men and women, and there are families.”
—Margaret Thatcher

"Patriotism is not short, frenzied outbursts of emotion, but the tranquil and steady dedication of a lifetime."
—Adlai Stevenson

“Freedom lies in being bold.”
—Robert Frost

"In the truest sense, freedom cannot be bestowed; it must be achieved."
—Franklin D. Roosevelt

“Freedom is one of the deepest and noblest aspirations of the human spirit.”
—Ronald Reagan

Liberty consists of doing anything which does not harm others: thus, the exercise of the natural rights of each man has only those borders which assure other members of the society the fruition of these same rights.
—Marquis De Lafayette

"America is another name for opportunity."
—Ralph Waldo Emerson

"Liberty is the breath of life to nations."
—George Bernard Shaw

“Ask not what your country can do for you, but what you can do for your country.”
—John F. Kennedy

"...The larger the slice taken by government, the smaller the cake available for everyone."

—Margaret Thatcher

"Those who won our independence believed liberty to be the secret of happiness and courage to be the secret of liberty."

—Louis D. Brandeis

It's not enough that we do our best; sometimes we have to do what's required.

—Winston Churchill

"Loyalty to country ALWAYS. Loyalty to government, when it deserves it."

—Mark Twain

"The will of the people is the only legitimate foundation of any government, and to protect it's free expression should be our first object."

—Thomas Jefferson

"I should like to be able to love my country and still love justice."

—Albert Camus

"A love for tradition has never weakened a nation, indeed it has strengthened nations in their hour of peril."

—Winston S. Churchill

"All wars are civil wars because all men are brothers... Each one owes infinitely more to the human race than to the particular country in which he was born."

—Francois de Salignac de La Mothe- Fenelon

Farewell to the Highlands, farewell to the North,
The birth-place of Valour, the country of Worth;
Wherever I wander, wherever I rove,
The hills of the Highlands forever I love.

—Robert Burns

"There can be no liberty unless there is economic liberty."
—Margaret Thatcher

I declare before you all that my whole life, whether it be long or short, shall be devoted to your service and the service of our great imperial family to which we all belong.
—Queen Elizabeth II

"Liberty, once lost, is lost forever."
—John Adams

"We fight not for glory, nor for wealth, nor honour but only and alone for freedom which no good man surrenders but with his life."
—Robert the Bruce

"If the freedom of speech is taken away then dumb and silent we may be led, like sheep to the slaughter."
—George Washington

"I am a Canadian, free to speak without fear, free to worship in my own way, free to stand for what I think right, free to oppose what I believe wrong, or free to choose those who shall govern my country. This heritage of freedom I pledge to uphold for myself and all mankind."
—John G.Diefenbaker

There is a certain enthusiasm in liberty, that makes human nature rise above itself, in acts of bravery and heroism.
—Alexander Hamilton

"It is not possible to be in favor of justice for some people and not be in favor of justice for all people."
—Martin Luther King Jr.

Our hopes are high. Our faith in the people is great. Our courage is strong. And our dreams for this beautiful country will never die.
—Pierre Trudeau

"Any society that would willingly give up a little liberty to gain a little security will deserve neither and loose both."
—Benjamin Franklin

"The Constitution is not a document for the government to restrain the people: it is an instrument for the people to restrain the government."
—Patrick Henry

"Those who deny freedom to others, deserve it not for themselves; and, under a just God, cannot long retain it."
—Abraham Lincoln

"It isn't enough to talk about peace. One must believe in it. And it isn't enough to believe in it. One must work at it."

—Eleanor Roosevelt

"The life of the nation is secure only while the nation is honest, truthful, and virtuous."

—Frederick Douglas

I have cherished the ideal of a democratic and free society in which all persons live together in harmony and with equal opportunities. It is an ideal which I hope to live for and to achieve. But if needs be, it is an ideal for which I am prepared to die.

-Nelson Mandela

"To be free is better than to be unfree – always. Any politician who suggests the opposite should be treated as suspect."

-Margaret Thatcher

"Give me liberty, or give me death!"

—Patrick Henry

Veteran Poets

All of these poets have either fought in a war or served in the military.
You can find their

Rupert Brooke, England,
Royal Navy, WWI

Paterson, Andrew Barton
"Banjo", Australia,
Major in the Army, WWI

Robert Graves, England,
Royal Army WWI

Ivor Gurney, England,
Gloucestershire Regiment,
WWI

Juliette Hiller, USA,
Specialist, United States
Army

Joyce Kilmer, USA
National Guard,WWI

Francis Ledwidge, Ireland,
infantry,WWI

John Mc Crea, Canada,
Canadian Field Artillery,
Second Boar War, WWI

Wilfred Edward Salter Owen,
England, Artists Artillery,
Second Lieutenant.
WWI

Isaac Rosenberg, England,
British Army, WWI

Siegfried Sassoon, England,
British Army. WWI

Charles Hamilton Sorley,
Scotland,
Captain, British Army, WWI

Henry Vaughn, Wales,
British Civil War

Julien Vocance, France,
French Army, WWI

George Washington, USA,
French and Indian War &
Revolutionary War

Hedd Wyn, Wales,
Royal Welsh Fusiliers, WWI

poetry throughout this book.

Mini Poet Bios

Adams, Francis William Lauderdale – 1862–1893 – Malta
In 1884 Adams was published in Australia where he lived. Later he moved to England. He continued to be published in both Australia and England. His most popular work was *Songs of the Army of the Night* in 1887.

Addison, Joseph — 1672-1719 — England
Addison excelled in his study of the classics. He was known for his ability to write Latin verses and he translated Virgil's Georgics and published it in 1694. He was an essayist, playwright, poet, and politician. He was the co-creator of The Spectator magazine in 1711 where his popular church Hymn *The Spacious Firmament on High* was published a year later. His most popular play was Cato in 1713. His first major work was about the lives of English poets.

Akiko Yosano — 1878-1942 — Japan
Yosano was responsible for running the family yōkan (a type of confection) business at age 11. She loved reading books from her father's library and often submitted poetry to the Myōjō poetry magazine. She is well known and considered to be a controversial poet for her time.

Alger Jr., Horatio – 1823–1899 – Massachusetts, USA
Alger, an American novelist, is known for writing rags-to-riches stories about boys who worked their way up to the middle class. He emphasized ideals of hard work, courage, and determination. He gained popularity with his book *Ragged Dick*. His novel themes were known as a "Horatio Alger myth."

Baker, Ella — b. 2008 — Utah, USA
Baker enjoys roller skating, doodling, reading and acting in her free time. Her favorite things are peanut butter, dark chocolate and her dog Remy.

Bates, Katharine Lee — 1859-1929 — Massachusetts, USA
Bates' father died shortly after she was born and was raised by her mother. She had a full education and graduated with a B.A. and in 1889 won a novel writing contest for her book Rose and Thorn. Later she used the prize money to travel to England and studied at Oxford University and then

returned to the US and worked her way up to being a professor at Wellesley College where she earned her degree. She never married in order to keep her position at the college. She is known for her anthem *America the Beautiful* and popularizing Mrs. Clause in *Goody Santa Claus on a Sleigh Ride.*

Becker, Lucy — b. 2002 — Kentucky, USA
Lucy Becker is an avid learner and the best older sister you could ask for ;). In her free time, Lucy likes to read, ride her horses, and play piano.

Blake, William – 1754–1827 – England
Blake was born in Soho, London. He grew up to be an English poet, printmaker, and painter. He attended school long enough to learn to read and write. After that, he learned at home, read books of his choosing, and at this point he became interested in poetry. He attended a drawing school at age ten. He was also a great artist in his time and was proclaimed by Johnathan Jones to be "far and away the greatest artist Britain has ever produced." Blake was considered idealistic and a bit mad for his views on politics and religion.

Boyer, Nellie — b. 1981 — Virginia, USA
Boyer's earliest memories of hearing poetry stems back to when she was a child and her grandmother would read Childcraft books to her. When she was in the third grade she would hide in her closet and read Shel Silverstein in her closet with a flashlight. is a lover of poetry, nature, good movies, and all beautiful things. She and her husband A US Air Force Vet) have 4 children and they love traveling, adventures, camping, playing soccer, and being together. She has homeschooled her own children for 10 years.

Bronson, Ruth Muskrat — 1897-1982 — Delaware, USA
Muskrat was born into the Cherokee tribe on the Delaware National Reservation in Indian Territory. Her ancestors were some of the Native Americans who were forced to walk the "Trail of Tears" from Georgia to Indiana. Her mother was Irish-English and her father was Cherokee. She strongly advocated for better education for Native Americans. She served as the Executive Secretary for the National Congress of American Indians in Washington DC for twenty Years before she moved to Arizona where she continued working for the rights of the Native Americans. She received her BA in English and was also a prolific poet and wrote many books.

Brooke, Rupert —1887-1915 — England — **WWI**
Brookes attended Cambridge (then called King's College, Cambridge) to study the Classics in 1906. He became one of the members of a group called The Apostles and helped start a drama club. He enjoyed both acting and writing poetry. He also belonged to a group called the Georgian Poets where both Robert Frost and Edward Thomas were members. At the outbreak of WWI, he enlisted in the military in 1914. He soon became known as a war poet in 1915 when two of his sonnets were published. In that same year his most famous collection of poetry was *1914 & Other Poems*.

Burns, Robert – 1759–1796 – Scotland
Burns was born in Alloway, Scotland in a house that was built by his father. William Burnes (his father) was a tenant farmer and his mother, Agnes Broun, was the daughter of a tenant farmer. He was the eldest of seven children. When he was seven his family moved to the Mount Oliphant farm where his father did the same work. Burns grew up doing manual farm labor and in poverty. He had very little formal education and gained most of his learning from his father. His father taught all of his children math, geography, history, reading, writing, and even wrote a *A Manual of Christian Beliefs*. He did attend an "adventure school" where he learned some Latin and French from John Murdock and later spent three weeks living with Murdock to study Latin, French and grammar more in depth. At age fifteen he was the main laborer at the farm and he met Nelly Kilpatrick who introduced him to poetry. His first attempt at a poem was "O, Once I Lov'd A Bonnie Lass." He became a poet and lyricist who wrote in both English and Scots dialect. Burns is still very popular in Scotland, and in 2009, a public vote won him the title of "Greatest Scot" He was a collector of folk songs. His poem turned song "Auld Lang Syne" is popular around the world.

Bush-Banks, Olivia Ward — 1869-1944 — New York, USA
Bush-Banks was born to parents who were African American and Montaukett Native American. Her mother died when she was nine months old and after her father remarried she was raised by her aunt who shared her mother's Montaukett heritage. She grew up to feel strongly about her Native American heritage. As an adult she was married twice and had 2 children. As a single parent she worked had to support her small family. She managed to still find time to write poetry and published her first collection of poetry, *Original Poems* in 1899. She enjoyed theater and every place she moved she was involved in it. In 1914 her most popular collection of poetry, *Driftwood*, was published. She became a recurring

contributor to the *Colored American* magazine and was active in supporting the "New Negro Movement."

Carleton, Caroline — 1811-1874 — Australia
Carleton was born in England and was a very bright child and had a good education. She learned to speak both Italian and French and was very familiar with Latin. She also played the pianoforte and harp. After getting married and having two children she moved to Southern Australia in 1839. In 1859 she entered a poetry contest and entered with the poem *The Song of Australia*. After her husband's death she started a girls school.

Castilla, Ethel — 1861-1937 — Australia
Castilla was named Ethelirita Ramos de Castilla in Kyenton Australia. She was a poet who was often published in *The Australian* and the *Sydney Mail*.

Cawein, Madison Julius — 1865-1914 — Kentucky, USA
Cawein was born to a father who made herbal medicines which developed a love of nature in Cawein. After primary education he worked in a pool hall for six years just to save money so he could return home and write. His first publication was *Blooms of the Berry* in 1887. The era of poetic modernism was kicked off with his poem *The Waste Land* published in 1922. He is believed to be an influence of T.S. Elliot's.

Chindongo, Amelie — b. 2014 — South Africa
Chindango wrote her poem *Malawi* in 2021. Her mother read poetry to her when she was a baby and developed such a love for it that she would sis sit attentively and listen to every word. She is an avid reader and loves the arts. She loves to write short stories, poetry and spends a lot of time drawing. She hopes to one day own an art gallery and publish many books.

Crowther, Melissa – b. 1981 – Utah, USA
Crowther is a cellist and loves to play music with her family and local chamber orchestra. She enjoys gardening, hiking, and reading poetry while having tea.

Daley, Victor James – 1858–1905 – Australia
Daley was born in Armagh, Ireland. He received his education in England. In 1878 he immigrated to Australia and became a freelance journalist and writer. He helped establish clubs for poets and writers. He also used the

pseudonym Creeve Roe (Red Branch in Irish). Best known poem is "A Sunset Fantasy."

Davis, Thomas Osborne — 1814-1845 — Ireland
Davis was born to a Welsh father and Irish mother. His father died while traveling to the serve in the Peninsular War one month before he was born. His mother was wealthy enough to take care of their family and she moved them to Dublin. Davis attended Trinity College and graduated with a degree in Logic and then studied law in Europe and London but he never practiced law. He was an Irish nationalist and spoke out for Irelands independence. He started a newspaper, *the Nation.*

De La Mare, Walter — 1873-1956 — England
De La Mare received his education at the St. Paul's Cathedral School. His maternal grandfather, Dr. Colin Arrott Browning, was a naval surgeon and author. De La Mare didn't like his name and asked people to call him Jack. He believed that there are two types of imagination. He was known to say "children are, in short, visionaries." He said that a child's thoughts are full of both creative and ingenuity. But the more exposure they have to the world the more their imagination fades away. His first collection of poetry was Songs of Childhood in 1902.

Dickinson, Emily – 1830–1886 – Massachusetts, USA
Dickinson was born in Amherst, Massachusetts on the family homestead. Her father was a lawer and her grandfather helped found Amherst College. Dickinson's father wanted his children to have a very good education, so much that even when he was away, he wrote letters to the children to encourage them to learn lots so they could tell him all about it when he returned home. She attended an all-girls school, Amherst Academy for seven years and was a very good student and she was considered a well-behaved child. A family friend, Benjamin Franklin Newton, introduced Dickinson (now an adult) to the writings of William Wordsworth and once gifted her a book of poetry written by Ralph Waldo Emerson which had a "liberating effect" on her. She preferred being alone and she wrote over 1800 poems of which only about ten were published while she was alive.

Doyle, Sir Arthur Conan – 1859–1930 – Scotland
Doyle started writing short stories while attending medical school. In 1879 his first published short story was titled *The Mystery of Sasassa Valley*. He was a practicing doctor on ships such as the Greenland whaler *Hope of Peterhead* and eventually opened his own practice. At age twenty-seven, his first Sherlock Holmes story was published.

Drake, Joseph Rodman — 1795-1820 — New York, USA
Drake was orphaned as a young child. As a young child he displayed a talent for writing poetry. He received his education at Columbia College. He practiced medicine after studying at a physician's office in 1816. In 1819 he and Fitz-Greene Halleck write satirical poems for the *New York Evening Post*. They used the penname "The Croakers." As a poet he was considered to be a part of the "Knickerbocker group" with other poets such as Washington Irving, Lydia M. Child and many more.

Dunkerley, William Arthur — 1852-1941 — England
Dunkerley spent a short time in the US after he was married. He then moved to London. There he was a Deacon and Teacher at the Ealing Congregational Church. He then was mayor of Worthing in Sussex. He wrote under his own name as well as under the penname John Oxenham and Julian Ross when doing journalism. His first publication was a murder mystery, A Mystery of the Underground. He also co-founded a magazine, The Idler.

Dyson, Louise — b.1987 — England
Dyson was Born in Aylesbury, Buckinghamshire, England. She was raised in England regularly traveled the United States to visit family in Indiana. She had two children and later emigrated to Indiana in 2021.

Emerson, Ralph Waldo – 1803–1882 – Massachusetts, USA
Emerson was born in Boston, Massachusetts and. is father died just before his eighth birthday. His mother raised he and his siblings with the assistance from other female family members. His aunt Mary Moody Emerson would even live with the family on and off. At age 9 he attended a Latin school and went to Harvard at age 14. As a student he kept a journal of all the books he read and called the collection of notebooks "Wide World." He was class poet of Harvard's 1821 graduating class. He grew up to be known as a philosopher, poet, essayist, and lecturer who led the transcendentalist movement.

Emerson, William Ralph — 1833-1917 — Illinois, USA
Emerson is the cousin of the famous author and transcendentalist Ralph Waldo Emerson. He was an architect known for his Shingle Styled houses and Inns. You can still see his architecture in Bar Harbor, Maine. He also worked with Olmsted in creating many of the building in the National Zo in Washington D.C.

Evans, Evan (Geirionydd, Levan Glan) — 1795-1855 —Wales
Evans was born in a farmhouse and he received his early education at a nearby church school. He then started to work on his parent's farm but after the rent was increased, they lost the farm. In 1816 he became a schoolmaster in Tal-y-Bont even without any higher education. And before the age of 26 he was an Elder at the Methodist Church. HE did lots of journalism and magazine editing in his time but is best known for his poetry. His father was also a poet. He won "The Chair" (the winner) at the National Eisteddfod competition three times. This is a largest music and poetry contest in Europe.

Fields, Barron — 1786-1846 — Australia
Fields was born in England and received the education needed to work in law. He became a barrister. He was also a great poet and contributed often to the press. In 1816 he emigrated to New South Wales, Australia to be a judge. In 1819 First Fruits of Australian Poetry was published. It was his first publication and only 12 pages.

Flanagan, Mary — b. 2007 — Georgia, USA
Flanagan was 14 years old when she wrote her poem Reign of Our Voice. She is homeschooled and has a passion for poetry and writing. Flanagan enjoys writing poetry, taking walks in nature and playing with her cat. Her favorite book is Little Women.

Freneau, Philip — 1752-1832 — New York, USA
Frenear was raised a Calvinist and after grammar school he attended Princeton University (then called College of New Jersey. He became friends with James Madison. After graduating he spent some time in the West indies. On his return home he become a revolutionary privateer crew member and was held captive on a British prison ship. This inspired his writing "The British Prison Ship" and lead to his writing many patriotic poems. This gained him the title "The Poet of the American Revolution." Some poems that influenced the future of poetry are *The House of Night, The Wild Honey Suckle, and The Indian Burying Ground.*

Fortune, Timothy Thomas — 1856-1928 — Florida, USA
Fortune was born into slavery to Emanuel and Sarah Jane Fortune in Marianna, Florida. After the Civil War he began his education at the first African American school in his town. His family moved to Jacksonville where he continued his education and he worked as a page in the State Senate and as an apprentice printer at a local newspaper. Even though he was mostly self-educated he was accepted to study law but then switched

to journalism. In 1905 a book of poems titled *Dreams of Life: Miscellaneous Poems* was published.

Gilbert, William Schwenck — 1836-1911 — England
Gilbert was born in London to a father who was a naval surgeon for a short time and an author. He attended King's College and then planned on joined the military but with the end of the Crimean War he joined the Civil Serve and then the Militia where he became a Captain. He left that career and gave a try at being a barrister but had so little success he had to turn to writing and illustration to make ends meet. His humorous poetry was found to be very enjoyable. This led to the poems being printed in a book, *Bab Ballads*. This led to him writing plays and comic operas.

Goethe, Johann Wolfgang von – 1749–1832 – Germany
Goethe was multitalented in writing both epic and lyrical poetry. During law school he preferred to learn about poetry rather than law. He was well known by age twenty-five after the success of his book *The Sorrow of Young Werther*. He sat on a council under the Duke of Saxe-Weimar, Karl August, who ennobled him. As the modern era's literary genius, he not only wrote poetry, but also worked in science and politics and wrote novels, and dramas, including his play *Faust*.

Graves, Robert – 1895–1985 – England — **WWI**
Graves was the son of Charles Graves, an Irish poet, who wrote the song "Father O'Flynn." During school he was good at boxing and began to write poetry. During WWI he wrote even more poetry while in the British Army and he came to be known as the war poet.

Gurney, Ivor — 1890-1937 — England — **WWI**
Gurney was born to a father who was a tailor and a mother who was a seamstress. He enjoyed music as a young child and displayed musical ability. He even sang in the Gloucester Cathedral from 1900-1906. He started college but WWI led to his enlisting into the British military. He started to write poetry when he was on the front lines and would mail them to friends. He was working on a book of poetry when he shoulder was injured. He recovered and returned to active duty where he finished the book, *Severn and Somme*, for publication in the Fall of 1917.

Hall, Lily — b. 2010 — Georgia, USA
Hall's father is active duty in the US Army. She has a sister and lives with both parents in Virginia. She lived in Georgia at the time her poem *Love For My Country*. During her early childhood her mother has read poetry to

her. Her favorite poet is Shel Silberstein and she enjoys books written by Tui T. Sutherland. She likes to draw, skate, play games, and enjoys watching movies.

Harper, Frances Ellen Watkins — 1825-1911 — Maryland, USA
Harper was born to free African American parents. She was orphaned at age three and was then raised by her aunt and uncle Wilkins. William Wilkins was a big influence in her life. He was an abolitionist and was not scared to speak up about it. She attended his school, Wilkin's Academy for Negro Youth. At age 13 she worked for a family who owned a book shop and she did the seamstress and nursemaid. In her free time, she would read books in the shop. Her first collection of poetry, *Forest Leaves* was completed at age twenty in 1845. She moved to Wilberforce, Ohio to be the first woman instructor at a school for African Americans. She was then a teacher in York, Pennsylvania. Because of a law passed in Maryland she could not return home or she would risk being sold into slavery. She moved in with William and Letita Still. Still is known to be the father of the underground Railroad. Harper then dedicated her efforts towards fighting against slavery. She published over 80 poems in her life time.

Hartley, John — 1839-1915 — England
Hartley was born in Halifax, West Yorkshire, England. He was famous for writing poetry and prose in the Yorkshire dialect. His poetry often focuses on the poverty of the district he lived in.

Hiller, Juliette — b. 1983 — Washington, USA — **US ARMY**
Hiller's family growing up moved very often all along the west coast. They eventually settled in Washington when she was 12. As a child she enjoyed poetry. With dyslexia, she found the rhymes poetry to be easy to understand and enjoyable. She was. Dr. Seuss fan and enjoyed the books Marvin K. Moonie and Cat in the Hat. As an adult she had her own adventures traveling the world in the military and as a missionary. After getting married she returned to Washington to start her family. She had 7 children and enjoys running, teaching ballet, leading worship at church, and homeschooling her children.

Homan, L. Allen, Dr. — b. 1953 — Canada
Homan was born and raised among the corn fields of rural Michigan, USA. After marrying his love, Jerrie, he moved his small family to serve Jesus Christ as a missionary in Canada. Since that time, he has ministered in some of the largest and most rural churches in Canada. His life has been one of committed loving sacrifice for his family, friends, and Savior.

Horton, George Moses — 1798-1867 — North Caroline, USA
Horton grew up to be known as "the Black Bard of North Carolina." He was born into slavery, sixth of ten children, on the William Horton plantation. He and his siblings were gifted to James Horton. After a division of this estate the sibling group was split up. He writes about this in his poem "Division of an Estate." He was known as a poet but all of his attempts to use poetry as an income was not fruitful. He was married in 1830's and had two children. He gained his freedom at age 68 and continued to write poetry. He emigrated to Liberia but it is unknown where he last lived.

Hunter, Richard — N.D.
Unfortunately, after much research, no bio information could be found on this poet.

Jefferson, Thomas —1743-1826 — Virginia, USA
Jefferson became the third President of the United States. His self-taught father wanted his children to have a better education than he had. Jefferson started with a tutor along with his sibling at age five. His mother and father died while he was a child and this led to him inheriting Monticello. He wrote the Declaration of Independence which led to the United States gaining its independence from England. He held many different political positions in his life time. He enjoyed playing the violin and did a lot of experimenting with gardening, and loved to read books. He died on July 4th 1826 on the 50th anniversary of the country's independence.

Johnson, Emily Pauline — 1861-1913 — Canada
Johnson was born near Brantford, Ontario on the Six Nations reservation. Her mother was English and her father was Mohawk Indian. She was an ill child and gained most of her education from her mother at home and by reading from the family's extensive library. Her paternal grandfather was a story teller and shared traditional Mohawk stories. His talent for performing rubbed off on Johnson. Her parents raised her and her three other siblings to fit into high society. This served her well in life. She performed on stage and was known to be a native American beauty. Her first poem *My Little Jean* was published in 1883 and best known for her collections of poetry.

Kilmer, Joyce — 1886-1918 — New Jersey, USA- **WWI**
Kilmer attended grammar school at age 8 and was the school paper editor. He won the
Lane Classic Prize for oration and won a scholarship for Rutgers College Grammar School. He had trouble with mathematics, yet managed to stay at the head of his class. From 1904-1906 he attended Rutgers University (earlier called Rutgers College). His most famous poem is *Trees* published in 1913 and was later published in his book *Trees and Other Poems* in 1914. After the U.S. entered into WWI Kilmer joined the New York National Guard. He gained the rank of Sergeant and was offered to become an officer but refused it because he would rather be a sergeant in the "Fighting 69th" then an officer in another unit. He went to France where he asked to serve in dangerous missions and did well at them. But his luck ran out and unfortunately, he died in Germany.

Lazarus, Emma — 1849–1887 — New York, USA
Lazarus is best known for her poem "The New Colossus" written in 1883. It was so popular; it was engraved on the Statue of Liberty. It also inspired the song "Give Me Your Tired" by Irving Berlin, and a 1985 song, "The Lady of the Harbor." She also wrote translations and prose. She was an activist for the Jewish people. She was educated at home and started writing poetry at age eleven and learned German, French, and Italian.

Ledwidge, Francis — 1887-1917 — Ireland —**WWI**
Ledwidge was born in Janeville, Slane, Ireland and he was called Frank. His parents wanted to provide the best education they could for their 9 children (Ledwidge being #9) but his father died when he was only five. This made it so the entire family had to go to work. Ledwidge received some formal education and was done at age thirteen and continued to educated himself as he worked at any work he could get. He started to be published at age 14 in the Drogheda Independent as well as two other papers. He was often unpaid. His first published collection of poems was titled *Songs of the Fields*. At the start of WWI, he joined the Army where he quickly gained the rank of lance Corporal. As a result of being injured he was inspired to write many poems about his experiences. His poems expressed his pride in being a soldier. He died a soldier while taking a tea break from building roads to help advance the troops.

Lawson, Henry – 1867–1922 – Australia
At age ten, an ear infection left him partially deaf. He was totally deaf by fourteen. His school teacher taught him all he could about poetry and later became one of Australia's best-known poets and short story writers. His

first poem published was "A Song of the Republic" in 1887. His mother Louisa Lawson, also a poet, published his first collection of poems in 1904. He focused most of his poetry on the Australian bush and aimed for realism in his writing.

Lazarus, Emma – 1849–1887 – New York, USA
Lazarus is best known for her poem "The New Colossus" written in 1883. It was so popular; it was engraved on the Statue of Liberty. It also inspired the song "Give Me Your Tired" by Irving Berlin, and a 1985 song, "The Lady of the Harbor." She also wrote translations and prose. She was an activist for the Jewish people. She was educated at home and started writing poetry at age eleven and learned German, French, and Italian.

Lindsay, Vachel — 1879-1931 — Illinois, USA
Lindsay was born in Springfield, Illinois and his family lived across the street from the state's Governor. This influenced his poetry, for instance *The Eagle Forgotten* when here refers to the governor John P. Altgeld. He went to medical school because his parents wanted him to but he wanted to be a painter. So went to Chicago to pursue art. In 1905 he started to take poetry more seriously and started to self-publish and sell it on the streets. Between 1906 and 1914 he traveled all over, from the East coast, to the mid-West, and even as far as New Mexico. He traded his poetry for food and lodging. Towards the end of his trekking, he started to gain fame. His two most famous poems are *The Congo* and *General William Booth Enters into Heaven*. He wrote his songs to be read as a chant or to be music.

Longfellow, Henry Wadsworth — 1807–1882 — Massachusetts, USA
As a young child, Longfellow was bright and studious and learned Latin. In his lifetime he studied many languages. He is most popular for his poems "Paul Revere's Ride" and "The Song of Hiawatha," and was the first to translate *Dante's Divine Comedy*. In 1820 his first poem, "The Battle of Lovell's Pond, "was published.

Lowell, James Russell — 1819-1891 — Massachusetts, USA
Lowell is an eighth-generation descendant of Percival Lowell who settled in Newbury, Massachusetts in 1639. His mother helped develop his love for literature, as well as tales from the Orkney islands, ballads, and especially poetry. At age 15 he attended Harvard College but he was not the best student. He was in a theatrical club called Hasty Pudding here he was a poet and secretary. It is surprising that he graduated at all. He even admitted that he did poorly at his studies. He was the class poet but lost that title since he was exiled from the school for not taking his studies

seriously and was forced to live in Concord Massachusetts with a Reverend. But while there he met Ralph Waldo Emerson and learned about Transcendentalism. His first poem was published in 1840 and then in started his own literary Journal with Robert Carter called *The Pioneer*. He wanted to produce a journal that only contained new literature and the first publication included the first printing of Edgar Allen Poe's *The Tell-Tale Heart*. Unfortunately, it only lasted three months. But Lowell didn't give up on writing. He wrote for the National Anti-Slavery Standard of New York, published book length poems, published a collection titles Fireside Journey about his time in Europe, was an editor, performed his poem *Commemoration Ode* at Harvard after President Lincolns assassination, dedicated to the fallen of the Civil War, was one of Longfellow's friends who helped him translate Dante's Divine Comedy, and published more poetry collections. After a time being a professor at Harvard, he entered politics and served as a delegate to the Republican National Convention. The newly voted President Hayes asked him to be an ambassador which he did from 1877 to 1885.

Machar, Agnes Maule — 1837-1927 — Canada
Machar is of Scottish decent and was educated by her father at home. She was studied Latin and Greek at age ten and not much later she learned French Greek and Italian. She was a veracious writer and published many books, her most popular novel being For *King and Country*. Her poetry can be read in the 1899 collection, *Lays of "True North" and Other Canadian Poems*. She was a strong advocate of Christianity and believed that evolution and Creationism went hand in hand. She also advocated for churches to help the poor more, prohibition, and better working conditions for woman and children.

Mckellar, Dorothea — 1885-1968 — Australia
Mackellar was born in the Sydney, Australia family home. In 1925 she commissioned a home to be built at Lovett Bay that one could only reach by boat. She supported herself and wrote poetry and more from 1908 and 1926. She was active in the Sydney Publishers, Editors, and Novelist Club, Sydney P.E.N. Club and the Bush Book Club of New South Wales. Her poetry was considered "Bush Poetry". Her poetry was inspired by the time she spent on her brother's farm. Her most well-known poem is *My Country* (included in this book) which she wrote at age 19. Her first collection of poems was published in 1911 titled *The Closed Door*.

Madison, James — 1751-1836 — Virginia, USA
Madison was born on the Belle Grove Plantation in Virginia. He was the oldest of 12 children but only six lived to be adults. From ages 11 to 16 he studied under the tutelage of Donald Robertson who taught many prominent families in the South. He continued his education with Reverend Thomas Martin who prepared him to attend Princeton (earlier names College of New Jersey). His family did not send him to the College of William and Mary because they felt it would not be good for his health. He became very good at speech and debate and adopted strong political views on civil and political liberty influenced by the Age of Enlightenment. After graduating her returned home to teach his younger siblings and started to study law on his own. He did it for his own knowledge but not to become a lawyer even though his education was good enough to pass the bar exam. He attended the Constitutional Convention and a signer of the Constitution. Madison wrote 29 of Federalist Paper essays and Madison's essays #10 and #51 speak of a "representative democracy" and the idea fs checks and balances to prevent any one area of the government becoming too powerful. He also later advocated for the Bill of Rights. He and Thomas Jefferson organized the Democratic-Republican Party. Madison became the fourth President of the United States. He was the president during the War of 1812.

Major DREWE, of Exeter — alive in 1796 — England
Known for writing the poem "Receipt To Make A Sally Lun" about the Sally Lunn bun made popular in Bath, England.

Mathers, Edward Powys — 1892-1939 — England
Mathers was a translator, poet and a creator of advanced crossword puzzles. He is known for his translation of the French version of *One Thousand Nights and One Night*. Mathers also translated The Garden of Bright Waters: One Hundred and Twenty Asiatic Love Poems in 1920. He used the pseudonym "Torquemada" for his crossword puzzles published in The Observer.

Matsuo Basho – 1644–1694 – Japan
Matsuo Basho was born in Japan and introduced to poetry at a young age. He was the most famous poet during Japan's Edo period. He wrote in a special form of poetry named haiku (hokku). He was considered the master of haiku, but he felt that his true genius lay in another poetry form called renku.

Melville, Anicka — b. 2005 — Utah, USA
Melville was born and raised in Southern Utah, surrounded by red mountains, and lots of desert. She loves to read, especially about history. She is a quiet but thoughtful thinker, and loves to play games of all sorts. She likes to try new things, and branch out in new hobbies. Some of her most loved hobbies are art, graphic design, juggling, and gardening.

McCrea, John — 1872-1918 — Canada — **Second Boar War & WWI**
McCrea was born in Ontario Canada to Lieutenant-Colone David McCrea and Janet Simpson Eckford. He attended Guelph Collegiate Vocational Institute where he was being trained to be an artilleryman. In 1894 he taught math and English at the Ontario Agricultural College. He returned to Toronto ad earned his B.A. And studied medicine on a scholarship. To make money he tutored other medical students to include two of the first female doctors in Ontario. After graduating he working in tow hospitals and then served as a lieutenant in South Africa in the Royal Canadian Artillery in the Second Boer War. When he returned to Canada, he became a professor of Pathology. IN 1905 he started his own practice and continued teaching and was the appointed physician for different hospitals. At the outbreak of WWI Canada was instantly involved when Britain declared war on Germany. McCrea became the Major and Medical officer of the 1st Brigade Canadian Field Artillery. Being a trained artillery man, he was agitated when he was pulled away from his guns to do medical duties. "all the…doctors in the world will not win this bloody war: what we need is more and more fighting men." His poem In Flanders Field was first published anonymously in Punch in 1915. Later he was given credit for the poem in the index. The poem became one of the most popular poems from the war. HE died in active duty from pneumonia in France.

McKay, Claude —1890-948 — Jamaica
McKay was Born Festus Claudius and raised in Jamaica. At age four he moved to live with his brother who was a teacher and he fell in love with literature, philosophy, science, and theology. But in his free time, he would read poems, to include Shakespeare which lead to him writing poetry by the age of 10. While doing a carriage and cabinet making apprenticeship, he met Walter Jekyll who encouraged McKay to focus on his writing. He also helped him publish his first book of poems, *Songs of Jamaica* in 1912. It was the first book of poetry published in his home dialect of Jamaican Patois. After this he moved to the United States. He was surprised at the segregation that existed and this eventually led to him joining a group of back radicals. He continued to write poetry and pub. He and worked many different jobs. One of his most popular poems, *If We*

Must Die was published in 1919 in The Liberator. This was during an intense summer of racial tension and violence in the US referred to as the "Red Summer." He traveled to the UK, Russia, Europe and North Africa over an 11-year period of time and used it as inspiration for a lot of his writing. He became a US citizen in 1940. His most famous poem, Home to Harlem, in 1928.

Michel, Sharon K. — b. 1979 — Canada
Michel was born in Michigan and her family moved to Ontario , Canada when she was two. Her father was always writing and her mom was an English college professor, so writing was a family culture and writing came naturally to her. She started writing poetry as a young teenager. She is a wife, Homemaker and Homeschool mom to 4 children for 13 years. She is lover of books, curriculum, and tea. She desires to be a friend to all and serve like Christ. She has a Bachelors Education degree.

Milne, A. A. – 1882–1956 – England
Well known for his beloved children's book *Winnie the Pooh* (1926). In 1903, Milne graduated from Cambridge with a mathematics degree. He served in both the First and Second World Wars. He wrote for *Punch* magazine and wrote eighteen plays and three books, one being *The Red House Mystery*. In 1924, two years after his son was born, he wrote a collection of poetry titled *When We Were Very Young*. His second collection of poetry, *Now We Are Six* was published in 1927.

Moore, Thomas — 1779-1852 — Ireland
Moore was born in Dublin in his family's home over their grocery shop. He loved music and theater and wanted to be an actor when he grew up. He would put together his own little plays with friends. He went to an English grammar school where he learned about Greek and Latin and learned to speak French and Italian. At age fourteen his first poem was published in the Anthologia Hibernica. His poetry popularized Irish culture since he wrote English lyric to Irish tunes. HE was referred to as a "squib" (no, not like in Harry Potter), a person who writes for the aristocratic Whigs. He is best known for his Irish themed poems set to music.

Muir, Alexander — 1830-1906 — Canada — Battle of Ridgeway
Muir was born in Scotland and his family immigrated to Toronto, Canada when he was three years old. He grew up to be an elementary school teacher and took a children's choir in 1874 to perform The Maple Leaf Forever for the very first time for the laying of the Newmarket Christian

Church corner stone. He wrote *The Maple Leaf Forever* after he fought with the Queen's Own Rifles of Canada.

Naomi, Ellie — b. 2001 — Idaho, USA
Naomi resides in the beautiful state of Idaho, She is a poet, author and writing instructor at Story Quest Academy. She can often be found reading, cooking, gardening and planting new clues for her web story The Hannah Anderson Mysteries.

Newbolt, Henry John, Sir — 1862-1938 — England
Newbolt attended both grammar School and Clifton College.
He studied law and graduated from Corpus Christi College, Oxford. He practiced law from 1887-1899. In 1897 he published a collection of ballads titles Admirals All which included his most well-known poem *Vitai* Lampada which means "the torch of life." Another popular poem of his is *Drake's Drum*. At the beginning of WWI he and 19 other authors were hired on to help promote a positive view of Britain's involvement in the war. *The War Films* was a poem to help ease the pain people felt when seeing the war reels before a movie.

Nichols, H. P. — 1816-1890 — Massachusetts, USA
Nichols ran a successful publishing company in Boston, Massachusetts during the mid-1800's. His partner was William Crosby. Later the publishing company was renamed Nichols & Noyes.

Niven, Frederick — 1878-1944 — Canada
Niven was born in Chile and lived there till he was school age when he moved to Scotland with his mother and attended school in Glasgow. He worked in his father's muslin factory, in a jewelry shop, and even a librarian. He moved to British Columbia for his health and worked for a railroad until 1915 when he returned to Scotland. His first volume of poetry, Maple Leaf Song was published in 1917. After getting married he permanently settled in Canada. Niven also wrote novels.

Noyes, Alfred — 1880-1958 — England
Noyes was born in England but his family moved to Wales when he was four years old. He attended Exeter College but did not get his degree because he was meeting with a publisher about his first volume of poetry titled *The Loom of Years* in 1903. He would publish five more volumes of poetry over the next ten years. The most popular poem of all his published works is *The Highwayman*. Noyes was also a playwright and short story writer. Noyes spoke out against war violence but with WWI being an ever-

present danger he concluded that when faced with a unreasonable and aggressive enemy that “a nation could not but fight. Because of poor eye sight he was not allowed to serve on the front lines so he worked in propaganda and helped create good moral through poetry when just a 1913 he had published a very strong anti-war poem titled *The Wine Press*.

Ouchi Yoshitaka — 1507-1551 — Japan
Ōuchi was a daimyo (feudal lord) of the Suo Province and head of the Ōuchi clan. The Ōuchi clan was a prominent and powerful family in Western Japan. This was during the reign of the Ashikaga shogunate and the Ōuchi clan supported the Ashikaga during the Nanboku-cho Wars. Ōuchi came from a long line of conquers to include his father Yoshioki. After his father died in battle in 1528 he gained control of the Kyūshū area by defeating the Shōni clan. Unfortunately his other attempts to follow in his father's footsteps did not end well. Ōuchi decided to focus his time on the arts and culture. The arts and foreign trade grew and the province prospered. Ōuchi also allowed Portuguese missionaries to preach to his people. He even developed a close relationship with the emperor. When the emperor was in trouble Ōuchi devised a plan to save the people and move the capital in a non-confrontational way. It was working but his lead Samurai felt he was being week and lead a revolt against him resulting in him no longer being the head of the Ōuchi clan.

Owen, Wilfred Edward Salter — 1893-1918 — England — **WWI**
Owens' father passed away when he was only four and as a result, he formed a close relationship with his mother. He discovered his aptitude for poetry in 1904 when on holiday. His influences were the Bible, and romantic poets, especially Wordsworth and John Keats. In order to complete his education, he had to work in order to have a place to live and to pay for tuition. He studied botany and the head of the English department suggested that he take some free classes in Old English. In 1913 he moved to France to tutor English and French in Bordeaux. When WWI broke out, he contemplated joining the French army, but in the end, he returned to England and the Artists Artillery where he was Promoted to Second Lieutenant. Once he fell into a shell bast hole and gained a concussion as well as part of a trench mortar shell blast that left him unconscious. He was removed from active duty where he was to recover. He wrote lots of poetry during this time, about his experiences, and met Siegfried Sassoon. After being approved for duty, he learned that Sassoon had been severally injured. He decided to return to active duty to continue documenting the war through poetry. He died in action on 4 November 1918.

Parker, Dorothy — 1893-1967 — New York, USA
Parker was born in New Jersey and before age five her family moved to Manhattan, New York. Her father was Scottish and her mother was both Scottish and Jewish. She sold her first poem in in 1914 to *Vanity Fair* magazine. Not to long after that she was hired to be an editorial assistant at *Vogue* magazine and a couple years later, she moved over to *Vanity Fair*. She was known for her witty criticism when writing as a critic. Her first collection of poetry Enough Rope, was published in 1926.

Paterson, Andrew Barton "Banjo" — 1864-1914 — Australia — **WWI**
Paterson was born on a property named "Narrambia" in New South Wales, Australia. He was known as a "bush poet." Most of his poetry reflects upon the rural outback where he grew up near Orange, New South Wales. During his younger years he was educated by a governess but as soon as he could ride a pony, he went to a bush school in Binalong. HE then attended a grammar school till he was 16. He became a journalist and wrote poetry. During the Second boar war he was a war correspondent. During WWI he was an Ambulance driver and later traveled to Africa, Egypt and China. He was discharged from the Australian Army in 1919 at rank of Major. His first poetry collection, The Man from Snowy River and Other Versus, was published in 1895.

Payne, Annabel — b.2010 — North Carolina, USA
Payne is a Christian author from Stockdale North Carolina. She was homeschooled as a child and is the 2nd of four children. Besides poetry she also enjoys baking, painting, and most of all, reading.

Perrine, Niccole – b. 1983 – Idaho, USA
Perrine was born in Upstate New York, raised in Southern California and Southcentral Alaska. She made her home in Southwestern Idaho and is the mother of five and author of T*he Joy Series*.

Poe, Edgar Allen – 1809–1849 – Virginia, USA
Poe was born in Boston, Massachusetts, and then after his father left and mother died, he moved to Virginia with the Allen family. He released his first forty-page book of poetry at age eighteen titled, *Tamerlane and other Poems*. He was a poet, writer, editor, and a literary critic. He is most famous for his poem "The Raven" and he is said to be the originator of the detective story. His poetry is known for being dark and strange.

Pung, Joshua — b. 2009 — New Jersey, USA
Pung lives in NJ and is educated at home by his parents. They enjoy reading lots of poetry. Pung especially enjoys poetry written in rhyme. His favorite poet is Christina Rossetti. He loves soccer, building things, games, and all vegetables. In his free time, he plays outside or plays video games. He is an obedient child.

Riley, James Whitcomb – 1849–1916 – Indiana, USA
Riley started out by submitting poems to newspapers. He eventually became more popular with a little help from Henry Wadsworth Longfellow. He did poetry reading tours. He was known as a best-selling author by the 1890s. His most famous publication was a collection of children's poetry titled *Rhymes of Childhood* and it was illustrated by Howard Chandler Christy.

Rosenberg, Isaac — 1890-1918 — England — **WWI**
Rosenberg was born in Bristol, England to Lithuanian Jewish parents who had immigrated from Latvia (then called Dvinsk). He lived in, and attended schools, with prominently Jewish populations. He later attended a school of art and started an apprenticeship with an engraver. In 1911 he left to attend the Slade School of Fine arts to pursue poetry and art. In 1912 he published 10 poems in a pamphlet titled Night and Day. He moved to Cape Town in South Africa, where his siter was, with hopes of improving his difficulties with bronchitis. While there he wrote the poem *On Receiving News of the War* after hearing about the start of WWI. After feeling his health was improving, he returned to England. Unable to find work he enlisted in the British Army in 1915. Before his enlistment, he published a collection of poetry titled *Youth*. He was not for the war but had said "I never joined the army for patriotic reasons. Nothing can justify war. I suppose we must all fight to get the trouble over." Unfortunately, he wrote his last poem, "Through These Pale Cold Days" (March 1918), in a letter before being sent to the front lines where he was killed in action at the rank of Private.

Ryan, Abram Joseph — 1838-1886 — Maryland, USA
Ryan was born to Irish immigrant parents both from Clogheen, Tipperary. Being a very good-natured boy, his mother and teachers encouraged him to pursue a spiritual career. He attended St. Mary's of the Barron and in 1855 pursued the Holy Order and cut off his relationship with his childhood sweetheart. He continued his religious studies and his classmates found his poetry to be entertaining. He went on religious tours and was highly liked for his style of preaching. His superiors felt that his messages were not all

spiritually based and he was sent back to St. Mary's to teach theology. He did not like that he was not able to share his thoughts publicly and decided to leave his station at the church. He and his brother wanted to support the confederacy. He never enlisted but was a supporter of the Confederate army and was a freelance Chaplin to the Confederate soldiers. To poems written after his brother's death in uniform are considered some of his best work. They are *In Memoriam* and *In Memory of My Brother*, written in 1863. His most famous post war poem was *The Conquered Banner*.

Sassoon, Siegfried — 1886-1967 — England
Sasoon was born into a wealthy family. His father was Jewish and his mother Anglo-Catholic. He was the second of three boys. He gained a primary education and attended a few different colleges. His first poem to be successful was *Daffodil Murderer* in 1913. With the threat of WWI Sassoon joined the Army and was a member of the Sessex Yeomanry. While serving in France he met Robert Graves and they became friends. After experiencing war first hand his poetry tone changed.

Schkrohowsky, Thomasin — 2005 — Washington, USA
Schkrohowsky was born in Pittsburg, PA. Currently lives on an island in Alaska. She is the oldest of 4 siblings. Her mother would read poetry aloud to her when she was little. Her favorite was Disobedience by AA Milne. She loves it so much, she put it to memory and she still recites it to this day. Her current favorite poet is Edward Rowland Sill. Current interests include writing, drawing, playing and listening to music, and exploring the beach at low tide.

Service, Robert William – 1874–1958 – England
Service is known as the "Bard of the Yukon." This poet of Scottish descent was a banker but later traveled to the United States and Canada. His first poems were inspired by the Klondike Gold Rush and became popular. He continued to write poetry and published a collection titled *Songs of Sourdough.*

Setian, Alitsa — b. 2009 — South Carolina, USA
Setian was born in Greenville, South Carolina to parents of Armenian descent. Both parents speak Armenian which has made it so Setian, her older sister and younger brother are fluent in Armenian. She loves reading, writing, playing (indoors and outdoors!), exploring, and learning as much as she can. She likes to hike, snowboard, act and play piano. She hopes to someday be an author, horse breeder and maybe even do some real estate like her father. She enjoys traveling and has visited many parts of the

United States, Canada and has even been to Armenia. She has always enjoyed writing and poetry. Her main influence is her mother.

Shackleford, Mason — about 2013 — Missouri

Shelley, Percy Bysshe – 1792–1822 – England
Shelley is an English, Romantic poet who was known for his radical views both in his poetry and life. In the English language he is believed to be one of the best philosophical and lyrical poets. Some of the best-known poems are "Ozymandias", "The Skylark," and "The Cloud." He received his early education at home.

Simpson, Joshua McCarter — 1820-1876 — Ohio, USA
Simpson was an African-American and lover of both song and poetry. Many of his poems are written to be read with song. He was an abolitionist and wrote lots about emancipation He only has three months of education and taught himself to write and read. He published his first pamphlet of his poetry ten years after singing a poem for the first time in public. His song-poems became very popular in the Underground Road since the words of protest were disguised by the cheerful hymns and patriotic songs. He did attend Oberin College from 1844-1848 because he wanted to become a teacher. In 1974 he published 53 song-poems representing twenty years of writing. He is best known for his poem *Away to Canada* (included in this book).

Sorley, Charles Hamilton – 1895-1915 — Scotland —**WWI**
Sorley was born in Aberdeen, Scotland to father who was a Philosophy professor. Sorley had a college education and loved cross country running, especially in the rain. Some of his pre-war poems were *The Song of the Ungirt Runner*, and *Rain*. Before WWI he had traveled to Germany to study the language and local culture. Unfortunately, his study abroad was cut short by the start of WWI where he was detained in Trier and later that day released and told to leave Germany immediately. He returned to England and enlisted in the British Army. He arrived in France in May of 1915 as a lieutenant and promoted to captain in August of the same year. He lost his life to a sniper's bullet in October 1915. His last poem was recovered from his belongings
"When you see millions of mouthless dead
Across your dreams in pale battalions go"

Stevenson, Robert Louis – 1850–1894 – Scotland
Even though Stevenson had bronchial troubles his entire life, he enjoyed traveling. He wrote continually. Not only is he known for his novels, *Treasure Island, Kidnapped, Strange Case of Dr. Jekyll and Mr. Hyde*, he is also very well known for his collection of children's poems titled *A Child's Garden of Verses*.

Strong, Elijah — 2004 — Maryland, USA
Strong was born in Colorado and moved to Maryland shortly before he started Kindergarten. He is the oldest of six children, and enjoy reading, writing, ultimate frisbee, and marine science. He plans on becoming either a marine biologist or an author once he graduates college. He started writing poetry as a way to express his thoughts and feelings, and continue to do so whenever the mood strikes him. As a poet, he doesn't consciously model his work off of others, though I will occasionally take inspiration from a song I've listened to or something he has read.

Tennyson, Alfred Lord – 1850–1892 – England
During the reign of Queen Victoria, he was the Poet Laureate of England and earned the Chancellor's Gold Medal for the poem "Timbuktu." Classic mythological themes show up in much of his poetry. He wrote in the lyrical and blank verse styles and tried his hand at being a playwright, but that was not as successful. Many of his writings have held strong within the English language like "Tis better to have loved and lost, than never to have loved at all."

Tynan, Katharine — 1859-1931 — Ireland
Tynan was born into a farming family within the county od Dublin. She attended school at St. Catherine's convent school. She is believed to have written 100 or more novels. Her first poem was published in 1875.

Urso, Isabel — b. 2008 — Kentucky, USA
Urso was born in Fort Worth, TX Bio: Some of my hobbies are writing, baking, crafting, theater, and playing video games with my younger brother. Writing has always been something I have enjoyed, but during Covid I started writing a lot in my free time. When I write, I often find inspiration in Mother Nature.

Vocance, Julien — 1878-1954 — France — **WWI**
Vocance was born Joseph Seguin and became famous for writing haiku, a for of poetry traditionally written in Japan. The Haiku for was introduced to Europe by a fellow French man Couchoud. Vocance strived to perfect

this form of short poetry. At the start of WWI Vocance joined the French Army and compiled a large quantity of poems that were published as Cent Visions of Guerre (One Hundred Visions of War) in 1916. During the war he lost one of his eyes, resulting in migraines the rest of his life.
Vaughan, Henry — 1621-1695 — Wales — **British Civil War**
Vaughn was a twin born in the Llansantiffread parish of Brecknockshire, Wales. His brother's name was Thomas who was an alchemist and philosopher. His mother was an heir and only daughter of David and Gwenllian Morgan of Llansantiffread. He had many important family ties to sigh society to include the Welsh knight Dafydd Gam (the same knight mentioned in the Shakespeare play Henry V). His family also had both Catholic and Protestant ties. His grandmother Frances was imprisoned for her catholic beliefs. He and his brother were educated by Mathew Herbert and later attended Jesus College. At the start of the British Civil War, he left London to go home and he worked as a secretary to Sir Marmaduke Lloyd. Vaughn is believed to have served briefly in the Royalist Army and when he returned, he began to study medicine. Vaughn's first published volume of poetry was titled *Poems, with the Tenth Satire of Juvenal Englished.* Included in this collection is the poem "Upon the Priory Grove" where he reflects upon his first wife. He loved his Welsh heritage and the mountains he lived among. The area is now a part of the Brecon Beacon National Park and the River Usk valley. During the British Civil War his poetry portrays a dislike for the Royalists even though he was one himself. He went through a lot of loss at the time to include losing his grandfather and being forced out of his home. His family chose to move to the countryside. You can view this time period through his eyes in his poetry collection Silex Scintillans, his most well-known publication. His poetry went through a change before this collection from secular to a more sacred influence. He is an "example of a poet who can write both graceful and effective prose".

Wackler, Elijah — b. 2004 — Michigan, USA
Wackler writes his poetry from an apartment under the stairs in Michigan. Wackler is inspired by music, nature, and art. In his free time, he plays guitar, runs cross country, and participates in JOAD archery. He also serves on an Advisory Committee for a local, non-profit, swing dance club. One of Wackle's favorite events is volunteering and entering projects into the Oakland County Fair. His dream is to own a Christmas tree farm and deliver holiday cheer to people. Wackler has ancestors who served in the Revolutionary War, Civil War, WWI, and WWII.

Washington, George — 1732-1799 — Virginia, USA
French and Indian war & Revolutionary War
Washington was born in Virginia and was the oldest of six children and he had four older half siblings. He did not have the formal education his older half-brother had but he went to school and learned and surveying. This skill helped him earn a living and fill his want for adventure. During the French and Indian War, he had command of his own regiment where he was able to gain experience and respect that helped him eventually to gain the title of Commanding General of the Continental Army. He had a large role in ratifying and adopting the Constitution of the United Sates. He also served two terms as the First President of the United States.

Welgan, Maddox —b. 2008 — California, USA
Welgan was 12 years old when he wrote his poem Freedom Fighters when living in Japan while his father was serving in the US Navy. Growing up he has moved to many places. At the time of publication, he was residing in California with his family, parents and two brothers. He enjoys spending time with his sibling's playing games and building with LEGO.

Wheatley, Phillis – 1753–1784 – West Africa (most likely Gambia or Senegal)
Born in West Africa and sold into slavery at age seven or eight, Wheatley was purchased by the Wheatley family who named her after the slave ship that brought her to America, *The Phillis*. The Wheatley family members taught her how to read and write and by age twelve she could read classics in both Greek and Latin. Her level of education was considered untraditional for a female, let alone a slave. She wrote her first poem at age fourteen. After her book of poetry was published in 1773 the Wheatley's emancipated Phillis. She was the first African-American woman recorded to publish a book of poetry.
Whitman, Walt – 1819–1892 – New York, USA
Whitman had to leave his formal education at age eleven to work, but later on in life he became a journalist, essayist, and poet. He combined the ideas of both Transcendentalism and realism in his literature. He is well known for his poem "O Captain! My Captain!" (Written after the death of Abraham Lincoln) and his poetry collection *Leaves of Grass*, published in 1855.

Wilde, Oscar – 1854–1900 – Ireland
Wilde was educated at home as a young child and also learned French and German from a nursemaid and governess. He joined his brother at school where he excelled academically. In 1881 a collection of sixty-one of his

poems were published in a book: *Poems*. He wrote poetry and is known for his *The Picture of Dorian Grey*, *The Happy Prince and Other Tales*, and his play *The Importance of Being Earnest*.

Wilds, Myra Viola – N.D. – Kentucky, USA
Wilds was an African American woman who was born in Mount Ollie, Kuntucky. She published her collection of poetry in 1915 titled Thoughts of Idle Hours through the National Baptist Publishing Board. She was known as the "blind verse writer" because she wrote her entire book when she was blind. It is believed she lost her site in 1911 from eye strain as a dress maker. In 1914 she wrote her first poem, Sunshine, and it took her eleven months to complete her book. Her poetry reflects her life living in the American South.

Wordsworth, William – 1770–1850 – England
Wordsworth's mother taught him how to read. His first published work was a sonnet in 1787 in the *European Magazine*. He attended Cambridge to continue his education and enjoyed doing "walking tours" of many European countries. In 1793 his first collection of poems, *An Evening Walk and Descriptive Sketches*, was published. In 1798 he collaborated with Coleridge and created *Lyrical Ballads* which included Wordsworth's famous poem "Tintern Abbey."

Wyn, Hedd – 1887—1917 – Wales - WWI
Wyn was born Ellis Humphrey Evans to Evan and Mary Evans and was the eldest of seven children. He grew up on his father's family from the majority of his life. His education started at age 6 at the local primary and Sunday school and his education stopped at age 14 when he became a shepherd on the farm. Even his meager education he was talented at writing poetry. He wrote his firt poem at age 11 titled "Y Das Fawn" or The Peat Stack. He enjoyed writing in both English and Welsh. His favorite poet was Percy Bysshe Shelley and enjoyed writing bout religion and nature. He participated in many poetry contests and he was given the name Hedd Wyn (hedd means "peace" and wyn means "pure" or white) at a poets meeting. At the out brake of WWI, he was among those who were against war but when the family we required to send one person to fight in the was Ellis went in his younger brothers stead. Within a month he became a casualty of war.

Yeats, William Butler –1865–1939 – Ireland
Yeats studied poetry from a young age. He received the Nobel Prize in Literature in 1923. He also wrote plays like *The Player Queen* and *On*

Baile's Strand. Another notable poem is "The Wild Swans at Coole." He was also an active participant in Irish politics.

Zesiger, Brock — b. 2012 — Utah, USA
Zesiger was born in Great Falls, Montana and later his family moved to Utah. Zesiger's favorite activity is wrestling and he hopes to be an Olympic gold medalist for the USA team someday. He like to cook, ride his bike, play piano and is learning sign language. He enjoys building and creating things and would love to invent something in the future! Zesiger has one brother, one sister, one dog, one cat, 3 fish and 4 tarantula spiders! He enjoys poetry and is delighted by humorous poems. He pulls inspiration from nature.

Zesiger, Jake — b.2010 — Utah, USA
Zesiger was born in Salt Lake City, Utah and the oldest of two siblings, a brother and sister. His family had moved to both Montana (where his brother was born) and Oregon). His family then moved back to Utah, his state of birth. He loves wrestling and is working towards being a wrestler at Penn State University in Pennsylvania. Zesiger also enjoys art, sports, guitar and piano. He is studying sign language and finds it very interesting! His mother has inspired his interest in poetry. His travels are also inspirational fuel for things he chooses to write about.

Glossary

abash—to make someone feel ashamed or embarrassed; disconcerted
Hope is the Thing with Feathers (DEC) 256

Abhorred—feeling of hatred and discuss towards something or someone
1942 (AUG) 176

abiding—an object or feeling that lasts a long time like a rock or a memory.
A Nation's Strength (FEB) 71

abreast—facing the same direction side by side with others
The Present Crisis (JAN) 43
The King of England (JUNE) 148

accolade—an award given to acknowledge great merit as a special honor. This can be an award or a ceremony like being knighted.
Mark Twain and Joan of Arc (JAN) 60

adorned—to make more appealing or attractive with decoration or objects.
Foreign Lands (APR) 118

aforesaid—something mentioned beforehand
A Mixed Battle Song (MAY) 138

aggrieved—when someone feels as if they have been treated unfairly or feel resentment towards a person or specific outcome.
Balto (JAN) 56

albeit—same meaning as although
The Present Crisis (Jan) 43

Alderney—a breed of dairy cow that is extinct
The King's Breakfast (FEB) 77
allegiance—showing loyalty
To My Country (APR) 109

anarchies—when there is no law or government in power
Sonnet to Liberty (FEB) 85

anemones—a flower
The Invaders (JUN) 152

anomalous—deviating from what is expected or normal
The Kangaroo (MAR) 96

asphodel—a Eurasian lily plant
A Pot of Tea (NOV) 244

asunder—to be put into pieces; divided apart
The Union (APR) 114

auspicious—conducive to success
On Virtue (NOV) 232

austere—very strict attitude or deminer
To My Country (APR) 109

auxiliars—a soldier who is serving along-side a nation other than his own
The French Revolution as It Appeared to Enthusiasts at Its Commencement (MAY) 128

azure—a blue hugh like a sky on a clear day
The Song of Australia (JAN) 61
The American Flag (MAR) 86
The King of England (JUN) 148
The Valley of Unrest (OCT) 230

Baal—an ancient Middle Eastern God
God Save the Flag (MAR) 102

babbling—the bubbling sound of running water.
Liberty – A Fragment (MAR) 91

bairnie—small child
Goody Santa Clause on a Sleigh Ride (DEC) 260

baldric—a strap or belt worn over the shoulder to hold a weapon like a sword, drum or bugle.
The American Flag (MAR) 86

balm—an ointment to place on the skin or wound to aid in healing.
On Liberty and Slavery (FEB) 75
Men of England (JUN) 141
The Mocking Bird (SEPT) 199

barbarous—primitive, uncivilized, and very brutal; savage
Occasioned by George Washington's Arrival in Philadelphia(FEB) 68

barrack—typically housing for soldiers or when someone is shouting and making fun of someone who is performing, speaking or doing a play.
At the Tug-O-War (MAR) 98
Paul Revere's Ride (APR) 103

bayonet—a pointed weapon that can be attached to the end of a rifle.
The American Flag (MAR) 86
Arms and the Boys (AUG) 177

bearer—a person who holds something
The American Flag (MAR) 86

befitting—appropriate for a situation
A Monument for the Soldier (NOV) 241

behemoth—a very large creature
Boston Hymn (JUL) 159

benighted—a state of moral ignorance; a state of pitifulness
On Being Brought from Africa to America (FEB) 66

bequeath—leave something to a person
A Monument for the Soldier (NOV) 241

bereave—actively suffering from the loss of a loved one.
Character of the Happy Warrior (Jan) 46

bereft—deprived or lacking in something; sad or lonely
Gone to the War (JUN) 145
Cotton King (FEB) 66

betwixt—between two things or two people
Cavalry Crossing the Ford (JUN) 144

beying—a howling sound made by a dog
Away to Canada (MAY) 133

bier—a place where a coffin is placed before burial or to be moved to the grave.
The Death of Lincoln (APR) 177

bivouac—to camp outside without any tent; to sleep out under the stars; temporary campsite like a soldier or mountaineer would use
A Song for the Irish Militia (JULY) 167
A Psalm of Life (DEC) 254

blanched—being dipped in boiling water
The Mountains (DEC) 253

blight—a plant disease caused by a fungus
The Present Crisis (Jan) 43

bliss(ful)—being perfectly happy
Choice (MAR) 100
Morning on the Shinnecock (MAY) **140**

blithe—cheerful and casual indifference; joyous
I Hear America Singing (JUNE) 144
Halloween (OCT) 214

blypes—Scottish for shred or piece of skin
Halloween (OCT) 214

Boadicea—Queen of the British Iceni and led and uprising against the Roman Empire about 60AD.
A Daughter of the States (JUL) 162

boast—to brag pridefully out ones self
Cannon Fodder (MAR) 89

bosom—a woman's chest
Mrs. Earth (APR) 115
Niagara (NOV) 236

bough—the larger branches of a tree
Sailing to Byzantium (Jan) 49
On Liberty and Slavery (FEB) 75
Spring in War-Time (APR) 109
Boston Hymn (JUL) 159
At the Melting of the Snow (SEPT) 200
Laura Secord (Tales of Bravery) 297
Autumn (OCT) 206
Pilgrim (NOV) 243

bowers—a shady place under a tree
The French Revolution as It Appeared to Enthusiasts at Its Commencement (MAY) 128

bramble—a prickly bush like a berry or wild thorned bush
The Fairies Dancing (APR) 115

brazier—a portable heater with a place to hold coals
A Pot of Tea (NOV) 244

bridegrooms—the title given to a man on his wedding day
Cannon Fodder (MAR) 89

bridle—the headgear used to control a horse that includes
Paul Revere's Ride (APR) 103

bristling—hairs that are stiff and spiky
The Old Soldier (MAY) 131

Britannia—derived from the Latin word "Britannicae" and was the term the Romans used when speaking of the British Isles.
The Maple Leaf Forever (FEB) 82

bulwarked—a defense created by an embankment or wall
1942 (AUG) 176

busby—a black fur military hat
At Home (MAY) 134

Byzantium—later known as Constantinople, Byzantium was an ancient Greek city that existed during the classical antiquity.
Sailing to Byzantium (Jan) 49

caffy—a fairhaired victor
A Pot of Tea (NOV) 244

Cain—biblical name of a person who killed his own brother.
On Being Brought from Africa to America (FEB) 66

Caledonia—a Latin name used by the Roman Empire to refer to the area in Great Britain North of the River Forth including the majority of Scotland.
Liberty – A Fragment (MAR) 91

calvaries—referring to a representation of the crucifixion of Christ.
The Present Crisis (Jan) 43

camelopard—a giraffe
The Kangaroo (MAR) 96

cannonades—continuous gun fire
Sonnet to Liberty (FEB) 85

carbineers—a soldier armed with a carbine
A Song for the Irish Militia (JULY) 167

carcass—a dead animals body or remains
A Poem Against the Tories (MAR) 99

celestial—related to heaven; heavenly
The American Flag (MAR) 86

centaur—mythological Greek creature that is half man on top and half horse on bottom.
The Kangaroo (MAR) 96

Cherokee—the largest Native American Indian Tribe in the United States
The Hunter's Wooing (FEB) 80

chimeras—mythological Greek monster part lion, goat, and dragon that breaths fire.
The Kangaroo (MAR) 96

churning—agitate; to move about vigorously
The Land of the Free (APR) 117

Circe— a minor Greek mythology goddess
Newton (APR) 119

circumscribed—restricted within limits
The Power of Armies is a Visible Thing (MAR) 92

clad—clothed
Mark Twain and Joan of Arc (JAN) 60

clave—cleaver
Drummer's Lament (JUL) 174

cock—a rooster
The Dead Kings (MAR) 90
Paul Revere's Ride (APR) 103

Colossus—it's referring to "The Colossus of Rhodes" an antient statue of the Greek sun-god Helios located on the island of Rhodes.
The New Colossus (OCT) 205

commonweal—public welfare
To My Country (APR) 109

communion—thoughts and feelings on an intimate level, often related to spirituality. A Christian worship service in many religions
The Union (APR) 114

comrade—another person who belongs to or participates in the same group or organization like the military, a club or a society.
D-Day (JUN) 142
At The Melting Of The Snow (SEPT) 200
Niagara (NOV) 236

condone—permit or approve
To My Country (APR) 109

conquest—seeking after control of an geographical area or people using the military.
To Germany (APR) 111

contortionists—a performer who twists their body into strange shapes.
The Troop Ship (OCT) 207

contradiction—two opposing ideas
The Kangaroo (MAR) 96

contumelious – acting insulting, scornful and/or insulting
The Present Crisis (Jan) 43

converse—the reverse of something
The Kangaroo (MAR) 96

convex—when something is curved outwards like the exterior of a circle or like the lens of a telescope or glasses.
Occasioned by George Washington's Arrival in Philadelphia (FEB) 68

cooed—A soft sound a dove or pigeon makes; talking with a soft gentle voice
On Liberty and Slavery (FEB) 75

coom—smut or soot
The Marsh Of Rhuddlan (AUG) 180

coothie—genial; kind; agreeable
Halloween (OCT) 214

Copernicus—a Polish mathematician of the Renaissance who created a model of the solar system with the sun at the center.
Newton (APR) 119

coppice—an area of bushes and trees cleared or cut back
My Country (NOV) 238

cowers—to act or shrink away in fear.
The Present Crisis (Jan) 43

Cowskin—a creek in Eastern Oklahoma
The Hunter's Wooing (FEB) 80

credo—This is a Latin word referring to a statement of beliefs, a creed
The Present Crisis (Jan) 43

condone—permit or approve
To My Country (APR) 109

coy—To act shy or modest in the effort to draw attention.
Address to Edinburgh (Jan) 51

culminant—the highest point; reaching full development
To My Country (APR) 109

curpin—buttocks
Halloween (OCT) 214

dappled—marked with spots or splotches of color
Sunlight and Sea (JUN) 155

dauntless—*to have no fear, nothing holds you back, unstoppable.*
The Maple Leaf Forever (FEB) 82

decrepitude—A state of being decrepit, frail and worn out because of age or neglect.
Greater Love (FEB) 74

defiance—choosing to be disobedient
Paul Revere's Ride (APR) 103

Delphic—related to the antient Greek oracle Delphi
The Present Crisis (Jan) 43

deluding—to be deceived by a misleading belief; foolish
George Washington (JAN) 62

deluge—a flood; to be inundated with a large quantity of something
God Save the Flag (MAR) 102

democracies—government run by the people
Sonnet to Liberty (FEB) 85

desolate—void of people; empty
God Save the Flag (MAR) 102
desolation—destruction and complete emptiness
The Kangaroo (MAR) 96

destined—something unfolding as if it was planned; fate
On the Death of Dr. Benjamin Franklin (APR) 113

dew(s)—droplets of water left on a surface from moisture in the air.
The Wild Honeysuckle (APR) 112
The Fairies Dancing (APR) 115
Both the Victor and the Vanquished (MAY) 140

diabolical—unpleasant, extremely bad; like the devil
On Being Brought from Africa to America (FEB) 66

dirge—a song or lament for the dead
The Marsh Of Rhuddlan (AUG) 180

discord—a disagreement
The Kangaroo (MAR) 96

disdain—feeling that a person does not deserve respect; to hold someone in contempt.
A Poem Against the Tories (MAR) 99

disentangled—untangled; free of knots
Newton (APR) 119

disgorge—to pour out
Ghosts of the New World (OCT) 221

dishevelled (disheveled)—unkept; disorderly and messy
Newton (APR) 119

dissolute—not having restraint, over indulgent and with little morals
Newton (APR) 119

dower—a widows share in her husband's estate. Noun for the word dowery.
Character of the Happy Warrior (Jan) 46

downtrodden—treated poorly
The Land of the Free (APR) 117

Dulce et decorum est Pro patria mori—a Latin phrase meaning "It is sweet and fitting to die for the homeland."
Dulce Et Decorum Est (OCT) 213

dunce–a person who is slow to learn
A Poem Against the Tories (MAR) 99

eager—when someone really wants something or wants to do something
Paul Revere's Ride (APR) 103
O Captain! My Captain! (APR) 108

ebbing—something that is becoming less or moving away or receding
The Present Crisis (Jan) 43

Eire—the Gaelic word for Ireland
The Dead Kings (MAR) 90

embattled—either preparing for or involved in war; surrounded by enemies
Concord Hymn (APR) 116

emulation(s)—when someone or something is imitated
A Song of Sydney (MAY) 135

enfranchised—given the right to vote
To My Country (APR) 109

enraptured—extremely pleasant; full of joy or pleasure
George Washington (JAN) 62

erect—very upright and strait
Cannon Fodder (MAR) 89

Eryri—either Welsh for eagle or Latin for "to rise"
The Marsh Of Rhuddlan (AUG) 180

extorted—to obtain something in an unfair way like threatening or by force.
Occasioned by George Washington's Arrival in Philadelphia (FEB) 68

exulting—feeling elation
O Captain! My Captain! (APR) 108

faggots—a bundle of sticks to use as fuel.
The Present Crisis (Jan) 43

fair Burnet—this is referring to Eliza Burnett (1766-1790) who was the daughter of a Scottish philosopher (Lord Monboddo) and she was one of the most popular young ladies of Edinburgh.
Address to Edinburgh (Jan) 51

fane—a temple or church
A Nation Once Again (MAR) 95

federation—A group of geographical areas with a central government while still retaining autonomy to a certain degree
The Union (APR) 114

fetters—chains and shackles used to bind the hands and feet of a prisoner.
Swiss Air-"Ranz Des Vaches (FEB) 81
The Death of Lincoln (APR) 177

Feudalism—a class system in medieval Europe where nobility held land and serfs were indebted
William Wallace (AUG) 179

Flanders Field—one of the eight World War I American cemeteries that are oversees. Located in Belgium.
In Flanders Field (MAY) 126

flaxen—a pale yellow color
The Fairies Dancing (APR) 115

fodder—food
Cannon Fodder (MAR) 89

foe—enemy
The American Flag (MAR) 86
God Save the Flag (MAR) 102
Concord Hymn (APR) 116

forebears—an ancestor
Newton (APR) 119

foreboding—having a feeling that something bad will happen
The Present Crisis (Jan) 43

forge—a space to heat metal
Men of England (JUN) 141

forlorn—lonely or pitifully sad
Ghosts of the New World (OCT) 221

furrow—a long trench plowed into the ground for planting
The Dead Kings (MAR) 90

gale—a very strong wind
The American Flag (MAR) 86
Hope is the Thing with Feathers (DEC) 256

Galileo—an Italian astronomer and scientist and referred to as the father of astronomy.
Newton (APR) 119

gallant—to be brave or heroic
Balto (JAN) 56
The American Flag (MAR) 86
A Mixed Battle Song (MAY) 138

garret—attic or top floor room
Goody Santa Clause on a Sleigh Ride (DEC) 260

gaunt—a person who is thin and suffering from age, hunger, or neglect.
Cotton King (FEB) 66

gay(ly)—happy
Address to Edinburgh (Jan) 51
The Wild Honeysuckle (APR) 112
A Song of Sydney (MAY) 135
Cavalry Crossing the Ford (JUN) 144
Beethoven In Central Park (AUG) 185
Joining the Colours (AUG) 188

girdle(d)—a garment that wraps around one's mid-section from the torso down to the hips; to be gird about, wrapped
Songs for the People (FEB) 78
A Song of Sydney (MAY) 135

girdling—to encircle like a belt
The Song of Australia (JAN) 61

gilded—covered in gold, traditionally thought of as gold leaf (real gold). gold paint.
Address to Edinburgh (Jan) 51
Paul Revere's Ride (APR) 103
Sea Magic (JUL) 169

gilt—covered in gold, traditionally thought of as gold leaf (real gold). gold paint.
A Soldier's Valentine (FEB) 73

guidon—a flag that narrows to a point, often used by a cavalry regiment
Cavalry Crossing the Ford (JUN) 144

falter(ed)—loosing strength
Gone to the War (JUN) 145

firmament—the sky or the heavens
Newton (APR) 119
The Spacious Firmament on High (SEPT) 203

fluttered—flapping wings quickly
Morning on the Shinnecock (MAY) 140

grace—showing goodwill
Cannon Fodder (MAR) 89

Grecian—referring to ancient Greece and often refers to the architecture of the time.
Sailing to Byzantium (Jan) 49

grenadiers—soldiers that are armed with a grenade launcher
Paul Revere's Ride (APR) 103

gropers—A large warm sea fish in the bass family
To Germany (APR) 111

gyre—to whirl or gyrate
Sailing to Byzantium (Jan) 49

Hebrides—islands off the West coast of Scotland
The Valley of Unrest (OCT) 230

hallowed—a holy place
Swiss Air-"Ranz Des Vaches" (FEB) 81

hapless—unfortunate
Address to Edinburgh (Jan) 51

harbinger—a person or thing that announces when a person arrives or approaches.
The American Flag (MAR) 86

harmony (ies)—a combination of notes sounded at the same time to create cords having a pleasant sound to the ear.

The Song of Australia (JAN) 61
Swiss Air-"Ranz Des Vaches" (FEB) 81

heaths—uncultivated land characteristic of Britain that would grow heather and grasses.

Liberty – A Fragment (MAR) 91

heinous—an absolutely horrible act

War (MAY) 132

heretic—beliefs different than those commonly accepted or believing and doing things contrary to religious beliefs.

The Present Crisis (Jan) 43

hippogriff—a feathered creature with an eagles head and a horse like body with talons on its front legs.

The Kangaroo (MAR) 96

hireling—a person who does low level/menial work

Boston Hymn (JUL) 159
Defence of Fort M'Henry (SEPT) 194

honey-fugle (honeyfuggle)—to cheat or deceive

Aunt Cloe's Politics (FEB) 80

hue—shades of color

The American Flag (MAR) 86

hurdies—the buttocks

Address to a Haggis (JAN) 54

iconoclast—a person who attacks popular beliefs or destroys religious images.

The Present Crisis (Jan) 43

idolatry—love or admiration for something or someone or the worship of anything other than God.
	To My Country (APR) 109

ignorance—lacking or not having knowledge
	Choice (MAR) 100

imminent—something that is anticipated or about to happen
	We are America (JAN) 62

immingled—mixed or blended together
	Liberty – A Fragment (MAR) 91

imperious—arrogant and domineering authoritarian power
	A Daughter of the States (JUL) 162

impetuous—acting without contemplating the consequences; forceful and rapid movement
	Paul Revere's Ride (APR) 103
	Dead Man's Dump (OCT) 208

inanities—nonsensical action or remark; silliness
	The Best School of All (SEPT) 196

incongruous—not keeping in harmony with its surroundings
	The Kangaroo (MAR) 96

Indiana—a state in the Unites States of America
	Dual (MAY) 137

indigenous—something that is native to a certain area
	The Power of Armies is a Visible Thing (MAR) 92

indigo—a dark blue color created from the indigo plant
	Newton (APR) 119

indomitable—Impossible to defeat or subdue
	Washington's Monument, February, 1885 (FEB) 72

inly—inwardly
The Dead Kings (MAR) 90

insolent—being arrogant and rude; showing disrespect
God Save the Flag (MAR) 102

inviterate (inveterate)—a habit that someone has had for a long time and unlikely to change.
George Washington (JAN) 62

jaunty—self-confident, cheerful and lively
Meadowlark (SEPT) 202

jeer—to make mocking or rude remarks towards someone
America (FEB) 65

jest—joke
Mark Twain and Joan of Arc (JAN) 60

keel—a ridge or blade that runs along the bottom of a boat for stability
O Captain! My Captain! (APR) 108

Kepler—a German astronomer best known for his study of planetary movement.
Newton (APR) 119

knoll—a small mound or hill
The Song of Australia (JAN) 61

knout—*a punishment inflicted by a whip*
Sonnet to Liberty (FEB) 85

kythe—Scottish for "make known"
Halloween (OCT) 214

lair—where a wild animal lives
The Hunter's Wooing (FEB) 80

lark—a small song bird
The Fairies Dancing (APR) 115

laments—deep grief; mourning
On the Death of Dr. Benjamin Franklin (APR) 113

lance—a long pointed weapon for jousting
The American Flag (MAR) 86

languished—lacking vitality; something or someone loosing strength or feeble
On Liberty and Slavery (FEB) 75

lark—a small song bird
The Dead Kings (MAR) 90

laureat(e)—a person who receives an honor or receives recognition for a great achievement
A Poem Against the Tories (MAR) 99

liberty—the ability to do be free to make choices without the fear of oppression.
On Liberty and Slavery (FEB) 75

lilting—when someone is speaking or singing and their voice rises and falls pleasantly
The Fairies Dancing (APR) 115

loins—the space between the hip bone and the false ribs; the area where your reproductive organs are.
The Jew (SEPT) 194

luster—a gentle sheen or glow or luster often from light reflecting off an object.
A Nation's Strength (FEB) 71

luxuriant—lavish or lush growth
The Song of Australia (JAN) 61

Lydia Darragh—a Quaker from Philadelphia who was a spy during the American Revolution for the Patriot side.
Unsung (SEPT) 193

lyre—an ancient Greek harp
A Prophecy to George Keats in America (MAY) 124
malice—wanting to do evil; ill will
America (FEB) 65
Arms and the Boy (AUG) 177

mammon—A biblical term for riches
The Song of Australia (JAN) 61

marmalade—A jelly preserve made with orange or other citrus rind and juice.
The King's Breakfast (FEB) 77

martyr—a person who is killed for what they believe.
The Present Crisis (Jan) 43

melancholy—feeling of sadness for no apparent reason
The Best School of All (SEPT) 196

melisma—music notes sung to a single syllable of text
Meadowlark (SEPT) 202

mellifluous(ly)—a smooth rich sound like a voice, soothing
Balto (JAN) 56

mess-tin—mess kit
A Pot of Tea (NOV) 244

minstrelsy—a wandering musician of medieval time
The Song of Australia (JAN) 61

mirth—amusement often expressed in laughter
Tipperary (JUN) 151

monarch—a ruler of a land such as a king, queen, or emperor

Cotton King (FEB) 66
Occasioned by George Washington's Arrival in Philadelphia (FEB) 68
The American Flag (MAR) 86
On the Death of Dr. Benjamin Franklin (APR) 113
To the King's Most Excellent Majesty 1768 (JUN) 157

monotone—a sound that is unchanging in pitch

Marshland (AUG) 186

moorings—the place a boat is docked or the items used to dock a boat.

Paul Revere's Ride (APR) 103

mould(y)—another spelling of moldy

The Present Crisis (Jan) 43
A Mixed Battle Song (MAY) 138
William Wallace (AUG) 179
Marshland (AUG) 186

mourn(ing)—deep sorrow over the loss of someone

Mark Twain and Joan of Arc (JAN) 60
The Land of the Free (APR) 117
Anthem for Doomed Youth (JUN) 147

murmuring—a person or group of people talking quietly about their dislike of something; complaining

Greater Love (FEB) 74
The Wild Honeysuckle (APR) 112

muse—the Greek goddesses over science and art and the daughters of Zeus.

A Poem Against the Tories (MAR) 99

muster—collect; gather before battle

Paul Revere's Ride (APR) 103

myrtle—an evergreen shrub

The Song of Australia (JAN) 61

native—naturally from a specific geographical area
Tipperary (JUN) 151

Nautch-girl—girls who dance for entertaining others in India. The dancing would be for royalty or cultural and religious ceremonies.
Sunlight and Sea (JUN) 155

ominous—The feeling or impression that something unpleasant is going to happen.
A Song of the Republic (JUN) 154
Ode for Trafalgar Day, 1905 (OCT) 222

onie—any
Address to a Haggis (JAN) 54

Old Glory—another name for the United States flag
Dual (MAY) 137

oppression—when anyone is treated unjustly or has cruel control forced upon them.
On Liberty and Slavery (FEB) 75

oracular—related to an oracle, something representing or holding the powers of an oracle.
The Present Crisis (Jan) 43

orisons—prayer
Anthem for Doomed Youth (JUN) 147

paddocks—a small field where horses and exercise or are kept
My Country (NOV) 238

painch—the first stomach section (rumen) of the sheep's digestive system.
Address to a Haggis (JAN) 54

pallor—pale appearance
Anthem for Doomed Youth (JUN) 147

palpitate—irregular or rapid heart rate
The Valley of Unrest (OCT) 230

patriot—a person devoted to supporting his country and willing to defend it.
Occasioned by George Washington…(FEB) 68
Washington's Monument, Feb 1885 (FEB) 72
America the Beautiful (JUL) 165
Love for My Country (JUL) 173
The Marsh of Rhuddlan (AUG) 180
Patriot Parade (SEPT) 191
Unsung (SEPT) 193
Canada's Resources (NOV) 240
After the Battle (NOV) 242

patriotism—devotion to one country
Love for My Country (JUL) 173

Pegasus—winged flying horse
The Kangaroo (MAR) 96

pendulums—an item swinging from a fixed point under the effects of gravity.
Marching (JUL) 164

penury—very poor, destitute
Opportunity (MAY) 130

perished—something that died suddenly
The Dead Kings (MAR) 90

perne—power, glory, rank
Sailing to Byzantium (Jan) 49

perseverance—never giving up to achieve a goal
Heavy is the Crown (MAY) 136

philosopher—a person who learns about philosophy; a deep thinker
On the Death of Dr. Benjamin Franklin (APR) 113

Picardy—a region of France
The Dead Kings (MAR) 90

pining—suffering a mental or physical decline often caused by a broken heart.
Gone to the War (JUN) 145
A Song for the Irish Militia (JULY) 167

pinions—the outer parts of a bird's wings; a wings pinions are cut to prevent a bird from flying.
On Liberty and Slavery (FEB) 75

piteous—causing or deserving pity
Greater Love (FEB) 74
Father Abe (SEPT) 189

pityless (pitiless)—cruel; showing no compassion
George Washington (JAN) 62
Ireland (MAR) 94

placable—forgiving, calmed, easily pacified
Character of the Happy Warrior (Jan) 46

plight—a situation that is challenging or difficult
Tipperary (JUN) 151

plucked—to be pulled out
The King of England (JUNE) 148

plucky—being determined and showing courage in difficulty
At the Tug-O-War (MAR) 98

pomp—elaborate ceremony meant for show that are ostentatious and boastful.
Occasioned by George Washington's Arrival in Philadelphia (FEB) 68
The New Colossus (OCT) 205
October (OCT)

pond'rous (ponderous)—very heavy in weight
Address to Edinburgh (Jan) 51

porringer—a shallow bowl no more than 6 inches in diameter and between 1.5 inches and 3 inches deep. Used in Europe during the Middle Ages.

The King's Breakfast (FEB) 77

prankt (ed)—when someone has had a trick or prank done upon them

The Fairies Dancing (APR) 115

preposterous—opposite of common sense; ridiculous and absurd

The Kangaroo (MAR) 96

prodigious—impressive by size

The Kangaroo (MAR) 96

progeny—a descendant

The Captain (JUL) 172

profaned—disrespected and irreverence

A Nation Once Again (MAR) 95

prophetic—something that is described or predicted to happen in the future.

The Present Crisis (Jan) 43

provoke—purposefully bother or annoy someone

The Wild Honeysuckle (APR) 112

quaffed—to drink in large quantities

The Song of Australia (JAN) 61

quaint—old-fashioned

Morning on the Shinnecock (MAY) 140

Quaker—a religion group who believed in pacifism and believed in spiritual equality of men and women.

Unsung (SEPT) 193

quarrel—a heated argument between two people
In Flanders Field (MAY) 126

quay—a platform used for loading cargo on and off a ship
A Song of Sydney (MAY) 135

queer—strange
On Cissarat Kalifa (MAY) 127
The Troop Ship (OCT) 207
The Cremation of Sam McGee (DEC) 258

ramparts—a castle or cities defensive wall
Defence of Fort M'Henry (SEPT) 194

rapture—an intense feeling of joy
Address to Edinburgh (Jan) 51

rapturous—expressing or feeling full of ecstatic delight; extreme joy
Father Abe (SEPT) 189

ratton—a rat
Halloween (OCT) 214

reaps—to cut or harvest a crop
Men of England (JUN) 141

reekin—not smelling good, stinking
Address to a Haggis (JAN) 54

Rembrandt—Dutch painter from the Baroque era
Newton (APR) 119

renown—fame; when lots of people know who you are
The King of England (JUNE) 148

respire—breath
On Liberty and Slavery (FEB) 75

ridding—getting rid of; setting free
A Nation Once Again (MAR) 95

Rosnaree—a small village in Ireland
The Dead Kings (MAR) 90

rousers—a person who rouses or stirs people up
A Mixed Battle Song (MAY) 138

roving—always wandering from one place to another
The Wild Honeysuckle (APR) 112

roystering— to be a part of a noisy revelry, merrymaking
Balto (JAN) 56

ruddy— a person having a healthy red color
The King of England (JUNE) 148
Marching (JUL) 164
Goody Santa Clause on a Sleigh Ride (DEC) 260

sable—a color that is dark brown or black
On Being Brought from Africa to America (FEB) 66

Sally Lun—this is a sweet bun mad popular in Bath, England made by Solange Luyon, a French immigrant who moved to Bath in 1680. Learn more about the sweet bun in the bread recipe section of this book.
Receipt To Make A Sally Lun (JAN) 57

sanctuary—a safe place to go
Expectans Expectavi (MAR) 88

sanguine—having a positive attitude, even in a bad situation
Receipt To Make A Sally Lun (JAN) 57

satire—humor that uses exaggeration, irony and bring attention to a persons stupidity. Often used in political humor and Shakespeare
A Poem Against the Tories (MAR) 99

saulchana—a plant native to Eastern Oklahoma
The Hunter's Wooing (FEB) 80

scanty—a very small amount
Tipperary (JUN) 151

scourge—a whip that is used to inflict pain as a punishment; something that causes trouble or suffering
Men of England (JUN) 141
Thoughts (DEC) 249

sceptres—a decorative and ornamental staff carried by rulers for ceremonies.
Occasioned by George Washington's Arrival in Philadelphia (FEB) 68
To the King's Most Excellent Majesty 1768 (JUN) 157
Dead Man's Dump (OCT) 208

sedges—a class of plant that is long and grass like
Marshland (AUG) 186

Senecas—a group of Native American Indians also known as the Mingo.
The Hunter's Wooing (FEB) 80

sensual—Having great satisfaction of the senses
Sailing to Byzantium (Jan) 49

sentinel—a soldier who stands guard
Paul Revere's Ride (APR) 103

sepulchre (sepulcher)—a small space built as a monument to bury a person
Men of England (JUN) 141

serpentine—snake shaped
Cavalry Crossing the Ford (JUN) 144

seraphim—a deity creature with two to three pairs of wings in by the Jewish, Christian, and Islamic literature.
To My Country (APR) 109

serene—calm and peaceful
A Daughter of the States (JUL) 162

servest—serve
The King of England (JUNE) 148

sevenfold—seven times more (X7)
Newton (APR) 119

shire—English countryside
Anthem for Doomed Youth (JUN) 147

shanties—a poorly built shack
War (MAY) 132

sheath(ing)—a covering for a blade or sword; a protective covering
God Save the Flag (MAR) 102
A Song for the Irish Militia (JULY) 167

shrine—a holy place to worship that contains a relic or representation of a deity or person
Expectans Expectavi (MAR) 88

shroud—shelter, covering
The American Flag (MAR) 86

skirmish—an unplanned fight between small armies or fleets
The Picnic Battle (JUL) 70

skulk—to hide out of sight; often for a sinister reason.
A Poem Against the Tories (MAR) 99

slighted—to feel disrespected by how someone speaks to or treats you
To God and the Soldier (APR) 113

smite—to hit hard
The Death of Lincoln (APR) 177

sodden—soaked or saturated with liquid
Vitai Lampada (AUG) 177

sombre—gloomy, dull color
Paul Revere's Ride (APR) 103

sonsie—Having a healthy and attractive look
Address to a Haggis (JAN) 54

sov'reign—(also spelt sovereign) A ruler such as a monarch such as a king, queen or emperor.
Address to Edinburgh (Jan) 51

Spavinaw—a creek in Eastern Oklahoma, USA
The Hunter's Wooing (FEB) 80

spectacle—something drawing attention; visually striking
Morning on the Shinnecock (MAY) 140

splendours—wonderful, grandeur
The American Flag (MAR) 86

spurn—to reject someone or something with great contempt
To My Country (APR) 109
1942 (AUG) 176
William Wallace (AUG) 179

squalling—constant noisy crying
A Mixed Battle Song (MAY) 138

stealthy—to move in a manner or behave in a way as to not be seen.
Paul Revere's Ride (APR) 103

strident—harsh and loud
To the Poet Before Battle (AUG) 188

subterranean—things occurring under the surface of the Earth
The French Revolution as It Appeared to Enthusiasts at Its Commencement (MAY) 128

succor—helping a person in a time of difficulty and distress
Boston Hymn (JUL) 159

sultry—humid and hot
Washington's Monument, February, 1885 (FEB) 72

Sumter—a city in South Carolina
Gone to the War (JUN) 145

sunder—to be taken or smashed apart
The Present Crisis (Jan) 43

swarthy—dark colored skin
On Cissarat Kalifa (MAY) 127

swathe (swath)—a long strip of land
A Prophecy to George Keats in America (MAY) 124

swathed—wrapped in layers
Marshland (AUG) 186

sylvan—a rural wooded area
Occasioned by George Washington's Arrival in Philadelphia (FEB) 68

tapering—shrinking from wide to narrow
To Germany (APR) 111

tarry—to stay or abide in a place
Expectans Expectavi (MAR) 88

tatter(ed)—when cloth is torn irregularly
Sailing to Byzantium (Jan) 49
Old Ironside (SEPT) 192

tempered—to be made stronger by heating and cooling, like with the metal of a sword.
Men of England (JUN) 141

tempestuous—strong turbulent feelings; confliction emotions; extremely story

The Swiss Alpes (DEC) 249

thairm—intestines, in this instance it is referring to a sheep's intestines.

Address to a Haggis (JAN) 54

throe—a struggle that is painful or a violent struggle

The Present Crisis (Jan) 43

Tipperary—A county in Ireland

Tipperary (JUN) 151

Tramp(ing)—noisy, heavy walking

The Dead Kings (MAR) 90
Foreign Lands (APR) 118

transmute— changes in form

Character of the Happy Warrior (Jan) 46

tremulous—when a voice is trembling or nervous

The Fairies Dancing (APR) 115

tressed—refers to hair long hair being arranged in some organized way.

The Fairies Dancing (APR) 115

trills—a rhythmic vibrating sound

O Captain! My Captain! (APR) 108

trump (ings)—a sound like a trumpet calling to all to hear.

On Liberty and Slavery (FEB) 75
The American Flag (MAR) 86

tyrant—a ruler that is cruel to his subjects
On Liberty and Slavery (FEB) 75
Ireland (MAR) 94
The Parting Before the Battle (MAR) 101
Men of England (JUN) 141

uncouth—bad behavior or poor manners
The Present Crisis (Jan) 43

undefiled—pure
To My Country (APR) 109

unerring—to always be right; not in error
America (FEB) 65

unquenchable—unable to be satisfied or extinguished
We are America (JAN) 62

unwittingly—unaware of the full facts
Expectans Expectavi (MAR) 88

usurpations—taking a throne illegally; usurping is wrongful seizure of a throne.
God Save the Flag (MAR) 102

Utopia—the idea of a society that lives in perfect harmony
The French Revolution as It Appeared to Enthusiasts at Its Commencement (MAY) 128

vainly—when something does not produce a result one hopes for no matter what you do.
God Save the Flag (MAR) 102

vanquished—defeated
Both the Victor and the Vanquished (MAY) 140
Old Ironside (SEPT) 192

vehemently—intense and passionate; strong feelings
Expectans Expectavi (MAR) 88

Vernon—the home of George Washington was named Mount Vernon located in Mount Vernon, Virginia.
Occasioned by George Washington's Arrival in Philadelphia (FEB) 68

venerable—respect because of age, character, or wisdom
Washington's Monument, February, 1885 (FEB) 72

vengeance—punishing someone out of revenge for doing something to you.
Swiss Air-"Ranz Des Vaches" (FEB) 81
The American Flag (MAR) 86

verdant—to be covered in green grass or other lush green vegetation
A Poem Against the Tories (MAR) 99

versemen—a person who writes in verse
To the Poet Before Battle (AUG) 188

vestige—a trace left behind, showing that something used to exist. Like a dead dried up flower stem after the flower has died off. It can also mean a very small amount.
The Wild Honeysuckle (APR) 112

vexed—troubled about something that is annoying or problematic; to be worried
Away to Canada (MAY) 133

vigil—waiting in prayer or peace
The Song of Australia (JAN) 61

vollies—many projectiles (bullets, arrows…) being released at the same time.
A Poem Against the Tories (MAR) 99

votive—something received in fulfillment of a vow like a candle.
Concord Hymn (APR) 116

wailing—crying out loud in great pain

Anthem for Doomed Youth (JUN) 147

Wallace—A famous historical hero of Scotland
Liberty – A Fragment (MAR) 91

wan—pale skin like someone who is sick
Cotton King (FEB) 66

warbling—a sting of softly sung notes
Morning on the Shinnecock (MAY) 140

welkin—heaven or the sky
The American Flag (MAR) 86

wheedle—to persuade someone to do something with flattery and coaxing
Goody Santa Clause on a Sleigh Ride (DEC) 260

winnower—a person who fishes for minnows.
The Present Crisis (Jan) 43

wintle—rolling or staggering motion
Halloween (OCT) 214

winze—Scottish for curse
Halloween (OCT) 214

woodbine—a common plant name
A Song of Sydney (MAY) 135

worset—a yarn made of tightly twisted; thread made from combed long-staple wool
Halloween (OCT) 214

wrought—to be formed and shaped
Character of the Happy Warrior (Jan) 46

Xerxes—known as Xerxes the Great and son of Darius the Great. The fourth king of kings from the Achaemenid Empire from 486-465 BC.

A Poem Written in a Journal (FEB) 79

yew—a conifer tree that can have little red berries with a very poisonous seed.

The Invaders (JUN) 152

yore—a long time past

The Maple Leaf Forever (FEB) 82

zealot—a person who is a fanatic about something like religion, politics or anything else he/she has strong feelings about

1942 (AUG) 176

Index

Search Poems By Subject

Native American

Nature

Navy

Night

Search by Poet

Search Poets by Country

Australia

Canada

England

USA

Made in the USA
Coppell, TX
09 July 2026

83947824R00273